The Philosophy of
Laughter and Humor

SUNY Series in Philosophy
Robert C. Neville, Editor

SUNY Series in Philosophy
Roert C. Neville, Editor

The Philosophy of Laughter and Humor

John Morreall, Editor

State University of New York Press

Published by
State University of New York Press, Albany

For information, address State University of New York
Press, State University Plaza, Albany, N.Y., 12246

Library of Congress Cataloging in Publication Data

The philosophy of laughter and humor.

   (SUNY series in philosophy)
   Bibliography: p. 264
   Includes index.
   1. Wit and humor—Philosophy.   I. Morreall, John,
1947-   .   II. Series.
√ PN6149.P5P48   1987   128'.3   86-14498
ISBN 0-88706-326-8
ISBN 0-88706-327-6 (pbk.)

10 9 8 7 6 5 4 3 2

Contents

For Slim

Preface

Philosophers, especially in our century, have often been charged with overlooking the important features of human life. By choosing topics that are of no interest to ordinary people, and by writing books that only other philosophers read, they guarantee themselves a minimal role in society. "As things now stand," a colleague once wrote to me, "professional philosophers rank well below hairdressers and football coaches in social influence. This is partly due to the difficulty in careful thought. But a good deal of the problem lies in the willful obscurity of our work. In choice of topics, style, or language, we seem determined to be unhelpful."

The last few years have seen some improvement here, especially in areas of applied ethics. But other important features of human life are still barely mentioned by philosophers, and one of them is laughter and humor. There are few things on which most people place more value than having a good laugh. Countless questionnaires have ranked "a sense of humor" as among the two or three things we find most essential in a spouse or friend. Humor abounds in our literature and art. And yet it takes a lot of searching through philosophy journals and university course catalogs to discover anything about laughter and humor being written or taught by a philosopher.

This gap in contemporary philosophy is all the more curious in light of the attention laughter and humor have recently received from scholars in other fields—psychology, literature, medicine, anthropology, sociology, linguistics, and religion, to name the most important. And it is not that laughter and humor are too simple or too well understood to generate any philosophical questions. Even as a biological phenomenon, laughter remains an anomaly; and, as work in other fields has shown, amusement is at least as complex a mental state as fear or jealousy, which are much discussed in philosophy. Furthermore, as an aspect of our social interaction, what is as complicated as sophisticated humor? Even technically minded philosophers interested in such things as presupposition and speech act theory could find much to analyze in our joking interactions.

A good deal of the philosophical neglect of humor, I will suggest in the Introduction, can be attributed to a longstanding prejudice that began with Plato and Aristotle. But whatever the reasons for this neglect, it is high time we gave humor the philosophical attention it deserves. I made an effort in this direction a few years ago by writing *Taking Laughter Seriously*. The enthusiastic response it received, from colleagues and readers in general, convinced me that this is an important topic about which more needs to be said. In this volume I aim to keep the discussion going by presenting what I consider the most important philosophical writings on laughter and humor, giving roughly equal space to the history of thought on the topic and to contemporary essays.

Part I consists of readings from Plato to Bergson, some of them complete essays but most excerpts from larger works. In the history of thought about laughter and humor represented here, three dominant theories emerge, the Superiority Theory, the Relief theory, and the Incongruity Theory. In part II, contemporary philosophers examine these three theories, suggest improvements in them, and extend the discussion to such topics as the relation between humor and aesthetic experience. The essays in part III attempt to deepen our understanding of humor by comparing and contrasting amusement to other mental states. And part IV focuses on the ethics of humor, an area which is of the greatest practical importance, but which, of all the topics considered in this book, has received the least careful attention.

As with any topic in philosophy, one of the best ways to discover the most discussable readings in the philosophy of laughter and humor is to teach courses on the subject and see which readings get the most response. I have done this, and I am grateful to the students in my classes at Hobart and William Smith Colleges, and at the University of Santa Clara, for serving as guinea pigs for this book. I might add that I find teaching courses in this area a joy. All kinds of topics come up quite naturally, topics in aesthetics and ethics, in philosophical and empirical psychology, and in literary and film criticism. We discuss Aristotle's views on happiness, psychological research on surprise, and anthropological studies of clowning. We watch Katharine Hepburn/Cary Grant comedies. And we try to answer what is for me the basic philosophical question: When is seriousness called for, and when isn't it? Of the twenty-odd courses I have taught, no other has been so enjoyable or has allowed for so much philosophizing about basic human concerns.

Permissions

Robert Sharpe, "Seven Reasons Why Amusement is an Emotion" originally appeared in the *Journal of Value Inquiry*, 9 (1975), 201–203.

John Morreall, "Humor and Emotion" originally appeared in the *American Philosophical Quarterly*, 20 (1983), 297–304.

Joseph Boskin, "The Complicity of Humor: The Life and Death of Sambo" originally appeared in *The Philosophical Forum*, 9 (1977–78), 371–382.

The Charles Addams cartoon in "Funny Ha-Ha, Funny Strange, and Other Reactions to Incongruity" originally appeared in *The New Yorker*, January 13, 1940, p. 13. copyright 1940, 1968 The New Yorker Magazine, Inc.

Introduction

Samuel Johnson, the story goes, ran into a college friend he had not seen for forty years, and in the course of their conversation they got to comparing their lives. "You are a philosopher," the man said to Dr. Johnson. "I have tried in my time, too, to be a philosopher, but I don't know how; cheerfulness was always breaking through." The idea that many people, including a good number of philosophers, have of philosophy is that it is the serious discipline par excellence. It is paradigmatically "heavy" stuff. In such a view, a philosophical discussion is the last place where humor — or for Johnson's friend even cheerfulness — would be appropriate. And for those who see humor as incompatible with philosophizing, it is often a short step to thinking that humor is not an appropriate subject for philosophical investigation. Though short, this step is faulty. Even if we were to assume that we should not philosophize humorously, that does not rule out humor as something to philosophize about. To take a simple analogy, we all agree that we should not use fallacies in our philosophical reasoning; but fallacies are nonetheless a perfectly respectable subject of philosophical investigation.

As the editor of a book with the title *The Philosophy of Laughter and Humor*, I am obviously convinced not simply that humor could be philosophically interesting, but that it actually is so. But I am convinced of much more. Far from seeing humor as incompatible with philosophy, I find that there is a special affinity between the two.

Wittgenstein said that a philosophy book could be written consisting of nothing but jokes: these would be based on fallacies, category mistakes, and other confusions about the logic of different concepts and arguments. We can even read certain humorous works not intended as philosophy books, such as Lewis Carroll's *Alice in Wonderland* and *Through the Looking Glass*, and find many philosophical lessons. Indeed, P. L. Heath's *The Philosopher's Alice* does just that. Wittgenstein, with his concern about measurement and checking procedures, would have much to say about Alice's behavior when she eats a special cake in the hope of changing her size:

1

She ate a little bit, and said anxiously to herself, "Which way?
Which way? holding her hand on the top of her head to feel
which way it was growing, and she was quite surprised to find that
she remained the same size.[1]

Wittgenstein's own example of a person's checking a story in the
newspaper by running out to buy a second copy of the same paper,
might easily have been something done by the March Hare.

But the connection between humor and philosophy goes deeper
than their frequent focusing on nonsense and faulty reasoning. For
they both involve a certain detachment from the practical aspects of
life. To think philosophically or to enjoy the humor in our experience, we must be without urgent practical concerns. To have
cultivated a philosophical spirit or a rich sense of humor is to have a
distanced, and, at least potentially, a more objective view of the
world. This aspect of philosophy long ago became an extended
meaning of the word "philosophical": "rational; sensibly composed;
calm, as in a difficult situation." Similarly, the person who faces life
with a sense of humor has a calmer attitude and can view things
more rationally. As the psychologist Penjon said of humor at the
turn of the century, it "frees us from vanity on the one hand, and
from pessimism on the other, by keeping us larger than what we do,
and greater than what can happen to us."[2]

There is also a conceptual flexibility, an imaginative use of
unusual perspectives, that characterizes both philosophy and
humor. William James captured this feature of philosophy nicely:
"Philosophy, beginning in wonder, as Plato and Aristotle said, is
able to fancy everything different from what it is. It sees the familiar
as if it were strange, and the strange as if it were familiar."[3] Except
perhaps for the reference to wonder here, this statement also
describes humor. Indeed, I can think of no better way to
characterize the comedy of someone like Jonathan Winters or
George Carlin than to say that it sees the familiar as if it were
strange, and the strange as if it were familiar. In both philosophy
and humor we shift mental gears and look at things in new ways.
And this departing from well-worn paths of thought brings a certain
mental liberation, which has long been counted as among the chief
values of philosophy and of humor. To read the *Alice* books or to
discuss a question like "Could you and I trade bodies?" is to break
out of our ordinary ways of thinking. For both the philosopher and

the humorist, nothing is to be taken for granted: everything can be looked at with a questioning, experimental, even irreverent eye.

Both humor and philosophy can become stale, of course, as when writers of TV "sitcoms" simply rework the same jokes over and over, or when a certain body of philosophical thinking is treated as a rigid system to be learned and applied. When humor becomes rigid, it is rather easy to tell, for people stop laughing. Rigid philosophy is not always as easy to detect, but one telltale sign is humorlessness. When the playful, critical spirit of humor goes out of philosophy, it usually loses its flexibility of perspective and its open-endedness. In his obituary article on Bertrand Russell, Gilbert Ryle wrote of the importance of Russell's and William James's humor to their philosophical legacy:

> James and Russell found out for themselves and so taught us at our best how to pop doctrinal bubbles without drawing blood; how to be illuminatingly and unmaliciously naughty; and how, without being frivolous, to laugh off grave conceptual bosh. Stuffiness in diction and stuffiness in thought were not, of course, annihilated, but they were put on the defensive from the moment when James and Russell discovered that a joke can be the beginning, though only the beginning, of a blessed release from a strangling theoretical millstone.[4]

But if I am right about this close affinity between humor and philosophy, how are we to explain the traditional neglect of humor as a philosophical topic? The answer, I think, is historical. In Greek thought a theory of laughter became entrenched that made humor ethically suspect. This was the so-called Superiority Theory, held by Plato and Aristotle, according to which, laughter is always directed at someone as a kind of scorn. Even wit, Aristotle said, is "educated insolence." Needless to say, in such a view, humor is at best a nasty business and should be kept in check. From this negative evaluation of humor, it does not immediately follow that humor is unfit as a topic of philosophical study; but because the activity of creating and enjoying humor was seen as somehow unworthy, there was little motivation to study it. The Superiority Theory turned out to be a classic case of a theory built on too few instances, and it was later recognized that there is no essential connection between laughter and scorn. But this recognition came only a few hundred years ago, after the Superiority theory had held the field for over two thousand years.

The sloppy theorizing that created and sustained the Superiority Theory has troubled the whole history of thought on laughter and humor, as we shall see in several of the historical selections. But first, lest we perpetuate this sloppiness, we should take a moment to clarify the terms we will be using.

"Laughter" seems the simplest term to start with. It denotes a combination of bodily events, including the spasmodic expulsion of air from the lungs, accompanying sounds, characteristic facial distortions, and in heavy laughter the shaking of the whole body. Except in pathological cases and cases where laughing is performed as an action, laughter is an involuntary or semi-voluntary response to a stimulus. The simplest such stimuli are merely sensory, as in laughter at being tickled, or the baby's laughter at being tossed into the air and caught. In such cases, it is important to note, there need be nothing humorous causing the laughter. A more complex stimulus for laughter, but again one which is not humorous, is a sudden change in one's perceptual field, as in the baby's laughter at peekaboo, or the adult's laughter at the magician's disappearing act. What makes humor different from these cases of nonhumorous laughter is the mental state we call "amusement." Put simply, a case of laughter involves humor when the laughter is caused by and expresses amusement. "Humor," according to the *Oxford English Dictionary*, is "that quality of action, speech, or writing which excites amusement." A comment is required here, for the word "amusement" has a wide and a narrow sense. In the wide sense we are amused when our attention is simply agreeably occupied, as when we pass the time on a car trip by singing. In the narrow sense of humorous amusement — with which we are concerned — we are amused when our attention is agreeably occupied in a particular way. To specify what this way is would require some commitment to a theory of humor. In "A New Theory of Laughter" I will offer such a theory, analyzing amusement as the enjoyment of a conceptual shift, analogous to the enjoyment of a shift in sensory input in the laugh of being tickled, and the enjoyment of a perceptual shift in the baby's laugh at peekaboo. But however we are to specify the nature of amusement, it is essential to distinguish between amusement as a mental state and laughter as a bodily phenomenon, and to notice that not all laughter is caused by amusement. I should also add that not all amusement issues in laughter; the amusement may be too mild, for example, or because of the situation we may suppress laughter.

These distinctions between laughter, amusement, and humor are essential, because without them we are in danger of conflating different kinds of laughter situations and different aspects of the same situation. Perhaps the most common mistake here is to treat all cases of laughter as cases of humor. Kant and Schopenhauer, for example, present their Incongruity Theories as if they were theories of laughter generally, when at most they could hope to serve as theories of humor. Bergson titles his book *Laughter*, when a more accurate title would have been *Humor*, or better, *Comedy*.

Adding to such lapses of precision in theories of laughter and humor, there are related problems of terminology. Most significant, perhaps, is that before the seventeenth century the words "humor" and "amusement" did not have their modern senses. Earlier words such as "comic" are sometimes rough equivalents for "humorous," but often they have narrower meanings. And other words like "ridiculous," "ludicrous," and especially "laughable" have connotations of derision which "humorous" need not have. Even the modern word "humor" has sometimes been used, by literary critics and others, in a narrowed sense — for the kind of humor that involves an amiable, sympathetic, non-sarcastic view of human foibles. Contemporary philosophers do not use the word in this way, but in the widest sense. And because they are usually looking for a general account of humor, they tend to skip over other literary distinctions such as those between farce, parody, satire, buffoonery, and burlesque.

Having sketched our basic categories of laughter, amusement, and humor, we can now briefly preview some of the questions that arise in this book in connection with these terms. Most prominent are the basic questions: "What is humor?", "What is laughter?", and "What is the relation of humor to laughter?" In answer to these questions, we have three traditional theories — the Superiority Theory already mentioned, the Relief Theory, and the Incongruity Theory.

According to the Superiority Theory, represented by the selections from Plato, Aristotle, and Hobbes, we laugh from feelings of superiority over other people, or over our own former position. While this theory does seem to cover many cases of laughter and humor, there are some counterexamples. As Hutcheson first pointed out in replying to Hobbes, we do not always respond with laughter when we see the failure of others or our own success; and conversely, much of our amusement does not seem to involve feelings of superiority.

The Relief Theory takes a more physiological approach to laughter, treating it as the venting of excess nervous energy. This theory, best represented by the selections from Spencer and Freud, has been very influential in contemporary psychology, where it takes the form of accounts like Daniel Berlyne's "arousal jag" theory of laughter. But like the Superiority Theory, the Relief Theory does not seem to capture the essence of laughter or humor. It simply seems false that every time we laugh we are working off excess energy. More importantly, even if some cases of laughter do involve the venting of excess energy, it does not seem that our amusement *is* just that venting of energy. As Roger Scruton suggests in his essay "Laughter," both the Relief and the Superiority Theories seem inadequate in capturing the essence of humor, because they focus on incidental benefits to the amused person rather than on what it is about amusing things that makes them amusing.

The Incongruity Theory, the most popular current philosophical theory of humor and the one most prominent in this book, seems more promising than its two competitors, simply because it attempts to characterize the formal object of amusement. It tries to say just what something has to have in order for us to find it amusing. This theory, found in Kant, Schopenhauer, Kierkegaard, and many since, holds that the formal object of amusement is "the incongruous." What amuses us is some object of perception or thought that clashes with what we would have expected in a particular set of circumstances. In the contemporary essays, Clark reformulates Schopenhauer's version of the Incongruity Theory, and then Martin suggests an improvement on Clark's version.

Besides the basic questions about the nature of laughter and humor, there are several others discussed in a number of the readings. One is the relationship between humor and the aesthetic point of view, an issue first raised by Kierkegaard (though not in the passages in this book). One tradition, seen here in Scruton's essay, holds that amusement is by nature a kind of aesthetic interest. Martin challenges this idea, insisting that much of our amusement is not aesthetic.

Another important question is the relationship between amusement and emotions. Is amusement itself an emotion? Plato, Sharpe, de Sousa and others say Yes; Bergson, Scruton, and Morreall say No. The debate here revolves around the similarities and dissimilarities between amusement and such standard emotions as fear, anger, and love. Whether we take a stand or simply call this debate "linguistic," the evidence on both sides should show us just how special a role amusement plays in our lives.

Because laughter is a social phenomenon, it prompts many ethical questions. These are concentrated in part IV, but come up in other selections too. What is the difference, so often appealed to in joking sessions among friends, between laughing *at* people and laughing *with* them? And why is it so offensive to be laughed at? What is it about sexist and racist jokes that makes them objectionable?

There are other ethical questions about humor that arise even apart from social considerations. Does the love of humor indicate a kind of irresponsibility or even — as Plato, Hartley, and Santayana suggest — a kind of irrationality? Or is our sense of humor an integral part of our rationality, as Scruton and Morreall claim?

Not all the issues in this book are crucial. Room is left for smaller questions, such as why puns are the lowest form of humor. But all the questions put together show, I think, that whether or not Samuel Johnson's friend was right that humorlessness is an occupational disease among philosophers, humor and laughter are certainly rich topics for philosophers to investigate.

Notes

1. Lewis Carroll, *Alice's Adventures in Wonderland*, in P. L. Heath, *The Philosopher's Alice* (New York: St. Martin's, 1974), p. 20.

2. Quoted in Max Eastman, *The Sense of Humor* (New York: Scribner's, 1921), p. 188.

3. William James, *Some Problems of Philosophy* (Cambridge, Mass: Harvard University Press, 1979), p. 11.

4. Gilbert Ryle, "Bertrand Russell 1872-1970," *Proceedings of the Aristotelian Society* 71 (1970-71): 77-78.

I. Traditional Theories of Laughter and Humor

1   Plato (428-348 B.C.)

As with so many topics, Western thought about humor and laughter begins with Plato. What we laugh at, in Plato's view, is vice, particularly self-ignorance, in people who are relatively powerless. Our amusement is a kind of malice toward such people, he thought, and this should make us wary of amusement, but so should the fact that amusement is an emotion in which we tend to lose rational control of ourselves. In his *Republic*, when setting up rules for the education of the young Guardians of the ideal state, Plato singles out laughter as something to be avoided. The guardians "must not be prone to laughter, for usually when we abandon ourselves to violent laughter, our condition provokes a violent reaction." So that the young Guardians are not given bad models to follow, literature should be censored to eliminate all mention of the gods or heroes as overcome with laughter. (*Republic*, 388e)

Philebus 48-50

SOCRATES:	And do you realize that when we see a comedy, here again the soul experiences a mixture of pain and pleasure.
PROTARCHUS:	I don't quite understand you.
SOC:	No, Protarchus, for it's somewhat difficult to see this mixture of feelings in our reaction to comedy.
PROT:	Yes, it does seem difficult.
SOC:	Yet the obscurity of this case should make us more eager to examine it, for that will make it easier to detect other cases of mixed pleasures and pain.
PROT:	Yes, go on.
SOC:	We mentioned malice just now [before this passage]. Would you call that a pain of the soul?
PROT:	Yes.
SOC:	And yet the malicious man is somehow pleased at his neighbor's misfortunes.
PROT:	Certainly.
SOC:	Now ignorance, or what we call stupidity, is an evil.

PROT: Surely.

SOC: Assuming that to be true, observe the nature of the ridiculous.

PROT: Please explain.

SOC: Taken generally, the ridiculous is a certain kind of evil, specifically a vice. It is that kind of vice which can be described by the opposite of the inscription at Delphi.

PROT: You mean "Know thyself," Socrates?

SOC: I do. And the opposite would read "Know not thyself."

PROT: Certainly.

SOC: Now, Protarchus, see if you can divide this into three parts.

PROT: How? I'm afraid I can't.

SOC: Do you mean that I must make this division for you?

PROT: Yes, and I beg you to do so.

SOC: Aren't there three ways in which someone may be ignorant of himself?

PROT: What are they?

SOC: First, about wealth; he may imagine himself richer than he is.

PROT: Yes, many people are like that, certainly.

SOC: But there are even more who imagine themselves taller or more handsome or physically better than they really are.

PROT: Quite so.

SOC: And yet surely the greatest number are mistaken about the third class of goods, that is possessions of the soul. They imagine themselves superior in virtue, when they are not.

PROT: Yes, indeed.

SOC: And of all the virtues, isn't wisdom the one most men are always claiming, disputing endlessly and lying about how wise they are?

PROT: Certainly.

SOC: And may not all this be truly called evil?

PROT: Surely.

SOC: Well now, Protarchus, we must make another
               two-fold division if we want to see the curious
               mixture of pleasure and pain that lies in the
               malice of amusement. How do we make this divi-
               sion? All who are foolish enough to hold this false
               conceit of themselves can be divided, like
               mankind in general, into two classes — those who
               are strong and powerful and those who are the
               opposite.

PROT: Certainly.

SOC: Then let this be the principle of division. Those
               who are weak and unable to retaliate when they
               are laughed at may rightly be called ridiculous;
               those who are strong and can defend themselves
               may be more truly called formidable and hateful.
               For ignorance in the strong is hateful, because it
               is hurtful to everyone both in real life and on the
               stage, but powerless ignorance may be considered
               ridiculous, which it is.

PROT: That's perfectly true, but I'm not yet clear about
               the mixture of pleasures and pains here.

SOC: Well, let's consider the nature of malice.

PROT: Go ahead.

SOC: Both pain and pleasure can be wrong, can't they?

PROT: Unquestionably.

SOC: And delighting in our enemies' misfortunes is
               neither malicious nor wrong?

PROT: Of course not.

SOC: But to feel delight instead of pain when we see our
               friends in misfortune — that is wrong, isn't it?

PROT: Certainly.

SOC: Now, didn't we say that ignorance is always an
               evil?

PROT: Yes.

SOC: Then if we find in our friends the three kinds of
               ignorance we outlined, imaginary wisdom, beau-
               ty and wealth, delusions which are ridiculous in
               the weak and hateful in the strong — if we find
               these in a harmless form in our friends, may we

	not say, as I was saying before, that these delusions are simply ridiculous?
PROT:	Yes, we may.
SOC:	And do we not agree that this state of mind, being ignorant, is evil?
PROT:	Certainly.
SOC:	And when we laugh at it, do we feel pain or pleasure?
PROT:	Clearly we feel pleasure.
SOC:	And we agreed that it is malice that is the source of the pleasure we feel at our friend's misfortune?
PROT:	Certainly.
SOC:	Then our argument shows that when we laugh at what is ridiculous in our friends, our pleasure, in mixing with malice, mixes with pain, for we have agreed that malice is a pain of the soul, and that laughter is pleasant, and on these occasions we both feel malice and laugh.

2 Aristotle (348–322 B.C.)

Aristotle agreed with Plato that laughter is essentially derisive and that in being amused by someone we are finding that person inferior in some way. To find someone's shortcomings funny, he added, we must count them as relatively minor; otherwise we would be disturbed by them. Though Aristotle did not go along with Plato's recommendation that we should suppress laughter generally, he did think that most people overdo joking and laughing. The moral ideal is to avoid the extremes of the humorless boor and the "anything for a laugh" buffoon: it is to be ready-witted but tactful. Besides his view of laughter as derision, Aristotle hinted at the later theory that laughter is a reaction to many kinds of incongruity, and not just human shortcomings. In the *Rhetoric* (3, 2) he mentions that a speaker can get a laugh by setting up a certain expectation in the audience, and then jolting them with something they did not expect. His example is from an unknown comedy: "And as he walked, beneath his feet were—chilblains." Jokes can work this way, too, he notes; consider those that involve word play or a change of spelling. This observation that surprise can make us laugh was not developed by Aristotle or followers like Cicero, however. It was not until Kant and Schopenhauer that the Incongruity Theory of laughter was worked out in any detail.

Poetics, ch. 5, 1449a

Comedy, as we have said, is an imitation of people who are worse than the average. Their badness, however, is not of every kind. The ridiculous, rather, is a species of the ugly; it may be defined as a mistake or unseemliness that is not painful or destructive. The comic mask, for example, is unseemly and distorted but does not cause pain.

Nicomachean Ethics, Book IV, ch. 8

Since life includes relaxation as well as activity, and in relaxation there is leisure and amusement, there seems to be here too the possibility of good taste in our social relations, and propriety in what we say and how we say it. And the same is true of listening. It will make a difference here what kind of people we are speaking or listening to. Clearly, here, too, it is possible to exceed or fall short of the mean. People who carry humor to excess are considered vulgar buffoons. They try to be funny at all costs, and their aim is more to raise a laugh than to speak with propriety and to avoid giving pain to the butt of their jokes. But those who cannot say anything funny themselves, and are offended by those who do, are thought to be boorish and dour. Those who joke in a tactful way are called witty, which implies a quick versatility in their wits. For such sallies are thought to be movements of one's character, and, like bodies, characters are judged by their movements. The ridiculous side of things is always close at hand, however, and most people take more fun than they should in amusement and joking. So even buffoons are called witty just as though they were fine wits. But it is clear from our discussion that they differ from the witty person, and to a considerable extent.

Tact also belongs to the middle state, and a man is tactful if he says and listens to the sort of thing that befits a good and well-bred man. For there are some things that are proper for such a man to say and to hear in joking, and there is a difference between the joking of a well-bred and a vulgar man, and between that of an educated and of an uneducated man. We can see this difference in the old and the new comedies: for the writers of old comedy it was indecent language that was ridiculous, while those writing new comedy prefer innuendo. Between these two there is quite a difference in propriety. Can we then define the man who jokes well as the one who says nothing unbecoming a well-bred man, or as one who does not give pain in his jokes, or even as one who gives delight to his listeners? Or is that definition itself undefinable, since different things are hateful or pleasant to different people? The kind of jokes he will listen to will be the same, for the kind of jokes a person can put up with are also the kind he seems to make. There are, then, jokes he will not make, for a joke is a kind of abuse. There are some kinds of abuse which lawgivers forbid; perhaps they should have forbidden certain kinds of jokes.

Such, then, is the man who follows the mean—he being as it were a law unto himself—whether we call him tactful or witty. The buffoon, however, cannot resist any temptation to be funny, and spares neither himself nor others if he can get a laugh. He says things that no cultivated man would say, and some which he would not even listen to. The boor, by contrast, is useless in such social relations, for he contributes nothing and takes offense at everything, despite the fact that relaxation and amusement are a necessary element in life.

3 Cicero (106–43 B.C.)

Though best known as an orator and statesman, Cicero was also keenly interested in philosophy, and believed that philosophy and rhetoric should be combined. In his work *On the Orator* he examines the use of humor in public speaking, discussing such techniques as exaggeration, sarcasm, and punning, and such philosophical topics as the nature of humor and the ethics of its use. In large part he follows what Aristotle had said, but he adds at least one new idea of some theoretical importance, the distinction between humor in what is being talked about, and humor arising from the language used. This distinction is similar to that made today between the comedian, who says funny things, and the comic, who says things funny.

On the Orator, Book II

Ch. 58

The seat and province of the laughable, so to speak, lies in a kind of offensiveness and deformity, for the sayings that are laughed at the most are those which refer to something offensive in an inoffensive manner. . . . But very careful consideration must be given to how far the orator should carry laughter . . . for neither great vice, such as that of crime, nor great misery is a subject for ridicule and laughter. People want criminals attacked with more forceful weapons than ridicule, and do not like the miserable to be derided, unless, perhaps, when they are insolent. You must also be considerate of people's feelings, so that you do not speak rashly against those who are personally beloved.

Ch. 59

There are two kinds of jokes, one of which is based on things, the other on words.

Ch. 60

Whatever is wittily expressed consists sometimes in an idea, sometimes only in the language used. But people are most delighted with a joke when the laugh is raised by the idea and the language together.

Ch. 63

The most common kind of joke is that in which we expect one thing and another is said; here our own disappointed expectation makes us laugh. But if something ambiguous is thrown in too, the effect of the joke is heightened.

4   Thomas Hobbes (1588-1679)

The Superiority Theory of laughter, which got its start in Plato and Aristotle, was put into a stronger form by Hobbes. Human beings, in his view, are in constant struggle with one another for power and what power can bring. In this struggle the failure of our competitors is equivalent to our success. And so we are all constantly watching for signs that we are better off than others, or, what counts as the same thing, that others are worse off than we are. Laughter is nothing but an expression of our sudden glory when we realize that in some way we are superior to someone else.

From Leviathan, *Part I, ch. 6, in* English Works, *vol. 3, ed. Molesworth (London: Bohn, 1839)*

Sudden glory, is the passion which makes those grimaces called laughter; and is caused either by some sudden act of their own, that pleases them; or by the apprehension of some deformed thing in another, by comparison whereof they suddenly applaud themselves. And it is incident most to them, that are conscious of the fewest abilities in themselves; who are forced to keep themselves in their own favor by observing the imperfections of other men. And therefore much laughter at the defects of others, is a sign of pusillanimity. For of great minds, one of the proper works is, to help and free others from scorn; and compare themselves only with the most able.

From Human Nature, *ch. 8, §13, in* English Works, *vol. 4, ed. Molesworth (London: Bohn, 1840)*

There is a passion that has no name; but the sign of it is that distortion of the countenance which we call laughter, which is always joy: but what joy, what we think, and wherein we triumph when we laugh, is not hitherto declared by any. That it consists in wit, or, as they call it, in the jest, experience confutes: for men laugh at mischances and indecencies, wherein there lies no wit nor jest at all. And forasmuch as the same thing is no more ridiculous when it grows stale or usual, whatsoever it be that moves laughter, it must be new and unexpected. Men laugh often, especially such as are greedy of applause from every thing they do well, at their own actions performed never so little beyond their own expectations; as also at their own jests: and in this case it is manifest, that the passion of laughter proceeds from a sudden conception of some ability in himself that laughs. Also men laugh at the infirmities of others, by comparison wherewith their own abilities are set off and illustrated. Also men laugh at jests, the wit whereof always consists in the elegant discovering and conveying to our minds some absurdity of another: and in this case also the passion of laughter proceeds from the sudden imagination of our own odds and eminency: for what is else the recommending of our selves to our own good opinion, by comparison with another man's infirmity or absurdity? For when a jest is broken upon ourselves, or friends of whose dishonor we participate, we never laugh thereat. I may therefore conclude, that the passion of laughter is nothing else but sudden glory arising from some sudden conception of some eminency in ourselves, by comparison with the infirmity of others, or with our own formerly: for men laugh at the follies of themselves past, when they come suddenly to remembrance, except they bring with them any present dishonor. It is no wonder therefore that men take heinously to be laughed at or derided, that is, triumphed over. Laughter without offence, must be at absurdities and infirmities abstracted from persons, and when all the company may laugh together: for laughing to one's self puts all the rest into jealousy and examination of themselves. Besides, it is vain glory, and an argument of little worth, to think the infirmity of another, sufficient matter for his triumph.

5   Descartes (1596-1650)

Descartes's treatment of laughter is found in *The Passions of the Soul,* part Two (art. 124–127) and part Three (art. 178–181). In part Two he offers a physiological explanation of laughter, and in part Three he considers the place of laughter in ridicule. No mention is made of humor or amusement. According to Descartes, there are only six basic emotions—wonder, love, hatred, desire, joy, and sadness—and laughter is found to accompany three of them, wonder, (mild) hatred, and joy. Laughter itself, according to Descartes, is the repeated rapid expulsion of air from the lungs caused by a sudden flow of blood into the lungs from the heart, with the attendant movements of the diaphragm and muscles of the chest and face.

Although Descartes goes beyond the Hobbesian account of laughter by acknowledging that there are other causes of laughter besides hatred, in Part 3, "Of Particular Passions," he considers laughter only as it occurs in scorn and ridicule. Indeed, he incorporates joy and wonder into scorn as the cause of scornful laughter. Had Descartes explored the relation of laughter to wonder itself, considered apart from scorn, he might well have developed a version of the Incongruity Theory of laughter. Aristotle and Cicero might also have done so, had they not taken ridicule as their paradigm case of laughter. Descartes wrote about wonder in some detail (Part 2, art. 53 and 70–78) as a surprised reaction to that which is "rare and extraordinary." Had he extended his theorizing by considering incongruity as a type of novelty, it would have been a short step to the idea of laughter as caused by our surprise at some incongruity.

From The Passions of the Soul, *in* The Philosophical Works of Descartes, *translated by Elizabeth Haldane and G. Ross (Cambridge: Cambridge University Press, 1911)*

Second Part

Article 124

Of Laughter

Laughter consists in the fact that the blood, which proceeds from the right orifice in the heart by the arterial vein, inflating the lungs suddenly and repeatedly, causes the air which they contain to be constrained to pass out from them with an impetus by the wind-pipe, where it forms an inarticulate and explosive utterance; and the lungs in expanding equally with the air as it rushes out, set in motion all the muscles of the diaphragm from the chest to the neck, by which means they cause motion in the facial muscles, which have a certain connection with them. And it is just this action of the face with this inarticulate and explosive voice that we call laughter.

Article 125

Why it does not accompany the greatest joys.

But although it seems as though laughter were one of the prin-cipal signs of joy, nevertheless joy cannot cause it except when it is moderate and has some wonder or hate mingled with it. For we find by experience that when we are extraordinarily joyous the subject of this joy never causes us to burst into laughter, and we cannot even be so easily induced to do so by some other cause as when we are sad. And the reason of this is that in great joys the lung is always so full of blood that it cannot be further inflated by repeated gushes.

Article 126

What are its principal causes.

And I can only observe two causes which make the lung thus in-flate suddenly. The first is the surprise of admiration or wonder, which, being united to joy, may open the orifices of the heart so quickly that a great abundance of blood suddenly entering on its right side by the *vena cava*, rarefies there, and, passing from thence by the arterial vein, inflates the lung. The other is the admixture of some liquor which increases the rarefaction of the blood, and I can find nothing which could do that but the most liquid part of that which proceeds from the spleen, which part of the blood being driven to the heart by some slight emotion of hatred, assisted by the surprise of wonder, and mingling itself there with the blood which proceeds from the other parts of the body which joy causes to enter there in abundance, may cause this blood to dilate there much more than usual. We observe the same thing in many other liquids which, when on the fire, suddenly dilate when we throw a little vinegar into the vessel where they are; for the most liquid portion of the blood which comes from the spleen is in nature similar to vinegar. Experience also causes us to see that in all the possible occurrences which can produce this explosive laughter which proceeds from the lung, there is always some little element of hatred, or at least of wonder. And those whose spleen is not in a very healthy condition are subject to being not alone more sad, but also at intervals more gay and more disposed to laughter than the others, inasmuch as the spleen sends two sorts of blood to the heart, the one thick and coarse, which causes sadness, the other very fluid and subtle, which causes joy. And often, after having laughed much, we feel ourselves naturally inclined to sadness because the more fluid portion of the blood of the spleen being exhausted, the other, more coarse, follows it towards the heart.

Article 127

Its cause in indignation.

As to the laughter which sometimes accompanies indignation, it is usually artificial and feigned; but when it is natural, it appears to proceed from the joy that we have in observing the fact that we cannot be hurt by the evil at which we are indignant, and, along with that, from the fact that we find ourselves surprised by the novelty or by the unexpected encountering of this evil. In this way joy, hatred and wonder contribute to it. At the same time I would fain believe that it may also be produced without any joy, by the movement of aversion alone, which sends blood from the spleen to the heart, where it is rarefied and driven from thence to the lung; and this it easily inflates when it finds it almost empty. And speaking generally, all that can suddenly inflate the lung in this way causes the outward action laughter, excepting when sadness changes it into that of groans, and the cries which accompany tears. In reference to which Vives writes of himself regarding a time when he had been long without eating, that the first pieces of food which he placed in his mouth caused him to laugh; and this might proceed from the fact that his lung, emptied of blood by lack of nourishment, was promptly inflated by the first juice which passed from his stomach to his heart, and which the mere imagination of eating could conduct there, even before the arrival of the food he was eating.

Third Part

Article 178

Of Scorn.

Derision or scorn is a sort of joy mingled with hatred, which proceeds from our perceiving some small evil in a person whom we consider to be deserving of it; we have hatred for this evil, we have joy in seeing it in him who is deserving of it; and when that comes upon us unexpectedly, the surprise of wonder is the cause of our bursting into laughter, in accordance with what has been said above of the nature of laughter. But this evil must be small, for if it is great we cannot believe that he who has it is deserving of it, unless when we are of a very evil nature or bear much hatred towards him.

Article 179

Why the least perfect are usually most given to mockery.

And we notice that people with very obvious defects such as those who are lame, blind of an eye, hunched-backed, or who have received some public insult, are specially given to mockery; for, desiring to see all others held in as low estimation as themselves, they are truly rejoiced at the evils which befall them, and they hold them deserving of these.

Article 180

Of the function of ridicule.

As regards the modest bantering which is useful in reproving vices by making them appear ridiculous, so long as we do not laugh at them ourselves or bear any hatred towards the individuals concerned, it is not a passion, but a quality pertaining to the well disposed man which gives evidence of the gaiety of his temper and the tranquility of his soul, which are characteristic marks of virtue; it often also shows the ingenuity of his mind in knowing how to present an agreeable appearance to the things which he ridicules.

Article 181

Of the function of laughter in ridicule.

And it is not wrong to laugh when we hear the jests of another; these jests may even be such that it would be difficult not to laugh at them; but when we ourselves jest, it is more fitting to abstain from laughter, in order not to seem to be surprised by the things that are said, nor to wonder at the ingenuity we show in inventing them. And that makes those who hear them all the more surprised.

6   Francis Hutcheson (1694–1746)

A century after Hobbes's account of laughter appeared in *Human Nature* and *Leviathan*, Hutcheson published the following critique of Hobbes, along with his own ideas on the nature and value of humor. In the first paper Hutcheson uses many counterexamples to show that there is no essential connection between having feelings of superiority and laughing or being amused. Or to put it in contemporary jargon, having feelings of superiority is neither a necessary condition nor a sufficient condition for laughter or amusement. In the second paper Hutcheson offers his own theory of humor, based on the association of ideas, a phenomenon much discussed in the eighteenth century. Hutcheson agrees with Addison that genius in serious literature consists in the ability to trigger ideas of greatness, novelty, and beauty in the reader through the use of apt metaphors and similes. *comic* genius, he continues, is largely the ability to use somewhat *inappropriate* metaphors and similes to trigger ideas that clash with each other. Here Hutcheson has at least the beginnings of an Incongruity Theory of humor. In the last paper Hutcheson discusses some of the values of humor, most notably the pleasure it brings, its role as social lubricant, and its ability to promote mental flexibility.

From Reflections Upon Laughter *(Glasgow, 1750)*

I

Aristotle, in his *Art of Poetry*, has very justly explained the nature of one species of laughter, viz. the Ridiculing of Persons, the occasion or object of which he tells us is . . . "some mistake, or some turpitude, without grevious pain, and not very pernicious or destructive." But this he never intended as a general account of all sorts of laughter.

But Mr. Hobbes, who very much owes his character of philosopher to his assuming positive solemn airs, which he uses most when he is going to assert some palpable absurdity, or some ill-natured nonsense, assures us that "Laughter is nothing else but sudden glory, arising from some sudden conception of some eminency in ourselves, by comparison with the infirmity of others, or with our own formerly: for men laugh at the follies of themselves past, when

26

they come suddenly to remembrance, except they bring with them any present dishonor." . . .

If Mr. Hobbes's notion be just, then, first, there can be no laughter on any occasion where we make no comparison of ourselves to others, or of our present state to a worse state, or where we do not observe some superiority to ourselves above some other thing: and again, it must follow, that every sudden appearance of superiority over another must excite laughter, when we attend to it. If both these conclusions be false, the notion from whence they are drawn must be so too.

First then, that laughter often arises without any imagined superiority of ourselves, may appear from one great fund of pleasantry, the parody, and burlesque allusion, which move laughter in those who may have the highest veneration for the writing alluded to, and also admire the wit of the person who makes the allusion. Thus many a profound admirer of the machinery in Homer and Virgil has laughed heartily at the interposition of Pallas, in *Hudibras*, to save the bold Talgol from the knight's pistol, presented to the outside of his skull:

> But Pallas came in shape of rust,
> And 'twixt the spring and hammer thrust
> Her Gorgon shield, which made the cock
> Stand stiff, as 'twere transform'd to stock.

And few, who read this, imagine themselves superior either to Homer or Butler; we indeed generally imagine ourselves superior in sense to the valorous knight, but not in this point, of firing pistols. And pray, would any mortal have laughed, had the poet told, in a simple unadorned manner, that his knight attempted to shoot Talgol, but his pistol was so rusty that it would not give fire? And yet this would have given us the same ground of sudden glory from our superiority over the doughty knight.

Again, to what do we compare ourselves, or imagine ourselves superior, when we laugh at this fantastical imitation of the poetical imagery, and similitudes of the morning?

> The sun, long since, had in the lap
> Of Thetis taken out his nap;
> And like a lobster boil'd, the morn
> From black to red began to turn.

Many an orthodox Scotch Presbyterian, which sect few accuse of disregard for the holy scriptures, has been put to it to preserve his gravity, upon hearing the application of Scripture made by his countryman Dr. Pitcairn, as he observed a crowd in the streets about a mason, who had fallen along with his scaffold, and was overwhelmed with the ruins of the chimney which he had been building, and which fell immediately after the fall of the poor mason: "Blessed are the dead which die in the Lord, for they rest from their labors, and their works follow them." And yet few imagine themselves superior either to the apostle or the doctor. Their superiority to the poor mason, I am sure, could never have raised such laughter, for this occurred to them before the doctor's consolation. In this case no opinion of superiority could have occasioned the laughter, unless we say that people imagined themselves superior to the doctor in religion: but an imagined superiority to a doctor in religion is not a matter so rare as to raise sudden joy; and with people who value religion, the impiety of another is no matter of laughter.

It is said that when men of wit make us laugh, it is by representing some oddness or infirmity in themselves, or others. Thus allusions made on trifling occasions, to the most solemn figured speeches of great writers, contain such an obvious impropiety, that we imagine ourselves incapable of such mistakes as the alluder seemingly falls into; so that in this case too there is an imagined superiority. But in answer to this, we may observe, that we often laugh at such allusions, when we are conscious that the person who raises the laugh knows abundantly the justest propriety of speaking, and knows, at present, the oddness and impropriety of his own allusion as well as any in company; nay, laughs at it himself. We often admire his wit in such allusions, and study to imitate him in it, as far as we can. Now, what sudden sense of glory, or joy in our superiority, can arise from observing a quality in another, which we study to imitate, I cannot imagine. I doubt if men compared themselves with the alluder, whom they study to imitate, they would rather often grow grave or sorrowful.

Nay, farther, this is so far from truth, that imagined superiority moves our laughter, that one would imagine from some instances the very contrary: for if laughter arose from our imagined superiority, then, the more that any object appeared inferior to us, the greater would be the jest; and the nearer anyone came to an equality with us, or resemblance of our actions, the less we should be moved with laughter. But we see, on the contrary, that some ingenuity in dogs and monkeys, which comes near to some of our own arts, very often makes us merry; whereas their duller actions, in which they are much below us, are no matter of jest at all. Whence the author in the *Spectator* drew his observation, that the actions of beasts, which move our laughter, bear a resemblance to a human blunder, I confess I cannot guess; I fear the very contrary is true, that their imitation of our grave, wise actions would be fittest to raise mirth in the observer.

The second part of the argument, that opinion of superiority suddenly incited in us does not move to laughter, seems the most obvious thing imaginable. If we observe an object in pain while we are at ease, we are in greater danger of weeping than laughing; and yet here is occasion for Hobbes's sudden joy. It must be a very merry state in which a fine gentleman is, when well dressed, in his coach, he passes our streets, where he will see so many ragged beggars, and porters, and chairmen sweating at their labor, on every side of him. It is a great pity that we had not an infirmary or lazar-house to retire to in cloudy weather, to get an afternoon of laughter at these inferior objects: Strange! — that none of our Hobbists banish all canary birds and squirrels, and lap-dogs, and pugs, and cats out of their houses, and substitute in their place asses, and owls, and snails, and oysters, to be merry upon. From these they might have higher joys of superiority, than from those with whom we now please ourselves. Pride, or an high opinion of ourselves, must be entirely inconsistent with gravity; emptiness must always make men solemn in their behavior; and conscious virtue and great abilities must always be upon the sneer. An orthodox believer, who is very sure that he is in the true way to salvation, must always be merry upon heretics, to whom he is so much superior in his own opinion; and no other passion but mirth should arise upon hearing of their heterodoxy. In general, all men of true sense, and reflection, and integrity, of great capacity for business, and penetration into the tempers and interests of men, must be the merriest little grigs imaginable; Democritus must be the sole leader of all the philosophers; and perpetual laughter must succeed into the place of the long beard,

> . . . To be the grace
> Both of our wisdom and our face.

It is pretty strange that the authors whom we mentioned above have never distinguished between the words laughter and ridicule: this last is but one particular species of the former, when we are laughing at the follies of others; and in this species there may be some pretence to allege that some imagined superiority may occasion it. But then there are innumerable instances of laughter where no person is ridiculed; nor does he who laughs compare himself to anything whatsoever. Thus how often do we laugh at some out-of-the-way description of natural objects, to which we never compare our state at all. . . .

And then farther, even in ridicule itself there must be something else than bare opinion to raise it, as may appear from this, that if anyone would relate in the simplest manner these very weaknesses of others, their extravagant passions, their absurd opinions, upon which the man of wit would rally, should we hear the best vouchers of all the facts alleged, we shall not be disposed to laughter by bare narration. Or should one do a real important injury to another, by taking advantage of his weakness, or by some pernicious fraud let us see another's simplicity, this is no matter of laughter: and yet these important cheats do really discover our superiority over the person cheated, more than the trifling impostures of our humorists. The opinion of our superiority may raise a sedate joy in our minds, very different from laughter; but such a thought seldom arises in our minds in the hurry of a cheerful conversation among friends, where there is often an high mutual esteem. But we go to our closets often to spin out some fine conjectures about the principles of our actions, which no mortal is conscious of in himself during the action; thus the same authors above-mentioned tell us that the desire which we have to see tragical representations is because of the secret pleasure we find in thinking ourselves secure from such evils; we know from what sect this notion was derived.

> Because to see what ills you are free from yourself is pleasant.
> — Lucretius

This pleasure must indeed be a secret one, so very secret, that many a kind compassionate heart was never conscious of it, but felt itself in a continual state of horror and sorrow; our desiring such sights flows from a kind instinct of nature, a secret bond between us and our fellow creatures.

It is by nature's law that we weep at the funeral of a full-grown
maiden or when the earth closes over an infant. . . . For what decent person thinks that any human ills are not his concern?

—Juvenal

II

If a painter chose to join a human head to a horse's neck, and to
spread feathers of many colors over limbs brought together from
everywhere, so that what was at the top a beautiful woman ended
below as an ugly black fish, would you, my friend, allowed to see
such a picture, be able to hold back your laughter?

— Horace

In my former letter, I attempted to show that Mr. Hobbes's account of laughter was not just. I shall now endeavor to discover some
other ground of that sensation, action, passion, or affection, I know
not which of them a philosopher would call it.

The ingenious Mr. Addison, in his treatise of the pleasures of
the imagination, has justly observed many sublimer sensations than
those commonly mentioned among philosophers: he observes, particularly, that we receive sensations of pleasure from those objects
which are great, new, or beautiful; and, on the contrary, that objects which are more narrow and confined, or deformed and irregular, give us disagreeable ideas. It is unquestionable that we have
a great number of perceptions which can scarcely reduce to any of
the five senses, as they are commonly explained; such as either the
ideas of grandeur, dignity, decency, beauty, harmony; or, on the
other hand, of meanness, baseness, indecency, deformity; and that
we apply these ideas not only to material objects, but to characters,
abilities, actions.

It may be farther observed, that by some strange associations of
ideas made in our infancy, we have frequently some of these ideas
recurring along with a great many objects, with which they have no
other connection than what custom and education, or frequent allusions, give them, or at most, some very distant resemblance. The
very affections of our minds are ascribed to inanimate objects; and
some animals, perfect enough in their own kind, are made constant
emblems of some vices or meanness: whereas other kinds are made
emblems of the contrary qualities. For instances of these associations, partly from nature, partly from custom, we may take the

following ones: sanctity in our churches, magnificence in public buildings, affection between the oak and ivy, the elm and vine; hospitality in a shade, a pleasant sensation of grandeur in the sky, the sea, and mountains, distinct from a bare apprehension or image of their extension; solemnity and horror in shady woods. An ass is the common emblem of stupidity and sloth, a swine of selfish luxury; an eagle of great genius; a lion of intrepidity; an ant or bee of low industry, and prudent economy. Some inanimate objects have in like manner some accessary ideas of meanness, either for some natural reason, or oftener by mere chance and custom.

Now, the same ingenious author observes, in the *Spectator*, Vol. I, No. 62, that what we call a great genius, such as becomes a heroic poet, gives us pleasure by filling the mind with great conceptions; and therefore they bring most of their similitudes and metaphors from objects of dignity and grandeur, where the resemblance is generally very obvious. This is not usually called wit, but something nobler. What we call grave wit consists in bringing such resembling ideas together, as one could scarce have imagined had so exact a relation to each other; or when the resemblance is carried on through many more particulars than we could have at first expected: and this therefore gives the pleasure of surprise. In this serious wit, though we are not solicitous about the grandeur of the images, we must still beware of bringing in ideas of baseness or deformity, unless we are studying to represent an object as base and deformed. Now this sort of wit is seldom apt to move laughter, more than heroic poetry.

That then which seems generally the cause of laughter is the bringing together of images which have contrary additional ideas, as well as some resemblance in the principal idea: this contrast between ideas of grandeur, dignity, sanctity, perfection, and ideas of meanness, baseness, profanity, seems to be the very spirit of burlesque; and the greatest part of our raillery and jest is founded upon it.

We also find ouselves moved to laughter by an overstraining of wit, by bringing resemblances from subjects of a quite different kind from the subject to which they are compared. When we see, instead of the easiness, and natural resemblance, which constitutes true wit, a forced straining of a likeness, our laughter is apt to arise; as also, when the only resemblance is not in the idea, but in the sound of the words. And this is the matter of laughter in the pun. . . .

Again, any little accident to which we have joined the idea of meanness, befalling a person of great gravity, ability, dignity, is a matter of laughter, for the very same reason; thus the strange contortions of the body in a fall, the dirtying of a decent dress, the natural functions which we study to conceal from sight, are matters of laughter when they occur to observation in persons of whom we have high ideas. Nay, the very human form has the ideas of dignity so generally joined with it, that even in ordinary persons such mean accidents are matter of jest; but still the jest is increased by the dignity, gravity, or modesty of the person, which shows that it is this contrast, or opposition of ideas of dignity and meanness, which is the occasion of laughter.

We generally imagine in mankind some degree of wisdom above other animals, and have high ideas of them on this account. If then along with our notion of wisdom in our fellows, there occurs any instance of gross inadvertence, or great mistake, this is a great cause of laughter. Our countrymen are very subject to little trips of this kind, and furnish often some diversion to their neighbors, not only by mistakes in their speech, but in actions. Yet even this kind of laughter cannot well be said to arise from our sense of superiority. This alone may give a sedate joy, but not be a matter of laughter, since we shall find the same kind of laughter arising in us, where this opinion of superiority does not attend it: for if the most ingenious person in the world, whom the whole company esteems, should through inadvertent hearing, or any other mistake, answer quite from the purpose, the whole audience may laugh heartily, without the least abatement of their good opinion. Thus we know some very ingenious men have not in the least suffered in their characters by an extemporary pun, which raises the laugh very readily; whereas a premeditated pun, which diminishes our opinion of a writer, will seldom raise any laughter.

Again, the more violent passions, as fear, anger, sorrow, compassion, are generally looked upon as something great and solemn; the beholding of these passions in another strikes a man with gravity. Now if these passions are artfully, or accidentally, raised upon a small or fictitious occasion, they move the laughter of those who imagine the occasions to be small and contemptible, or who are conscious of the fraud: this is the occasion of the laugh in biting, as they call such deceptions.

According to this scheme, there must necessarily arise a great diversity in men's sentiments of the ridiculous in actions or characters, according as their ideas of dignity and wisdom are various. A truly wise man, who places the dignity of human nature in good affections and suitable actions, may be apt to laugh at those who employ their most solemn and strong affections about what, to the wise man, appears perhaps very useless or mean. The same solemnity of behavior and keenness of passion, about a place or ceremony, which ordinary people only employ about the absolute necessaries of life, may make them laugh at their betters. When a gentleman of pleasure, who thinks that good fellowship and gallantry are the only valuable enjoyments of life, observes men, and with great solemnity and earnestness, heaping up money, without using it, or incumbering themselves with purchases and mortgages, which the gay gentleman, with his paternal revenues, thinks very silly affairs, he may make himself very merry upon them: and the frugal man, in his turn, makes the same jest of the man of pleasure. The successful gamester, whom no disaster forces to lay aside the trifling ideas of an amusement in his play, may laugh to see the serious looks and passions of the gravest business arising in the loser, amidst the ideas of a recreation. There is indeed in these last cases an opinion of superiority in the laughter; but this is not the proper occasion of his laughter; otherwise I see not how we should ever meet with a composed countenance anywhere. Men have their different relishes of life, most people prefer their own taste to that of others; but this moves no laughter, unless, in representing the pursuits of others, they do join together some whimsical image of the opposite ideas.

In the more polite nations, there are certain modes of dress, behavior, ceremony, generally received by all the better sort, as they are commonly called: to these modes, ideas of decency, grandeur, and dignity are generally joined. Hence men are fond of imitating the mode; and if in any polite assembly, a contrary dress, behavior, or ceremony appear, to which we have joined in our country the contrary ideas of meanness, rusticity, sullenness, a laugh does ordinarily arise, or a disposition to it, in those who have not the thorough good breeding, or reflection, to restrain themselves, or break through these customary associations.

And hence we may see, that what is counted ridiculous in one age or nation, may not be so in another. We are apt to laugh at Homer, when he compares Ajax unwillingly retreating to an ass driven out of a cornfield; or when he compares him to a boar; or

Ulysses tossing all night without sleep through anxiety to a pudding frying on the coals. Those three similes have got low mean ideas joined to them with us, which it is very probable they had not in Greece in Homer's days; nay, as to one of them, the boar, it is well known that in some countries of Europe, where they have wild boars for hunting, even in our times, they have not these low sordid ideas joined to that animal, which we have in these kingdoms, who never see them but in their dirty styes, or on dunghills. This may teach us how impermanent a great many jests are, which are made upon the style of some other ancient writings, in ages when manners were very different from ours, though perhaps fully as rational, and every way as human and just.

III

Joking often cuts through great obstacles better and more forceful-
ly than being serious would.

— Horace

To treat this subject of laughter gravely may subject the author to a censure like to that which Longinus makes upon a prior treatise of the Sublime, because wrote in a manner very unsuitable to the subject. But yet it may be worth our pains to consider the effects of laughter, and the ends for which it was implanted in our nature, that thence we may know the proper use of it: which may be done in the following observations.

First, we may observe, that laughter, like many other disposi-tions of our mind, is necessarily pleasant to us, when it begins in the natural manner, from one perception in the mind of something ludicrous, and does not take its rise unnaturally from external mo-tions in the body. Everyone is conscious that a state of laughter is an easy and agreeable state, that the recurring or suggestion of ludicrous images tends to dispel fretfulness, anxiety, or sorrow, and to reduce the mind to an easy, happy state; as on the other hand, an easy and happy state is that in which we are most lively and acute in perceiving the ludicrous in objects. Anything that gives us pleasure puts us also in a fitness for laughter, when something ridiculous oc-curs; and ridiculous objects, occurring to a soured temper, will be apt to recover it to easiness. The implanting then a sense of the ridiculous, in our nature, was giving us an avenue to pleasure, and an easy remedy for discontent and sorrow.

Again, laughter, like other associations, is very contagious: our whole frame is so sociable, that one merry countenance may diffuse cheerfulness to many; nor are they all fools who are apt to laugh before they know the jest, however curiosity in wise men may restrain it, that their attention may be kept awake.

We are disposed by laughter to a good opinion of the person who raises it, if neither ourselves nor our friends are made the butt. Laughter is none of the smallest bonds to common friendships, though it be of less consequence in great heroic friendships.

If an object, action or event, be truly great in every respect, it will have no natural relation or resemblance to anything mean or base; and consequently no mean idea can be joined to it with any natural resemblance. If we make some forced remote jests upon such subjects, they can never be pleasing to a man of sense and reflection, but raise contempt of the ridiculer, as void of just sense of those things which are truly great. As to any great and truly sublime sentiments, we may perhaps find that, by a playing upon words, they may be applied to a trifling or mean action, or object; but this application will not diminish our high idea of the great sentiment. . . .

Let any of our wits try their mettle in ridiculing the opinion of a good and wise mind governing the whole universe; let them try to ridicule integrity and honesty, gratitude, generosity, or the love of one's country, accompanied with wisdom. All their art will never diminish the admiration which we must have for such dispositions, wherever we observe them pure and unmixed with any low views, or any folly in the exercise of them.

When in any object there is a mixture of what is truly great, along with something weak or mean, ridicule may, with a weak mind which cannot separate the great from the mean, bring the whole into disesteem, or make the whole appear weak or contemptible: but with a person of just discernment and reflection it will have no other effect but to separate what is great from what is not so.

When any object either good or evil is aggravated and increased by the violence of our passions, or an enthusiastic admiration, or fear, the application of ridicule is the readiest way to bring down our high imaginations to a conformity to the real moment or importance of the affair. Ridicule gives our minds as it were a bend to the contrary side; so that upon reflection they may be more capable of settling in a just conformity to nature.

Laughter is received in a different manner by the person ridiculed, according as he who uses the ridicule evidences good-nature, friendship, and esteem of the person whom he laughs at, or the contrary.

The enormous crime or grievous calamity of another is not itself a subject which can be naturally turned into ridicule: the former raises horror in us, and hatred, and the latter pity. When laughter arises on such occasions, it is not excited by the guilt or the misery. To observe the contortions of the human body in the air, upon the blowing up of an enemy's ship, may raise laughter in those who do not reflect on the agony and distress of the sufferers; but the reflecting on this distress could never move laughter of itself. So some fantastic circumstances accompanying a crime may raise laughter; but a piece of cruel barbarity, or treacherous villany, of itself, must raise very contrary passions. A jest is not ordinary in an impeachment of a criminal, or an investive oration: it rather diminishes than increases the abhorrence in the audience, and may justly raise contempt of the orator for an unnatural affectation of wit. Jesting is still more unnatural in discourses designed to move compassion toward the distressed. A forced unnatural ridicule, on either of these occasions, must be apt to raise, in the guilty or the miserable, hatred against the laughter; since it must be supposed to show from hatred in him toward the object of his ridicule, or from want of all compassion. The guilty will take laughter to be a triumph over him as contemptible; the miserable will interpret it as hardness of heart, and insensibility of the calamities of another. This is the natural effect of joining to either of these objects mean ludicrous ideas.

If smaller faults, such as are not inconsistent with a character in the main amiable, be set in a ridiculous light, the guilty are apt to be made sensible of their folly, more than by a bare grave admonition. In many of our faults, occasioned by too great violence of some passion, we get such enthusiastic apprehensions of some objects, as lead us to justify our conduct: the joining of opposite ideas or images allays this enthusiasm; and, if this be done with good nature, it may be the least offensive, and most effectual, reproof.

Ridicule upon the smallest faults, when it does not appear to flow from kindness, is apt to be extremely provoking, since the applying of mean ideas to our conduct discovers contempt of us in the ridiculer, and that he designs to make us contemptible to others.

Ridicule applied to those qualities or circumstances in one of our companions, which neither he nor the ridiculer thinks dishonorable, is agreeable to everyone; the butt himself is as well pleased as any in company.

Ridicule upon any small misfortune or injury, which we have received with sorrow or keen resentment, when it is applied by a third person, with appearance of good-nature, is exceeding useful to abate our concern or resentment, and to reconcile us to the person who injured us, if he does not persist in his injury.

From this consideration of the effects of laughter it may be easy to see for what cause, or end, a sense of the ridiculous was implanted in human nature, and how it ought to be managed.

It is plainly of considerable moment in human society. It is often a great occasion of pleasure, and enlivens our conversation exceedingly, when it is conducted by good-nature. It spreads a pleasantry of temper over multitudes at once; and one merry easy mind may by this means diffuse a like disposition over all who are in company. There is nothing of which we are more communicative than of a good jest: and many a man, who is incapable of obliging us otherwise, can oblige us by his mirth, and really insinuate himself into our kind affections, and good wishes.

But this is not all the use of laughter. It is well-known that our passions of every kind lead us into wild enthusiastic apprehensions of their several objects. When any object seems great in comparison of ourselves, our minds are apt to run into a perfect veneration: when an object appears formidable, a weak mind will run into a panic, an unreasonable, impotent horror. Now in both these cases, by our sense of the ridiculous, we are made capable of relief from any pleasant, ingenious well-wisher, by more effectual means, than the most solemn, sedate reasoning. Nothing is so properly applied to the false grandeur, either of good or evil, as ridicule: nothing will sooner prevent our excessive admiration of mixed grandeur, or hinder our being led by that, which is, perhaps, really great in such an object, to imitate also and approve what is really mean.

I question not but the jest of Elijah upon the false deity, whom his countrymen had set up, had been very effectual to rectify their notions of the divine nature, as we find that like jests have been very seasonable in other nations. Baal, no doubt, had been represented as a great personage of unconquerable power; but how ridiculous does the image appear, when the prophet sets before them, at once, the poor ideas which must arise from such limitation of nature as could be represented by their statues, and the high ideas of omniscience, and omnipotence, with which the people declared themselves possessed by their invocation: "Cry aloud, either he is talking, or pursuing, or he is on a journey, or he is asleep."

This engine of ridicule, no doubt, may be abused, and have a bad effect upon a weak mind; but with men of any reflection, there is little fear that it will ever be very pernicious. An attempt of ridicule before such men, upon a subject every way great, is sure to return upon the author of it. . . .

The only danger is in objects of a mixed nature before people of little judgment, who, by jests upon the weak side, are sometimes led into neglect, or contempt, if that which is truly valuable in any character, institution, or office. And this may show us the impertinence, and pernicious tendency of general undistinguished jests upon any character, or office, which has been too much overrated. But, that ridicule may be abused, does not prove it useless, or unnecessary, more than a like possibility of abuse would prove all our senses and passions impertinent or hurtful. Ridicule, like other edged tools, may do good in a wise man's hands, though fools may cut their fingers with it, or be injurious to an unwary bystander.

The rules to avoid abuse of this kind of ridicule are, first, either never to attempt ridicule upon what is every way great, whether it be any great being, character, or sentiments; or, if our wit must sometimes run into allusions, on low occasions, to the expressions of great sentiments, let it not be in weak company, who have not a just discernment of true grandeur. And, secondly, concerning objects of a mixed nature, partly great, and partly mean, let us never turn the meanness into ridicule without acknowledging what is truly great, and paying a just veneration to it. In this sort of jesting we ought to be cautious of our company.

> For that which we deride teaches us more quickly and delightfully than what we approve and revere does.
> —Horace

Another valuable purpose of ridicule is with relation to smaller vices, which are often more effectually corrected by ridicule, than by grave admonition. Men have been laughed out of faults which a sermon could not reform; nay, there are many little indecencies which are improper to be mentioned in such solemn discourses. Now ridicule, with contempt or ill-nature, is indeed always irritating and offensive; but we may, by testifying a just esteem for the good qualities of the person ridiculed, and our concern for his interests, let him see that our ridicule of his weakness flows from love to him, and then we may hope for a good effect. This then is another necessary rule, that along with our ridicule of smaller faults we should always join evidences of good-nature and esteem.

As to jests upon imperfections, which one cannot amend, I cannot see of what use they can be: men of sense cannot relish such jests; foolish trifling minds may by them be led to despise the truest merit, which is not exempted from the casual misfortunes of our moral state. If these imperfections occur along with a vicious character, against which people should be alarmed and cautioned, it is below a wise man to raise aversions to bad men from their necessary infirmities, when they have a juster handle from their vicious dispositions.

7   David Hartley (1705–1757)

Although Hartley's observations on laughter and humor do not constitute a new theory, they are interesting for the way they bring together elements of the three traditional theories, and for their sketchy speculations regarding the physiology, sociology, and ethics of humor. A Hobbesian theorist would like Hartley's observation that we often laugh at the mistakes of children and what we take to be the mistakes of rustics and foreigners. Those who hold an Incongruity Theory would find Hartley talking their language when he discusses surprise, inconsistencies, and improprieties as causes of laughter. And those who hold a Relief Theory could point to Hartley as a precursor when he notes that laughter sometimes results from the sudden dissipation of fear or other negative emotions. Perhaps the most interesting idea that Hartley develops, in the next-to-last paragraph, is that there is an element of irrationality to humor and that people who are always looking for the humorous aspects of their experience thereby disqualify themselves from the search for truth.

"Of Wit and Humor," from Observations on Man, *5th edition (London, 1810), Part I, ch. 4, §1.*

I come now to examine the pleasures of mirth, wit, and humor.

But, first, it will be necessary to consider the causes of laughter, and particularly the mental ones.

Now it may be observed that young children do not laugh aloud for some months. The first occasion of doing this seems to be surprise, which brings on a momentary fear first, and then a momentary joy in consequence of the removal of that fear, agreeably to what may be observed of the pleasures that follow the removal of pain. This may appear probable, inasmuch as laughter is a nascent cry, stopped of a sudden; also because if the same surprise which makes young children laugh be a very little increased, they will cry. It is usual, by way of diverting young children, and exciting them to laughter, to repeat the surprise, as by clapping hands frequently, reiterating a sudden motion, etc.

This is the origin of laughter in children, in general; but the progress in each particular is much accelerated, and the occasions multiplied, by imitation. They learn to laugh, as they learn to talk and walk, and are most apt to laugh profusely, when they see others laugh; the common cause contributing also in a great degree to produce this effect. The same thing is evident even in adults, and shows us one of the sources of the sympathetic affections.

To these things it is to be added, that the alternate motions of the chest follow the same degrees of mental emotion with more and more facility perpetually, so that at last children (who are likewise more exquisitely sensible and irritable than adults) laugh upon every trifling occasion.

By degrees they learn the power of suspending the actions both of laughing and crying, and associate this power with a variety of ideas, such as those of decency, respect, fear, and shame: the incidents and objects which before occasioned emotion sufficient to produce laughter, now occasion little or none, from the transmutation of their associations: their new associated pleasures and pains are of a more sedate kind, and do not affect them so much by surprise; and, which is a principal cause in respect of individuals, their equals laugh less, and, by forming them to the same model with themselves, make the disposition to laughter decrease still faster. For whatever can be shown to take place at all in human nature, must take place in a much higher degree than according to the original causes, from our great disposition to imitate one another, which has already been explained.

It confirms this account of laughter that it follows tickling, as noted above, i.e., a momentary pain and apprehension of pain, with an immediately succeeding removal of these, and their alternate recurrency; also that the softer sex, and all nervous persons, are much disposed to laugh and cry profusely, and to pass quickly from one state to the other. And it may deserve to be inquired, how far the profuse, continued laughter and mirth on one hand, sorrow, hanging the lip, and crying, on the other, which occur in madness, agree with it.

As children learn the use of language, they learn to laugh at sentences or stories, by which sudden alarming emotions and expectations are raised in them, and again dissipated instantaneously. And as they learned before by degree to laugh at sudden unexpected noises, or motions, where there was no fear, or no distinguishable one, so it is after some time in respect of words. Children, and young persons, are diverted by every little jingle, pun, contrast, or coincidence, which is level to their capacities, even though the harshness and inconsistency with which it first strikes the fancy, be so minute as scarce to be perceived. And this is the origin of that laughter which is excited by wit, humor, buffoonery, etc.

But this species of laughter abates also by degrees, as the other before considered did, and, in general, for the same causes; so that adults, and especially those that are judges of politeness and propriety, laugh only at such strokes of wit and humor, as surprise by some more than ordinary degree of contrast or coincidence; and have at the same time a due connection with pleasure and pain, and their several associations of fitness, decency, inconsistency, absurdity, honor, shame, virtue, and vice; so as neither to be too glaring on the one hand, nor too faint on the other. In the first case, the representation raises dislike and abhorrence; in the last, it becomes insipid.

From hence may be seen, that in different persons the occasions of laughter must be as different as their opinions and dispositions; that low similitudes, allusions, contrasts, and coincidences, applied to grave and serious subjects, must occasion the most profuse laughter in persons of light minds; and, conversely, increase this levity of mind, and weaken the regard due to things sacred; that the vices of gluttony, lewdness, vain glory, self conceit, and covetousness, with the concomitant pleasures and pains, hopes, fears, dangers, etc. when represented by indirect circumstances, and the representation heightened by contrasts and coincidences, must be the most frequent subject of mirth, wit, and humor, in this mixed degenerate state, where they are censured upon the whole; and yet not looked upon with a due degree of severity, distance, and abhorrence; that company, feasting, and wine, by putting the body into a pleasurable state, must dispose to laughter upon small occasions; and that persons who give themselves much to mirth, wit, and humor, must thereby greatly disqualify their understandings for the search after truth; inasmuch as by the perpetual hunting after apparent and partial agreements and disagreements, as in words, and indirect accidental circumstances, while the true natures of the things themselves afford real agreements and disagreements, that are very different, or quite opposite, a man must by degrees pervert all his notions of things themselves, and become unable to see them as they really are, and as they appear to considerate sober-minded inquirers. He must lose all his associations of the visible ideas of things, their names, symbols, etc., with their useful practical relations and properties; and get, in their stead, accidental, indirect, and unnatural conjunctions of circumstances, that are really foreign to each other, or oppositions of those that are united; and after some time, habit and custom will fix these upon him.

The most natural occasions of mirth and laughter in adults seem to be the little mistakes and follies of children, and the smaller inconsistencies and improprieties which happen in conversation, and the daily occurrences of life; inasmuch as these pleasures are, in great measure, occasioned, or at least supported, by the general pleasureable state which our love and affection to our friends in general, and to children in particular, put the body and mind into. For this kind of mirth is always checked where we have a dislike; also where the mistake or inconsistency rises beyond a certain limit; for then it produces concern, confusion, and uneasiness. And it is useful not only in respect of the good effects which it has upon the body, and the present amusement and relaxation that it affords to the mind; but also because it puts us upon rectifying what is so amiss, or any other similar error, in one another, or in children; and has a tendency to remove many prejudices from custom and education. Thus we often laugh at children, rustics, and foreigners, when yet they act right, according to the truly natural, simple, and uncorrupted dictates of reason and propriety, and are guilty of no other inconsistency than what arises from the usurpations of custom over nature; and we often take notice of this, and correct ourselves, in consequence of being diverted by it.

8   Immanuel Kant (1724–1804)

In his work on aesthetics in *the Critique of Judgment*, Kant proposes a theory of jokes which can be taken for a general theory of humor. It is a kind of Incongruity Theory, though he emphasizes the physical side of amusement rather than the mental. The pleasure we take in humor, according to Kant, is not as high a pleasure as our delight in beauty or—a still higher satisfaction—our delight in moral goodness. Indeed, even though amusement is caused by the play of ideas, it is a kind of sensory gratification based on feelings of well-being, especially feelings of health. In listening to a joke, Kant says, we develop a certain expectation as to how it will turn out. Then, at the punch line, our expectation vanishes. This sudden mental movement is not enjoyed by our reason, for our desire to understand is frustrated. But accompanying our mental gymnastics at the punch line is the animation of our intestines and internal organs, and this bodily motion produces a feeling of health. The incongruity we experience in humor "gives a wholesome shock to the body."

Critique of Judgment, *translated by J.H. Bernard (London: Macmillan, 1892), Part I, Div. 1, 54*

As we have often shown, there is an essential difference between *what satisfies simply in the act of judging it*, and that which *gratifies* (pleases in sensation). We cannot ascribe the latter [kind of satisfaction] to every one, as we can the former. Gratification (the causes of which may even be situated in ideas) appears always to consist in a feeling of the furtherance of the whole life of the man, and consequently, also of his bodily well-being, i.e., his health; so that Epicurus, who gave out that all gratification was at bottom bodily sensation, may, perhaps, not have been wrong, but only misunderstood himself when he reckoned intellectual and even practical satisfaction under gratification. If we have this distinction in view we can explain how a gratification may dissatisfy the man who sensibly feels it (e.g., the joy of a needy but well-meaning man at becoming the heir of an affectionate but penurious father); or how a deep grief may satisfy the person experiencing it (the sorrow of a widow at the death of her excellent husband); or how a gratification can in addition satisfy (as in the sciences that we pursue); or how a grief (e.g., hatred, envy, revenge) can moreover dissatisfy. The satisfaction or dissatisfaction here depends on reason, and is the same as approbation or disapprobation; but gratification and grief can only rest on the feeling or prospect of a possible (on whatever grounds) well-being or its opposite.

All changing free play of sensations (that have no design at their basis) gratifies, because it furthers the feeling of health. In the judgment of reason we may or may not have any satisfaction in its object or even in this gratification; and this latter may rise to the height of an affection, although we take no interest in the object, at least none that is proportionate to the degree of the gratification. We may subdivide this free play of sensations into the play of fortune [games of chance], the play of tone [music], and the play of thought [wit]. The first requires an interest, whether of vanity or of selfishness; which, however is not nearly so great as the interest that attaches to the way in which we are striving to procure it. The second requires merely the change of sensations, all of which have a relation to affection, though they have not the degree of affection, and excite aesthetical ideas. The third springs merely from the change of representations in the judgment; by it, indeed, no thought that brings an interest with it is produced, but yet the mind is animated thereby.

How much gratification games must afford, without any necessity of placing at their basis an interested design, all our evening parties show; for hardly any of them can be carried on without a game. But the affections of hope, fear, joy, wrath, scorn, are put in play by them, alternating every moment; and they are so vivid that by them, as by a kind of internal motion, all the vital processes of the body seem to be promoted, as is shown by the mental vivacity excited by them, although nothing is gained or learnt thereby. But as the beautiful does not enter into games of chance, we will here set it aside. On the other hand, music and that which excites laughter are two different kinds of play with aesthetical ideas, or of representations of the understanding through which ultimately nothing is thought, which can give lively gratification merely by their changes. Thus we recognize pretty clearly that the animation in both cases is merely bodily, although it is excited by ideas of the mind; and that the feeling of health produced by a motion of the intestines corresponding to the play in question makes up that whole gratification of a gay party, which is regarded as so refined and so spiritual. It is not the judging the harmony in tones or sallies of wit — which serves only in combination with their beauty as a necessary vehicle — but the furtherance of the vital bodily processes, the affection that moves the intestines and the diaphragm, in a word, the feeling of health (which without such inducements one does not feel) that makes up the gratification felt by us; so that we can thus reach the body through the soul and use the latter as the physician of the former.

In music this play proceeds from bodily sensations to aesthetical ideas (the objects of our affections), and then from these back again to the body with redoubled force. In the case of jokes (the art of which, just like music, should rather be reckoned as pleasant than beautiful) the play begins with the thoughts which together occupy the body, so far as they admit of sensible expression; and as the understanding stops suddenly short at this presentment, in which it does not find what it expected, we feel the effect of this slackening in the body by the oscillation of the organs, which promotes the restoration of equilibrium and has a favorable influence upon health.

In everything that is to excite a lively convulsive laugh there must be something absurd (in which the understanding, therefore, can find no satisfaction). *Laughter is an affection arising from the sudden transformation of a strained expectation into nothing.* This transformation, which is certainly not enjoyable to the understanding, yet indirectly gives it very active enjoyment for a moment. Therefore its cause must consist in the influence of the representation upon the body, and the reflex effect of this upon the mind; not, indeed, through the representation being objectively an object of gratification (for how could a delusive expectation gratify?), but simply through it as a mere play of representations bringing about an equilibrium of the vital powers in the body.

Suppose this story to be told: an Indian at the table of an Englishman in Surat, when he saw a bottle of ale opened and all the beer turned into froth and overflowing, testified his great astonishment with many exclamations. When the Englishman asked him, "What is there in this to astonish you so much?" he answered, "I am not at all astonished that it should flow out, but I do wonder how you ever got it in." At this story we laugh, and it gives us hearty pleasure; not because we deem ourselves cleverer than this ignorant man, or because of anything in it that we note as satisfactory to the understanding, but because our expectation was strained [for a time] and then was suddenly dissipated into nothing. Again: The heir of a rich relative wished to arrange for an imposing funeral, but he lamented that he could not properly succeed; "for" (said he) "the more money I give my mourners to look sad, the more cheerful they look!" When we hear this story we laugh loud, and the reason is that an expectation is suddenly transformed into nothing. We must note well that it does not transform itself into the positive opposite of an expected object — for then there would still be something, which might even be a cause of grief — but it must be transformed into nothing. For if a man arouses great expectations in us when telling a story, and at the end we see its falsehood immediately, it displeases us; e.g., the story of the people whose hair in consequence of great grief turned gray in one night. But if a wag, to repair the effect of this story, describes very circumstantially the grief of the merchant returning from India to Europe with all his wealth in merchandise who was forced to throw it overboard in a heavy storm and who grieved thereat so much that his *wig* turned gray the same night — we laugh and it gives us gratification. For we treat our own mistake in the case of an object otherwise indifferent to us, or rather the idea which we are following out, as we treat a ball which we knock to and fro for a time, though our only serious intention is to seize it and hold it fast. It is not the mere dismissal of a liar or a simpleton that arouses our gratification; for the latter story told with assumed seriousness would set a whole company in a roar of laughter, while the former would ordinarily not be regarded as worth attending to.

It is remarkable that in all such cases the jest must contain something that is capable of deceiving for a moment. Hence, when the illusion is dissipated, the mind turns back to try it once again, and thus through a rapidly alternating tension and relaxation it is jerked back and put into a state of oscillation. This, because the strain on the cord as it were is suddenly (and not gradually) relaxed, must occasion a mental movement, and an inner bodily movement harmonizing therewith, which continues involuntarily and fatigues, even while cheering us (the effects of a motion conducive to health).

For if we admit that with all our thoughts is harmonically combined a movement in the organs of the body, we will easily comprehend how to this sudden transposition of the mind, now to one now to another standpoint in order to contemplate its object, may correspond an alternating tension and relaxation of the elastic portions of our intestines which communicates itself to the diaphragm (like that which ticklish people feel). In connection with this the lungs expel the air at rapidly succeeding intervals, and thus bring about a movement beneficial to health; which alone, and not what precedes it in the mind, is the proper cause of the gratification in a thought that at bottom represents nothing.

Voltaire said that heaven had given us two things to counterbalance the many miseries of life, *hope* and *sleep*. He could have added *laughter*, if the means of exciting it in reasonable men were only as easily attainable, and the requisite wit or originality of humor were not so rare, as the talent is common of imagining things which break one's head, as mystic dreamers do, or which break one's neck, as your genius does, or which break one's heart, as sentimental romance-writers (and even moralists of the same kind) do.

We may therefore, as it seems to me, readily concede to Epicurus that all gratification, even that which is occasioned through concepts, excited by aesthetical ideas, is animal, i.e., bodily sensation; without the least prejudice to the spiritual feeling or respect for moral ideas, which is not gratification at all but an esteem for self (for humanity in us), that raises us above the need of gratification, and even without the slightest prejudice to the less noble [satisfactions] of taste.

We find a combination of these two last in *naiveté*, which is the breaking out of the sincerity originally natural to humanity in opposition to that art of dissimulation which has become a second nature. We laugh at the simplicity that does not understand how to dissemble; and yet we are delighted with the simplicity of the nature which thwarts that art. We look for the commonplace manner of artificial utterance devised with foresight to make a fair show; and behold! it is the unspoiled innocent nature which we do not expect to find, and which he who displays it did not think of disclosing. That the fair but false show which generally has so much influence upon our judgment is here suddenly transformed into nothing, so that as it were, the rogue in us is laid bare, produces a movement of the mind in two opposite directions, which gives a wholesome shock to the body. But the fact that something infinitely better than all assumed manner, viz. purity of disposition (or at least the tendency thereto), is not quite extinguished yet in human nature, blends seriousness and high esteem with this play of the judgment. But because it is only a transitory phenomenon and the veil of dissimulation is soon drawn over it again, there is mingled therewith a compassion which is an emotion of tenderness; this, as play, readily admits of combination with a good-hearted laugh, and ordinarily is actually so combined, and withal is wont to compensate him who supplies the material therefor for the embarrassment which results from not yet being wise after the manner of men.

An art that is to be *naive* is thus a contradiction; but the representation of naiveté in a fictitious personage is quite possible, and is a beautiful though a rare art. Naiveté must not be confounded with open-hearted simplicity, which does not artifically spoil nature solely because it does not understand the art of social intercourse.

The *humorous* manner again may be classified as that which, as exhilarating us, is near akin to the gratification that proceeds from laughter; and belongs to the originality of spirit, but not to the talent of beautiful art. *Humor* in the good sense means the talent of being able voluntarily to put oneself into a certain mental disposition, in which everything is judged quite differently from the ordinary method (reversed, in fact), and yet in accordance with certain rational principles in such a frame of mind. He who is involuntrily subject to such mutations is called *a man of humors* [launisch]; but he who can assume them voluntarily and purposively (on behalf of a lively presentment brought about by the aid of a contrast that excites a laugh)—he and his exposition are called *humorous* [launigt]. This manner, however, belongs rather to pleasant than to beautiful art, because the object of the latter must always show proper worth in itself, and hence requires a certain seriousness in the presentation, as taste does in the act of judging.

9   Arthur Schopenhauer (1788-1860)

Like Kant, Schopenhauer has an Incongruity Theory of humor. But while Kant located the essence of humor in the evaporation of an expectation, Schopenhauer sees it in a mismatch between our sensory knowledge of things and our abstract knowledge of those same things. What we perceive through our senses, Schopenhauer says, are individual things with many characteristics. But when we organize our sense perceptions under abstract concepts, we focus on only a few characteristics of any individual thing, thus allowing ourselves to lump very different things under the same concept, and to refer to very different things by the same word. Humor arises when we are struck by some clash between a concept and a perception that are supposed to be of the same thing. Schopenhauer's discussion of humor shows a negative attitude toward abstract rational knowledge, at least to its use when uncorrected by experience in the world. He treats folly, of which pedantry is a special form, as a person's preoccupation with concepts to the neglect of perceptions, which concepts can never fully replace.

The World as Will and Idea, *translated by R.B. Haldane and John Kemp, 6th edition (London: Routledge and Kegan Paul, 1907-1909)*

Book I, §13

All these discussions of the advantages and disadvantages of the application of reason are intended to show, that although abstract rational knowledge is the reflex of ideas of perception, and is founded on them, it is by no means in such entire congruity with them that it could everywhere take their place: indeed it never corresponds to them quite accurately. And thus, as we have seen, many human actions can only be performed by the help of reason and deliberation, and yet there are some which are better performed without its assistance. This very incongruity of sensuous and abstract knowledge, on account of which the latter always merely approximates to the former, as mosaic approximates to painting, is the cause of a very remarkable phenomenon which, like reason itself, is peculiar to human nature, and of which the explanations that have ever anew been attempted, are insufficient: I mean *laughter*. On account of the source of this phenomenon, we cannot avoid giving the explanation of it here, though it again interrupts the course of our work to do so. The cause of laughter in every case is simply the sudden perception of the incongruity between a concept and the real objects which have been thought through it in some relation, and laughter itself is just the expression of this incongruity. It often occurs in this way: two or more real objects are thought through *one* concept, and the identity of the concept is transferred to the objects; it then becomes strikingly apparent from the entire difference of the objects in other respects, that the concept was only applicable to them from a one-sided point of view. It occurs just as often, however, that the incongruity between a single real object and the concept under which, from one point of view, it has rightly been subsumed, is suddenly felt. Now the more correct the subsumption of such objects under a concept may be from one point of view, and the greater and more glaring their incongruity with it, from another point of view, the greater is the ludicrous effect which is produced by this contrast. All laughter then is occasioned by a paradox, and therefore by unexpected subsumption, whether this is expressed in words or in actions. This, briefly stated, is the true explanation of the ludicrous.

I shall not pause here to relate anecdotes as examples to illustrate my theory; for it is so simple and comprehensible that it does not require them, and everything ludicrous which the reader may remember is equally valuable as a proof of it. But the theory is confirmed and illustrated by distinguishing two species into which the ludicrous is divided, and which result from the theory. Either, we have previously known two or more very different real objects, ideas of sense perception, and have intentionally identified them through the unity of a concept which comprehends them both; this species of the ludicrous is called *wit*. Or, conversely, the concept is first present in knowledge, and we pass from it to reality, and to operation upon it, to action: objects which in other respects are fundamentally different, but which are all thought in that one concept, are now regarded and treated in the same way, till, to the surprise and astonishment of the person acting, the great difference of their other aspects appears: this species of the ludicrous is called *folly*. Therefore everything ludicrous is either a flash of wit or a foolish action, according as the procedure has been from the discrepancy of the objects to the identity of the concept, or the converse; the former always intentional, the latter always unintentional, and from without. To seem to reverse the starting point, and to conceal wit with the mask of folly, is the art of the jester and the clown. Being quite aware of the diversity of the objects, the jester unites them, with secret wit, under one concept, and then starting from this concept he receives from the subsequently discovered diversity of the objects the surprise which he himself prepared. It follows from this short but sufficient theory of the ludicrous, that, if we set aside the last case, that of the jester, wit must always show itself in words, folly generally in actions, though also in words, when it only expresses an intention and does not actually carry it out, or when it shows itself merely in judgments and opinions.

Pedantry is a form of folly. It arises in this way: a man lacks confidence in his own understanding, and, therefore, does not wish to trust to it, to recognize what is right directly in the particular case. He, therefore, puts it entirely under the control of the reason, and seeks to be guided by reason in everything; that is to say, he tries always to proceed from general concepts, rules, and maxims, and to confine himself strictly to them in life, in art, and even in moral conduct. Hence that clinging to the form, to the manner, to the exprecion and word which is characteristic of pedantry, and which with it takes the place of the real nature of the matter. The incongruity then between the concept and reality soon shows itself here, and it becomes evident that the former never condescends to the particular case, and that with its generality and rigid definiteness it can never accurately apply to the fine distinctions of difference and innumerable modifications of the actual. Therefore, the pedant, with his general maxims, almost always misses the mark in life, shows himself to be foolish, awkward, useless. In art, in which the concept is unfruitful, he produces lifeless, stiff abortive mannerisms. Even with regard to ethics, the purpose to act rightly or nobly cannot always be carried out in accordance with abstract maxims; for in many cases the excessively nice distinctions in the nature of the circumstances necessitate a choice of the right proceeding directly from the character; for the application of mere abstract maxims sometimes gives false results, because the maxims only half apply; and sometimes cannot be carried out, because they are foreign to the individual character of the actor, and this never allows itself to be entirely discovered; therefore, inconsistencies arise. Since then

Kant makes it a condition of the moral worth of an action, that it shall proceed from pure rational abstract maxims, without any inclination or momentary emotion, we cannot entirely absolve him from the reproach of encouraging moral pedantry. This reproach is the significance of Schiller's epigram, entitled "Scruples of Conscience." When we speak, especially in connection with politics, of doctrinaires, theorists, savants, and so forth, we mean pedants, that is, persons who know the things well in the abstract, but not in the concrete. Abstraction consists in thinking away the less general predicates; but it is precisely upon these that so much depends in practice.

To complete our theory it remains for us to mention a spurious kind of wit, the play upon words, the *calembourg*, the pun, to which may be added the equivocation, the *double entendre*, the chief use of which is the expression of what is obscene. Just as the witticism brings two very different real objects under one concept, the pun brings two different concepts, by the assistance of accident, under one word. The same contrast appears, only familiar and more superficial, because it does not spring from the nature of things, but merely from the accident of nomenclature. In the case of the witticism the identity is in the concept, the difference in the reality, but in the case of the pun the difference is in the concepts and the identity in the reality, for the terminology is here the reality. It would only be a somewhat far-fetched comparison if we were to say that the pun is related to the witticism as the parabola (*sic*) of the upper inverted cone to that of the lower. The misunderstanding of the word or the *quid pro quo* is the unintentional pun, and is related to it exactly as folly is to wit. Thus the deaf man often affords occasion for laughter, just as much as the fool, and inferior writers of comedy often use the former for the latter to raise a laugh.

Supplement to Book I: Chapter 8, "On the Theory of the Ludicrous"

According to my explanation given in the first volume, the source of the ludicrous is always the paradoxical, and therefore unexpected, subsumption of an object under a conception which in other respects is different from it, and accordingly the phenomenon of laughter always signifies the sudden apprehension of an incongruity between such a conception and the real object thought under it, thus between the abstract and the concrete object of perception. The greater and more unexpected, in the apprehension of the laugher, this incongruity is, the more violent will be his laughter. Therefore in everything that excites laughter it must always be possible to show a conception and a particular, that is, a thing or event, which certainly can be subsumed under that conception, and therefore thought through it, yet in another and more predominating aspect does not belong to it at all, but is strikingly different from everything else that is thought through that conception. If, as often occurs, especially in witticisms, instead of such a real object of perception, the conception of a subordinate species is brought under the higher conception of the genus, it will yet excite laughter only through the fact that the imagination realizes it, i.e., makes a perceptible representative stand for it, and thus the conflict between what is thought and what is perceived takes place. Indeed if we wish to understand this perfectly explicitly, it is possible to trace everything ludicrous to a syllogism in the first figure, with an undisputed major and an unexpected minor, which to a certain extent is only sophistically valid, in consequence of which connection the conclusion partakes of the quality of the ludicrous.

In the first volume I regarded it as superfluous to illustrate this theory by examples, for every one can do this for himself by a little reflection upon cases of the ludicrous which he remembers. Yet, in order to come to the assistance of the mental inertness of those readers who prefer always to remain in a passive condition, I will accommodate myself to them. Indeed in this third edition I wish to multiply and accumulate examples, so that it may be indisputable that here, after so many fruitless earlier attempts, the true theory of the ludicrous is given, and the problem which was proposed and also given up by Cicero is definitely solved.

If we consider that an angle requires two lines meeting so that if they are produced they will intersect each other; on the other hand, that the tangent of a circle only touches it at one point, but at this point is really parallel to it; and accordingly have present to our minds the abstract conviction of the impossibility of an angle between the circumference of a circle and its tangent; and if now such an angle lies visibly before us upon paper, this will easily excite a smile. The ludicrousness in this case is exceedingly weak; but yet the source of it in the incongruity of what is thought and perceived appears in it with exceptional distinctness. When we discover such an incongruity, the occasion for laughter that thereby arises is, according as we pass from the real, i.e., the perceptible, to the conception, or conversely from the conception to the real, either a witticism or an absurdity, which in a higher degree, and especially in the practical sphere, is folly, as was explained in the text. Now to consider examples of the first case, thus of wit, we shall first of all take the familiar anecdote of the Gascon at whom the king laughed when he saw him in light summer clothing in the depth of winter, and who thereupon said to the king: "If your Majesty had put on what I have, you would find it very warm," and on being asked what he had put on, replied: "My whole wardrobe!" Under this last conception we have to think both the unlimited wardrobe of a king and the single summer coat of a poor devil, the sight of which upon his freezing body shows its great incongruity with the conception. The audience in a theatre in Paris once called for the "Marseillaise" to be played, and as this was not done, began shrieking and howling, so that at last a commissary of police in uniform came upon the stage and explained that it was not allowed that anything should be given in the theatre except what was in the playbill. Upon this a voice cried: "And you, sir, are you also on the playbill?"—a hit which was received with universal laughter. For here the subsumption of what is heterogeneous is at once distinct and unforced. The epigramme:

> Bav is the true shepherd of whom the Bible spake:
> Though his flock be all asleep, he alone remains awake

subsumes, under the conception of a sleeping flock and a waking shepherd, the tedious preacher who still bellows on unheard when he has sent all the people to sleep. Analogous to this is the epitaph on a doctor: "Here lies he like a hero, and those he has slain lie around him; it subsumes under the conception, honorable to the hero, of "lying surrounded by dead bodies," the doctor, who is supposed to preserve life. Very commonly the witticism consists in a single expression, through which only the conception is given, under which the case presented can be subsumed, though it is very different from everything else that is thought under it. So is it in "Romeo" when the vivacious Mercutio answers his friends who promise to visit him on the morrow: "Ask for me tomorrow, and you shall find me a grave man." Under this conception a dead man is here subsumed; but in English there is also a play upon the words, for "a grave man" means both a serious man and a man of the grave. Of this kind is also the well-known anecdote of the actor Unzelmann. In the Berlin theatre he was strictly forbidden to improvise. Soon afterwards he had to appear on the stage on horseback, and just as he came on the stage the horse dunged, at which the audience began to laugh, but laughed much more when Unzelmann said to the horse: "What are you doing? Don't you know we are forbidden to improvise?" Here the subsumption of the heterogeneous under the more general concept is very distinct, but the witticism is exceedingly happy, and the ludicrous effect produced by it excessively strong. . . .

Further, the ultimate subsumption, ludicrous to all, of what in one respect is heterogeneous, under a conception which in other respects agrees with it, may take place contrary to our intention. For example, one of the free negroes in North America, who take pains to imitate the whites in everything, quite recently placed an epitaph over his dead child which begins, "Lovely, early broken lily." If, on the contrary, something real and perceptible is, with direct intention, brought under the conception of its opposite, the result is plain, common irony. For example, if when it is raining hard we say, "Nice weather we are having today"; or if we say of an ugly bride, "That man has found a charming treasure"; or of a knave, "This honest man," and so on. Only children and quite uneducated people will laugh at such things; for here the incongruity between what is thought and what is perceived is total. Yet just in this direct exaggeration in the production of the ludicrous its fundamental character, incongruity, appears very distinctly. This species of the ludicrous is, on account of its exaggeration and distinct intention, in some respects related to *parody*. The procedure of the latter consists in this. It substitutes for the incidents and words of a serious poem of drama insignificant low persons or trifling motives and actions. It thus subsumes the commonplace realities which it sets forth under the lofty conceptions given in the theme, under which in a certain respect they must come, while in other respects they are very incongruous; and thereby the contrast between what is perceived and what is thought appears very glaring. There is no lack of familiar examples of this, and therefore I shall only give one, from the "Zobeide" of Carlo Gozzi, act iv., scene 3, where the famous stanza of Ariosto (*Orl. Fur., i. 22*), "*Oh gran bontà de' cavalieri antichi,*" etc., is put word for word into the mouth of two clowns who have just been thrashing each other, and tired with this, lie quietly side by side. This is also the nature of the application so popular in Germany of serious verses, especially of Schiller, to trivial events, which clearly contains a subsumption of heterogeneous things under the general conception which the verse expresses. . . .

In all the examples of wit given here we find that under a conception, or in general an abstract thought, a real thing is, directly, or by means of a narrower conception, subsumed, which indeed, strictly speaking, comes under it, and yet is as different as possible from the proper and original intention and tendency of the thought. Accordingly wit, as a mental capacity, consists entirely in a facility for finding for every object that appears a conception under which it certainly can be thought, though it is very different from all the other objects which come under this conception.

The second species of the ludicrous follows, as we have mentioned, the opposite path from the abstract conception to the real or perceptible things thought through it. But this now brings to light any incongruity with the conception which was overlooked, and hence arises an absurdity, and therefore in the practical sphere a foolish action. Since the play requires action, this species of the ludicrous is essential to comedy. Upon this depends the observation of Voltaire: "I believe I have noticed in the theatre that there is almost never a general outburst of laughter except on the occasion of a misapprehension (Preface to *L'Enfant Prodigue*). The following may serve as examples of this species of the ludicrous. When some one had declared that he was fond of walking alone, an Austrian said to him: "You like walking alone; so do I: therefore we can go together." He starts from the conception, "A pleasure which two love they can enjoy in common," and subsumes under it the very case which excludes community. Further, the servant who rubbed a worn sealskin in his master's box with Macassar oil, so that it might become covered with hair again; in doing which he started from the conception, "Macassar oil makes hair grow." The soldiers in the guard-room who allowed a prisoner who was brought in to join in their game of cards, then quarrelled with him for cheating, and turned him out. They let themselves be led by the general conception, "Bad companions are turned out," and forget that he is also a prisoner, i.e., one whom they ought to hold fast. Two young peasants had loaded their gun with coarse shot, which they wished to extract, in order to substitute fine, without losing the powder. So one of them put the mouth of the barrel in his hat, which he took between his legs, and said to the other: "Now you pull the trigger slowly, slowly, slowly; then the shot will come first." He starts from the conception, "Prolonging the cause prolongs the effect." Most of the actions of Don Quixote are also cases in point, for he subsumes the realities he encounters under conceptions drawn from the romances of chivalry, from which they are very different. For example, in order to support the oppressed he frees the galley slaves. Properly all Münchhausenisms are also of this nature, only they are not actions which are performed, but impossibilities, which are passed off upon the hearer as having really happened. In them the fact is always so conceived that when it is thought merely in the abstract, and therefore comparatively *a priori*, it appears possible and plausible; but afterwards, if we come down to the perception of the particular case, thus *a posteriori* the impossibility of the thing, indeed the absurdity of the assumption, is brought into prominence, and excites laughter through the evident incongruity of what is perceived and what is thought. For example, when the melodies frozen up in the posthorn are thawed in the warm room — when Münchhausen, sitting upon a tree during a hard frost, draws up his knife which has dropped to the ground by the frozen jet of his own water, etc. Such is also the story of the two lions who broke down the partition between them during the night and devoured each other in their rage, so that in the morning there was nothing to be found but the two tails.

There are also cases of the ludicrous where the conception under which the perceptible facts are brought does not require to be expressed or signified, but comes into consciousness itself through the association of ideas. The laughter into which Garrick burst in the middle of playing tragedy because of a butcher in the front of the pit, who had taken off his wig to wipe the sweat from his head, placed the wig for a while upon his large dog, who stood facing the stage with his fore paws resting on the pit railings, was occasioned by the fact that Garrick started from the conception of a spectator, which was added in his own mind. This is the reason why certain animal forms, such as apes, kangaroos, jumping hares, etc., sometimes appear to us ludicrous because something about them resembling man leads us to subsume them under the conception of the human form, and starting from this we perceive their incongruity with it.

Now the conceptions whose observed incongruity with the perceptions moves us to laughter are either those of others or our own. In the first case we laugh at others, in the second we feel a surprise, often agreeable, at the least amusing. Therefore children and uneducated people laugh at the most trifling things, even at misfortunes, if they were unexpected, and thus convicted their preconceived conception of error. As a rule laughing is a pleasant condition; accordingly the apprehension of the incongruity between what is thought and what is perceived, that is, the real, gives us pleasure, and we give ourselves up gladly to the spasmodic convulsions which this apprehension excites. The reason of this is as follows. In every suddenly appearing conflict between what is perceived and what is thought, what is perceived is always unquestionably right; for it is not subject to error at all, requires no confirmation from without, but answers for itself. Its conflict with what is thought springs ultimately from the fact that the latter, with its abstract conceptions, cannot get down to the infinite multifariousness and fine shades of difference of the concrete. This victory of knowledge of perception over thought affords us pleasure. For perception is the original kind of knowledge inseparable from animal nature, in which everything that gives direct satisfaction to the will presents itself. It is the medium of the present, of enjoyment and gaiety; moreover it is attended with no exertion. With thinking the opposite is the case; it is the second power of knowledge, the exercise of which always demands some, and often considerable, exertion. Besides, it is the conceptions of thought that often oppose the gratification of our immediate desires, for, as the medium of the past, the future, and of seriousness, they are the vehicle of our fears, our repentance, and all our cares. It must therefore be diverting to us to see this strict, untiring, troublesome governess, the reason, for once convicted of insufficiency. On this account then the mien or appearance of laughter is very closely related to that of joy.

On account of the want of reason, thus of general conceptions, the brute is incapable of laughter, as of speech. This is therefore a prerogative and characteristic mark of man. Yet it may be remarked in passing that his one friend the dog has an analogous characteristic action peculiar to him alone in distinction from all

other brutes, the very expressive, kindly, and thoroughly honest
fawning and wagging of its tail. But how favorably does this saluta-
tion given him by nature compare with the bows and simpering
civilities of man. At least for the present, it is a thousand times more
reliable than their assurance of inward friendship and devotion.

The opposite of laughing and joking is *seriousness*. Accordingly
it consists in the consciousness of the perfect agreement and congruity of the conception, or thought, with what is perceived, or the reality. The serious man is convinced that he thinks the things as they
are, and that they are as he thinks them. This is just why the transition from profound seriousness to laughter is so easy, and can be effected by trifles. For the more perfect that agreement assumed by
seriousness may seem to be, the more easily is it destroyed by the
unexpected discovery of even a slight incongruity. Therefore the
more a man is capable of entire seriousness, the more heartily can he
laugh. Men whose laughter is always affected and forced are in-
tellectually and morally of little worth; and in general the way of
laughing, and, on the other hand, the occasions of it, are very
characteristic of the person. That the relations of the sexes afford
the easiest materials for jokes always ready to hand and within the
reach of the weakest wit, as is proved by the abundance of obscene
jests, could not be if it were not that the deepest seriousness lies at
their foundation.

That the laughter of others at what we do or say seriously of-
fends us so keenly depends on the fact that it asserts that there is a
great incongruity between our conceptions and the objective
realities. For the same reason, the predicate "ludicrous" or absurd"
is insulting. The laugh of scorn announces with triumph to the baffled adversary how incongruous were the conceptions he cherished
with the reality which is now revealing itself to him. Our own bitter
laughter at the fearful disclosure of the truth through which our
firmly cherished expectations are proved to be delusive is the active
expression of the discovery now made of the incongruity between the
thoughts which, in our foolish confidence in man or fate, we entertained, and the truth which is now unveiled.

The *intentionally* ludicrous is the *joke*. It is the effort to bring
about a discrepancy between the conceptions of another and the
reality by disarranging one of the two; while its opposite,
seriousness, consists in the exact conformity of the two to each other,
which is at least aimed at. But if now the joke is concealed behind

seriousness, then we have *irony*. For example, if with apparent seriousness we acquiesce in the opinions of another which are the opposite of our own, and pretend to share them with him, till at last the result perplexes him both as to us and them. This is the attitude of Socrates as opposed to Hippias, Protagoras, Gorgias, and other sophists, and indeed often to his collocutors in general. The converse of irony is accordingly seriousness concealed behind a joke, and this is *humor*. It might be called the double counterpoint of irony. Explanations such as "Humor is the interpenetration of the finite and the infinite" express nothing more than the entire incapacity for thought of those who are satisfied with such empty phrases. Irony is objective, that is, intended for another; but humor is subjective, that is, it primarily exists only for one's own self. Accordingly we find the masterpieces of irony among the ancients, but those of humor among the moderns. For, more closely considered, humor depends upon a subjective, yet serious and sublime mood, which is involuntarily in conflict with a common external world very different from itself, which it cannot escape from and to which it will not give itself up; therefore, as an accommodation, it tries to think its own point of view and that external world through the same conceptions, and thus a double incongruity arises, sometimes on the one side, sometimes on the other, between these concepts and the realities thought through them. Hence the impression of the intentionally ludicrous, thus of the joke, is produced, behind which, however, the deepest seriousness is concealed and shines through. Irony begins with a serious air and ends with a smile; with humor the order is reversed. The words of Mercutio quoted above may serve as an example of humor. Also in "Hamlet"—*Polonius:* "My honorable lord, I will most humbly take my leave of you." *Hamlet:* You cannot, sir, take from me anything that I will more willingly part withal, except my life, except my life, except my life." Again, before the introduction of the play at court, Hamlet says to Ophelia: "What should a man do but be merry? for, look you, how cheerfuly my mother looks, and my father died within these two hours. *Ophelia:* Nay, 'tis twice two months, my lord. *Hamlet:* So long? Nay, then let the devil wear black, for I'll have a suit of sables." Again, in Jean Paul's "Titan," when Schoppe, melancholy and now brooding over himself, frequently looking at his hands, says to himself, "There sits a lord in bodily reality, and I in him; but who is such?" Heinrich Heine appears as a true humorist in his

"*Romancero.*" Behind all his jokes and drollery we discern a profound seriousness, which is ashamed to appear unveiled. Accordingly humor depends upon a special kind of mood or temper (German, *Laune*, probably from *Luna*) through which conception in all its modifications, a decided predominance of the subjective over the objective in the apprehension of the external world, is thought. Moreover, every poetical or artistic presentation of a comical, or indeed even a farcical scene, through which a serious thought yet glimmers as its concealed background, is a production of humor, thus is humorous. Such, for example, is a colored drawing of Tishbein's which represents an empty room, lighted only by the blazing fire in the grate. Before the fire stands a man with his coat off, in such a position that his shadow, going out from his feet, stretches across the whole room. Tishbein comments thus on the drawing: "This is a man who has succeeded in nothing in the world, and who has made nothing of it; now he rejoices that he can throw such a large shadow." Now, if I had to express the seriousness that lies concealed behind this jest, I could best do so by means of the following verse taken from the Persian poem of Anwari Soheili:

> If thou hast lost possession of a world,
> Be not distressed, for it is nought;
> Or hast thou gained possession of a world,
> Be not o'erjoyed, for it is nought.
> Our pains, our gains, all pass away;
> Get thee beyond the world, for it is nought.

That at the present day the word humorous is generally used in German literature in the sense of comical arises from the miserable desire to give things a more distinguished name than belongs to them, the name of a class that stands above them. Thus every inn must be called a hotel, every money-changer a banker, every concert a musical academy, the merchant's counting-house a bureau, the potter an artist in clay, and therefore also every clown a humorist. The word *humor* is borrowed from the English to denote a quite peculiar species of the ludicrous, which indeed, as was said above, is related to the sublime, and which was first remarked by them. But it is not intended to be used as the title for all kinds of jokes and buffoonery, as is now universally the case in Germany, without opposition from men of letters and scholars; for the true conception of that modification, that tendency of the mind, that child of the sublime and the ridiculous, would be too subtle and too high for their public, to please which they take pains to make everything flat and vulgar. Well, "high words and a low meaning" is in general the motto of the noble present, and accordingly nowadays he is called a humorist who was formerly called a buffoon.

10 William Hazlitt (1778–1830)

Although he was best known as an essayist and critic, Hazlitt began his career as a philosopher and showed considerable philosophical competence in all his writings. In the following lecture, published in the same year as the first edition of Schopenhauer's *World as Will and Idea*, Hazlitt develops a theory of humor which goes significantly beyond the Incongruity Theories of Kant and Schopenhauer. Like them, he sees intellectual processes at work in the creation and appreciation of humor. He also sees the relation between our response to incongruity in amusement and our response to it in emotions like fear and sadness. Hazlitt offers other interesting observations on the nature of wit, on the idea that ridicule is a test of truth, and on the ethics of humor.

From Lectures on the English Comic Writers *(London: George Bell, 1885)*

Lecture I — Introductory.

On Wit and Humor

Man is the only animal that laughs and weeps; for he is the only animal that is struck with the difference between what things are, and what they ought to be. We weep at what thwarts or exceeds our desires in serious matters: we laugh at what only disappoints our expectations in trifles. We shed tears from sympathy with real and necessary distress; as we burst into laughter from want of sympathy with that which is unreasonable and unnecessary, the absurdity of which provokes our spleen or mirth, rather than any serious reflections on it.

To explain the nature of laughter and tears, is to account for the condition of human life; for it is in a manner compounded of these two! It is a tragedy or a comedy — sad or merry, as it happens. The crimes and misfortunes that are inseparable from it, shock and wound the mind when they once seize upon it, and when the pressure can no longer be borne, seek relief in tears: the follies and absurdities that men commit, or the odd accidents that befall them, afford us amusement from the very rejection of these false claims upon our sympathy and end in laughter. If everything that went wrong, if every vanity or weakness in another gave us a sensible pang, it would be hard indeed: but as long as the disagreeableness of the consequences of a sudden disaster is kept out of sight by the immediate oddity of the circumstances, and the absurdity or unaccountableness of a foolish action is the most striking thing in it, the ludicrous prevails over the pathetic, and we receive pleasure instead of pain from the farce of life which is played before us, and which discomposes our gravity as often as it fails to move our anger or our pity!

Tears may be considered as the natural and involuntary resource of the mind overcome by some sudden and violent emotion, before it has had time to reconcile its feelings to the change of circumstances: while laughter may be defined to be the same sort of convulsive and involuntary movement, occasioned by mere surprise or contrast (in the absence of any more serious emotion), before it has time to reconcile its belief to contradictory appearances. If we hold a mask before our face, and approach a child with this disguise on, it will at first, from the oddity and incongruity of the appearance, be inclined to laugh; if we go nearer to it, steadily, and without saying a word, it will begin to be alarmed, and be half inclined to cry: if we suddenly take off the mask, it will recover from its fears, and burst out laughing; but if, instead of presenting the old well-known countenance, we have concealed a satyr's head or some frightful caricature behind the first mask, the suddenness of the change will not in this case be a source of merriment to it, but will convert its surprise into an agony of consternation, and will make it scream out for help, even though it may be convinced that the whole is a trick at bottom.

The alternation of tears and laughter, in this little episode in common life, depends almost entirely on the greater or less degree of interest attached to the different changes of appearance. The mere suddenness of the transition, the mere balking our expectations, and turning them aburptly into another channel, seems to give additional liveliness and gaiety to the animal spirits: but the instant the change is not only sudden, but threatens serious consequences, or calls up the shape of danger, terror supersedes our disposition to mirth, and laughter gives place to tears. It is usual to play with infants, and make them laugh by clapping your hands suddenly before them; but if you clap your hands too loud, or too near their sight, their countenances immediately change, and they hide them in the nurse's arms. Or suppose the same child grown up a little older, comes to a place, expecting to meet a person it is particularly fond of, and does not find that person there, its countenance suddenly falls, its lips begin to quiver, its cheek turns pale, its eye glistens, and it vents its little sorrow (grown too big to be concealed) in a flood of tears. Again, if the child meets the same person unexpectedly after long absence, the same effect will be produced by an excess of joy, with different accompaniments; that is, the surprise and the emotion excited will make the blood come into his face, his eyes sparkle, his tongue falter or be mute; but in either case the tears will gush to his relief, and lighten the pressure about his heart. On the other hand, if a child is playing at hide-and-seek or blindman's-buff, with persons it is ever so fond of, and either misses them where it had made sure of finding them, or suddenly runs up against them where it had least expected it, the shock or additional impetus given to the imagination by the disappointment or the discovery, in a matter of this indifference, will only vent itself in a fit of laughter.[1] The transition here is not from one thing of importance to another, or from a state of indifference to a state of strong excitement: but merely from one impression to another that we did not at all expect, and when we have expected just the contrary. The mind having been led to form a certain conclusion, and the result producing an immediate solution of continuity in the chain of our ideas, this alternate excitement and relaxation of the imagination, the object also striking upon the mind more vividly in its loose unsettled state, and before it has had time to recover and collect itself, causes that alternate excitement and relaxation, or irregular convulsive movement of the muscular and nervous system, which constitutes physical laughter. The *discontinuous* in our sensations produces a correspondent jar and discord in the frame. The steadiness of our faith and of our features begins to give way at the same time. We turn with an incredulous smile from a story that staggers our belief: and we are ready to split our sides with laughing at an extravagance that sets all common sense and serious concern at defiance.

To understand or define the ludicrous, we must first know what the serious is. Now the serious is the habitual stress which the mind lays upon the expectation of a given order of events, following one another with a certain regularity and weight of interest attached to

them. When this stress is increased beyond its usual pitch of intensity, so as to overstrain the feelings by the violent opposition of good
to bad, or of objects to our desires, it becomes the pathetic or
tragical. The ludicrous, or comic, is the unexpected loosening or
relaxing this stress below its usual pitch of intensity, by such an
abrupt transposition of the order of our ideas, as taking the mind
unawares, throws it off its guard, startles it into a lively sense of
pleasure, and leaves no time nor inclination for painful reflections.

The essence of the laughable then is the incongruous, the
disconnecting one idea from another, or the jostling of one feeling
against another. The first and most obvious cause of laughter is to
be found in the simple succession of events, as in the sudden shifting
of a disguise, or some unlooked-for accident, without any absurdity
of character or situation. The accidental contradiction between our
expectations and the event can hardly be said, however, to amount
to the ludicrous: it is merely laughable. The ludicrous is where there
is the same contradiction between the object and our expectations,
heightened by some deformity or inconvenience, that is, by its being
contrary to what is customary or desirable; as the ridiculous, which
is the highest degree of the laughable, is that which is contrary not
only to custom but to sense and reason, or is a voluntary departure
from what we have a right to expect from those who are conscious of
absurdity and propriety in words, looks, and actions.

Of these different kinds or degrees of the laughable, the first is
the most shallow and short-lived; for the instant the immediate surprise of a thing's merely happening one way or another is over, there
is nothing to throw us back upon our former expectation, and renew
our wonder at the event a second time. The second sort, that is, the
ludicrous arising out of the improbable or distressing, is more deep
and lasting, either because the painful catastrophe excites a greater
curiosity, or because the old impression, from its habitual hold on
the imagination, still recurs mechanically, so that it is longer before
we can seriously make up our minds to the unaccountable deviation
from it. The third sort, or the ridiculous arising out of absurdity as
well as improbability, that is, where the defect or weakness is of a
man's own seeking, is the most refined of all, but not always so pleasant as the last, because the same contempt and disapprobation
which sharpens and subtilises our sense of the impropriety, adds a
severity to it inconsistent with perfect ease and enjoyment. This last
species is properly the province of satire. The principle of contrast

is, however, the same in all the stages, in the simply laughable, the ludicrous, the ridiculous; and the effect is only the more complete, the more durably and pointedly this principle operates.

To give some examples in these different kinds. We laugh, when children, at the sudden removing of a pasteboard mask; we laugh when grown up more gravely at the tearing off the mask of deceit. We laugh at absurdity; we laugh at deformity. We laugh at a bottle-nose in a caricature; at a stuffed figure of an alderman in a pantomime; and at the tale of Slaukenbergius. A giant standing by a dwarf makes a contemptible figure enough. Rosinante and Dapple are laughable from contrast, as their masters from the same principle make two for a pair. We laugh at the dress of foreigners, and they at ours. Three chimneysweepers meeting three Chinese in Lincoln's-inn Fields, they laughed at one another till they were ready to drop down. Country people laugh at a person because they never saw him before. Anyone dressed in the height of the fashion, or quite out of it, is equally an object of ridicule. One rich source of the ludicrous is distress with which we cannot sympathize from its absurdity or insignificance. Women laugh at their lovers. We laugh at a damned author, in spite of our teeth, and though he may be our friend. "There is something in the misfortunes of our best friends that pleases us." We laugh at people on the top of a stage-coach, or in it, if they seem in great extremity. It is hard to hinder children from laughing at a stammerer, at a negro, at a drunken man, or even at a madman. We laugh at mischief. We laugh at what we do not believe. We say that an argument or an assertion that is very absurd, is quite ludicrous. We laugh to show our satisfaction with ourselves, or our contempt for those about us, or to conceal our envy or our ignorance. We laugh at fools, and at those who pretend to be wise — at extreme simplicity, awkwardness, hypocrisy, and affection. "They were talking of me," says Scrub, "for they laughed *consumedly*." Lord Foppington's insensibility to ridicule, and airs of ineffable self-conceit, are no less admirable; and Joseph Surface's cant maxims of morality, when once disarmed of their power to do hurt, become sufficiently ludicrous. We laugh at that in others which is a serious matter to ourselves; because our self-love is stronger than our sympathy, sooner takes the alarm, and instantly turns our heedless mirth into gravity, which only enhances the jest to others. Some one is generally sure to be the sufferer by a joke. What is sport to one, is death to another. It is only very sensible or very honest people, who laugh as freely at their own absurdities as at those of their neighbors. In general the contrary rule holds, and we only laugh at those misfortunes in which we are spectators, not sharers. The injury, the disappointment, shame, and vexation that we feel, put a stop to our mirth; while the disasters that come home to us, and excite our repugnance and dismay, are an amusing spectacle to others. The greater resistance we make, and the greater the perplexity into which we are thrown, the more lively and *piquant* is the intellectual display of cross-purposes to the bystanders. Our humiliation is their triumph. We are occupied with the disagreeableness of the result instead of its oddity or unexpectedness. Others see only the conflict of motives and the sudden alternation of events; we feel the pain as well, which more than counterbalances the speculative entertainment we might receive from the contemplation of our abstract situation.

You cannot force people to laugh: you cannot give a reason why they should laugh: they must laugh of themselves, or not at all. As we laugh from a spontaneous impulse, we laugh the more at any restraint upon this impulse. We laugh at a thing merely because we ought not. If we think we must not laugh, this perverse impediment makes our temptation to laugh the greater; for by endeavoring to keep the obnoxious image out of sight, it comes upon us more irresistibly and repeatedly; and the inclination to indulge our mirth, the longer it is held back, collects its force, and breaks out the more violently in peals of laughter. In like manner, anything we must not think of makes us laugh, by its coming upon us by stealth and unawares, and from the very efforts we make to exclude it. A secret, a loose word, a wanton jest, make people laugh. Aretine laughed himself to death at hearing a lascivious story. Wickedness is often made a substitute for wit; and in most of our good old comedies, the intrigue of the plot and the double meaning of the dialogue go hand-in-hand, and keep up the ball with wonderful spirit between them. The consciousness, however it may arise, that there is something that we ought to look grave at, is almost always a signal for laughing outright: we can hardly keep our countenance at a sermon, a funeral, or a wedding. What an excellent old custom was that of throwing the stocking! What a deal of innocent mirth has been spoiled by the disuse of it! It is not an easy matter to preserve decorum in courts of justice. The smallest circumstance that interferes with the solemnity of the proceedings, throws the whole place into an uproar of laughter. People at the point of death often say smart things. Sir Thomas More jested with his executioner. Rabelais and Wycherley both died with a *bon-mot* in their mouths.

Misunderstandings (*malentendus*), where one person means one thing, and another is aiming at something else, are another great source of comic humor, on the same principle of ambiguity and contrast. There is a highwrought instance of this in the dialogue between Aimwell and Gibbet, in the "Beaux Stratagem," where Aimwell mistakes his companion for an officer in a marching regiment, and Gibbet takes it for granted that the gentleman is a highwayman. The alarm and consternation occasioned by someone saying to him, in the course of common conversation, "I apprehend you," is the most ludicrous thing in that admirably natural and powerful performance, Mr. Emery's "Robert Tyke." Again, unconsciousness in the person himself of what he is about, or of what others think of him, is also a great heightener of the sense of absurdity. It makes it come the fuller home upon us from his insensibility to it. His simplicity sets off the satire, and gives it a finer edge. It is a more extreme case still where the person is aware of being the object of ridicule, and yet seems perfectly reconciled to it as a matter of course. So wit is often the more forcible and pointed for being dry and serious, for it then seems as if the speaker himself had no intention in it, and we were the first to find it out. Irony, as a species of wit, owes its force to the same principle. In such cases it is the contrast between the appearance and the reality, the suspense of belief and the seeming incongruity, that gives point to the ridicule, and makes it enter the deeper when the first impression is overcome. Excessive impudence, as in the "Liar"; or excessive modesty, as in the hero of "She Stoops to Conquer"; or a mixture of the two, as in the "Busy Body," are equally amusing. Lying is a species of wit and humor. To lay anything to a person's charge from which he is perfectly free, shows spirit and invention; and the more incredible the effrontery, the greater is the joke.

There is nothing more powerfully humorous than what is called *keeping* in comic character, as we see it very finely exemplified in Sancho Panza and Don Quixote. The proverbial phlegm and the romantic gravity of these two celebrated persons may be regarded as the height of this kind of excellence. The deep feeling of character strengthens the sense of the ludicrous. Keeping in comic character is consistency in absurdity; a determined and laudable attachment to

the incongruous and singular. The regularity completes the contradiction; for the number of instances of deviation from the right
line, branching out in all directions, shows the inveteracy of the
original bias to any extravagance or folly, the natural improbability,
as it were, increasing every time with the multiplication of chances
for a return to common sense, and in the end mounting up to an incredible and unaccountably ridiculous height, when we find our expectations as invariably baffled. The most curious problem of all, is
this truth of absurdity to itself. That reason and good sense should
be consistent, is not wonderful: but that caprice, and whim, and
fantastical prejudice, should be uniform and infallible in their
results, is the surprising thing. But while this characteristic clue to
absurdity helps on the ridicule, it also softens and harmonises its ex-
cesses: and the ludicrous is here blended with a certain beauty and
decorum, from this very truth of habit and sentiment, or from the
principle of similitude in dissimilitude. The devotion to nonsense,
and enthusiasm about trifles, is highly affecting as a moral lesson: it
is one of the striking weaknesses and greatest happinesses of our
nature. That which excites so lively and lasting an interest in itself,
even though it should not be wisdom, is not despicable in the sight of
reason and humanity. We cannot suppress the smile on the lip; but
the tear should also stand ready to start from the eye. The history of
hobby-horses is equally instructive and delightful; and after the pair
I have just alluded to, My Uncle Toby's is one of the best and
gentlest that "ever lifted leg!" The inconveniences, odd accidents,
falls, and bruises, to which they expose their riders, contribute their
share to the amusement of the spectators; and the blows and wounds
that the Knight of the Sorrowful Countenance received in his many
perilous adventures, have applied their healing influence to many a
hurt mind. In what relates to the laughable, as it arises from unforeseen accidents or selfwilled scrapes, the pain, the shame, the mor-
tification, and utter helplessness of situation, add to the joke, provided they are momentary, or overwhelming only to the imagination
of the sufferer. Malvolio's punishment and apprehensions are as
comic, from our knowing that they are not real, as Christopher Sly's
drunken transformation and short-lived dream of happiness are for
the like reason. Parson Adams's fall into the tub at the 'Squire's, or
his being discovered in bed with Mrs. Slipslop, though pitiable, are
laughable accidents: nor do we read with much gravity of the loss of
his "Æschylus," serious as it was to him at the time. A Scotch

clergyman, as he was going to church, seeing a spruce conceited mechanic who was walking before him, suddenly covered all over with dirt, either by falling into the kennel, or by some other calamity befalling him, smiled and passed on: but afterwards seeing the same person, who had stopped to refit, seated directly facing him in the gallery, with a look of perfect satisfaction and composure, as if nothing of the sort had happened to him, the idea of his late disaster and present self-complacency struck him so powerfully, that unable to resist the impulse, he flung himself back in the pulpit, and laughed till he could laugh no longer. I remember reading a story in an odd number of the "European Magazine," of an old gentleman who used to walk out every afternoon, with a gold-headed cane, in the fields opposite Baltimore House, which were then open, only with footpaths crossing them. He was frequently accosted by a beggar with a wooden leg, to whom he gave money, which only made him more importunate. One day, when he was more troublesome than usual, a well-dressed person happening to come up, and observing how saucy the fellow was, said to the gentleman, "Sir, if you will lend me your cane for a moment, I'll give him a good thrashing for his impertinence." The old gentleman, smiling at the proposal handed him his cane, which the other no sooner was going to apply to the shoulders of the culprit, than he immediately whipped off his wooden leg, and scampered off with great alacrity, and his chastiser after him as hard as he could go. The faster the one ran, the faster the other followed him, brandishing the cane, to the great astonishment of the gentleman who owned it, till having fairly crossed the fields, they suddenly turned a corner, and nothing more was seen of either of them. . . .

There is another source of comic humor which has been but little touched on or attended to by the critics—not the infliction of casual pain, but the pursuit of uncertain pleasure and idle gallantry. Half the business and gaiety of comedy turns upon this. Most of the adventures, difficulties, demurs, hair-breadth 'scrapes, disguises, deceptions, blunders, disappointments, successes, excuses, all the dexterous maneuvers, artful innuendoes, assignations, billets-doux, *double entendres*, sly allusions, and elegant flattery, have an eye to this—to the obtaining of those "favors secret, sweet, and precious," in which love and pleasure consist, and which when attained, and the *equivoque* is at an end, the curtain drops, and the play is over. All the attractions of a subject that can only be glanced at indirectly, that is a sort of forbidden ground to the imagination, except under severe restrictions, which are constantly broken through; all the resources it supplies for intrigue and invention; the bashfulness of the clownish lover, his looks of alarm and petrified astonishment; the foppish affectation and easy confidence of the happy man; the dress, the airs, the languor, the scorn, and indifference of the fine lady; the bustle, pertness, loquaciousness, and tricks of the chambermaid; the impudence, lies, and roguery of the valet; the match-making and unmaking; the wisdom of the wise; the sayings of the witty, the folly of the fool; "the soldier's, scholar's, courtier's eye, tongue, sword, the glass of fashion and the mold of form," have all a view to this. . . .

Humor is the describing the ludicrous as it is in itself; wit is the exposing it, by comparing or contrasting it with something else. Humor is, as it were, the growth of nature and accident; wit is the product of art and fancy. Humor, as it is shown in books, is an imitation of the natural or acquired absurdities of mankind, or of the ludicrous in accident, situation, and character: wit is the illustrating and heightening the sense of that absurdity by some sudden and unexpected likeness or opposition of one thing to another, which sets off the quality we laugh at or despise in a still more contemptible or striking point of view. Wit, as distinguished from poetry, is the imagination or fancy inverted, and so applied to given objects, as to make the little look less, the mean more light and worthless; or to divert our admiration or wean our affections from that which is lofty and impressive, instead of producing a more intense admiration and exalted passion, as poetry does. Wit may sometimes, indeed, be shown in compliments as well as satire; as in the common epigram:

> Accept a miracle, instead of wit:
> See two dull lines with Stanhope's pencil writ.

But then the mode of paying it is playful and ironical, and contradicts itself in the very act of making its own performance humble foil to another's. Wit hovers round the borders of the light and trifling, whether in matters of pleasure or pain; for as soon as it describes the serious seriously, it ceases to be wit, and passes into a different form. Wit is, in fact, the eloquence of indifference, or an ingenious and striking exposition of those evanescent and glancing impressions of objects which affect us more from surprise or contrast to the train of our ordinary and literal preconceptions, than from anything in the objects themselves exciting our necessary sympathy or lasting hatred. The favorite employment of wit is to add littleness to littleness, and heap contempt on insignificance by all the arts of petty and incessant warfare; or if it ever affects to aggrandise, and use the language of hyperbole, it is only to betray into derision by a fatal comparison, as in the mock-heroic; or if it treats of serious passion, it must do it so as to lower the tone of intense and high-wrought sentiment, by the introduction of burlesque and familiar circumstances. . . .

Wit or ludicrous invention produces its effect oftenest by comparison, but not always. It frequently effects its purposes by unexpected and subtle distinctions. For instance, in the first kind, Mr. Sheridan's description of Mr. Addington's administration as the fag end of Mr. Pitt's, who had remained so long on the treasury bench that, like Nicias in the fable, "he left the sitting part of the man behind him," is as fine an example of metaphorical wit as any on record. The same idea seems, however, to have been included in the old well-known nickname of the *Rump* Parliament. Almost as happy an instance of the other kind of wit, which consists in sudden retorts, in turns upon an idea, and diverting the train of your adversary's argument abruptly and adroitly into another channel, may be seen in the sarcastic reply of Porson, who hearing someone observe, that "certain modern poets would be read and admired when Homer and Virgil were forgotten," made answer: "And not till then!" Sir Robert Walpole's definition of the gratitude of place-expectants, "That it is a lively sense of *future* favors," is no doubt wit, but it does not consist in the finding out any coincidence or likeness, but in suddenly transposing the order of time in the common account of this feeling, so as to make the professions of those who pretend to it correspond more with their practice. It is filling up a blank in the human heart with a word that explains its hollowness at once. Voltaire's saying, in answer to a stranger who was observing how tall his trees grew — "That they had nothing else to do" — was a quaint mixture of wit and humor, making it out as if they really led a lazy, laborious life; but there was here neither allusion or metaphor. Again, that master-stroke in Hudibras is sterling wit and profound satire, where speaking of certain religious hypocrites he says, that they

> Compound for sins they are inclin'd to,
> by damning those they have no mind to;

but the wit consists in the truth of the character, and in the happy exposure of the ludicrous contradiction between the pretext and the practice; between their lenity towards their own vices, and their severity to those of others. . . .

In a word, the shrewd separation or disentangling of ideas that seem the same, or where the secret contradiction is not sufficiently suspected, and is of a ludicrous and whimsical nature, is wit just as much as the bringing together those that appear at first sight totally different. There is then no sufficient ground for admitting Mr. Locke's celebrated definition of wit, which he makes to consist in the finding out striking and unexpected resemblances in things as so to make pleasant pictures in the fancy, while judgment and reason, according to him, lie the clean contrary way, in separating and nicely distinguishing those wherein the smallest difference is to be found.[2] . . .

And, indeed, this may be considered as the best defense of the contested maxim: That *ridicule is the test of truth*, viz., that it does not contain or attempt a formal proof of it, but owes its power of conviction to the bare suggestion of it, so that if the thing when once hinted is not clear in itself, the satire fails of its effect and falls to the ground. The sarcasm here glanced at the character of the new or old French noblesse may not be well founded; but it is so like truth, and "comes in such a questionable shape," backed with the appearance of an identical proposition, that it would require a long train of facts and labored arguments to do away with the impression, even if we were sure of the honesty and wisdom of the person who undertook to refute it. A flippant jest is as good a test of truth as a solid bribe; and there are serious sophistries,

Soul-killing lies, and truths that work small good.

as well as idle pleasantries. Of this we may be sure, that ridicule fastens on the vulnerable points of a cause and finds out the weak sides of an argument; if those who resort to it sometimes rely too much on its success, those who are chiefly annoyed by it almost always are so with reason, and cannot be too much on their guard against deserving it. Before we can laugh at a thing, its absurdity must at least be open and palpable to common apprehension. Ridicule is necessarily built on certain supposed facts, whether true or false, and on their inconsistency with certain acknowledged maxims, whether right or wrong. It is, therefore, a fair test, if not of philosophical or abstract truth, at least of what is truth according to public opinion and common sense; for it can only expose to instantaneous contempt that which is condemned by public opinion, and is hostile to the common sense of mankind. Or to put it differently, it is the test of the quantity of truth that there is in our favorite prejudices. To show how nearly allied wit is thought to be to truth, it is not unusual to say of any person: "Such a one is a man of sense, for though he said nothing, he laughed in the right place." . . .

After all, verbal and accidental strokes of wit, though the most surprising and laughable, are not the best and most lasting. That wit is the most refined and effectual which is founded on the detection of unexpected likeness or distinction in things, rather than in words. It is more severe and galling—that is, it is more unpardonable though less surprising, in proportion as the thought suggested is more complete and satisfactory from its being inherent in the nature of the things themselves. *Haeret lateri lethalis arundo.* Truth makes the greatest libel; and it is that which barbs the darts of wit. The Duke of Buckingham's saying, "Laws are not, like women, the worse for being old," is an instance of a harmless truism and the utmost malice of wit united. This is, perhaps, what has been meant by the distinction between true and false wit. Mr. Addison, indeed, goes so far as to make it the exclusive test of true wit that it will bear translation into another language—that is to say, that it does not depend at all on the form of expression. But this is by no means the case. Swift would hardly have allowed of such a straitlaced theory to make havoc with his darling conundrums, though there is no one whose serious wit is more that of things, as opposed to a mere play either of words or fancy. I ought, I believe, to have noticed before, in speaking of the difference between wit and humor, that wit is often pretended absurdity, where the person overacts or exaggerates a certain part with a conscious design to expose it as if it were another person, as when Mandrake in the "Twin Rivals" says, "This glass is too big, carry it away, I'll drink out of the bottle." On the contrary, when Sir Hugh Evans says, very innocently, "'Od's plessed will, I will not be absence at the grace," though there is here a great deal of humor, there is no wit. This kind of wit of the humorist, where the person makes a butt of himself, and exhibits his own absurdities or foibles purposely in the most pointed and glaring lights, runs through the whole of the character of Falstaff, and is, in truth, the principle on which it is founded. It is an irony directed against one's self. Wit is, in fact, a voluntary act of the mind, or exercise of the invention, showing the absurd and ludicrous consciously, whether in ourselves or another. Cross-readings, where the blunders are designed, are wit; but if any one were to light upon them through ignorance or accident, they would be merely ludicrous.

It might be made an argument of the intrinsic superiority of poetry or imagination to wit, that the former does not admit of mere verbal combinations. Whenever they do occur, they are uniformly blemishes. It requires something more solid and substantial to raise admiration or passion. The general forms and aggregate masses of our ideas must be brought more into play to give weight and magnitude. Imagination may be said to be the finding out something similar in things generally alike, or with like feelings attached to them; while wit principally aims at finding out something that seems the same, or amounts to a momentary deception where you least expected it, namely, in things totally opposite. The reason why more slight and partial, or merely accidental and nominal resemblances serve the purposes of wit, and indeed characterize its essence as a distinct operation and faculty of the mind, is, that the object of ludicrous poetry is naturally to let down and lessen; and it is easier to let down than to raise up; to weaken than to strengthen; to disconnect our sympathy from passion and power, than to attach and rivet it to any object of grandeur or interest; to startle and shock our preconceptions by incongruous and equivocal combinations, than to confirm, enforce, and expand them by powerful and lasting associations of ideas, or striking and true analogies. A slight cause is sufficient to produce a slight effect. To be indifferent or sceptical, requires no effort; to be enthusiastic and in earnest, requires a strong impulse and collective power. Wit and humor (comparatively speaking, or taking the extremes to judge of the gradations by) appeal to our indolence, our vanity, our weakness, and insensibility; serious and impassioned poetry appeals to our strength, our magnanimity, our virtue, and humanity. Anything is sufficient to heap contempt upon an object; even the bare suggestion of a mischievous allusion to what is improper dissolves the whole charm, and puts an end to our admiration of the sublime or beautiful. Reading the finest passage in Milton's "Paradise Lost" in a false tone, will make it seem insipid and absurd. The cavilling at, or invidiously pointing out, a few slips of the pen, will embitter the pleasure, or alter our opinion of a whole work, and make us throw it down in disgust. The critics are aware of this vice and infirmity in our nature, and play upon it with periodical success. The meanest weapons are strong enough for this kind of warfare, and the meanest hands can wield them. Spleen can subsist on any kind of food. The shadow of a doubt, the hint of an inconsistency, a word, a look, a syllable, will destroy our best-formed convictions. What puts this argument in as striking a point of view as anything, is the nature of parody or burlesque, the secret of which lies merely in transposing or applying at a venture to anything, or to the lowest objects, that which is applicable only to certain given things, or to the highest matters. "From the sublime to the ridiculous there is but one step." The slightest want of unity of impression destroys the sublime; the detection of the smallest incongruity is an infallible ground to rest the ludicrous upon. But in serious poetry, which aims at riveting our affections, every blow must tell home. The missing a single time is fatal, and undoes the spell. We see how dificult it is to sustain a con-tinued flight of impressive sentiment: how easy it must be then to travesty or burlesque it, to flounder into nonsense, and be witty by playing the fool. It is a common mistake, however, to suppose that parodies degrade, or imply a stigma on the subject; on the contrary, they in general imply something serious or sacred in the originals. Without this, they would be good for nothing, for the immediate contrast would be wanting, and with this they are sure to tell. The best parodies are, accordingly, the best and most striking things reversed. Witness the common travesties of Homer and Virgil. Mr. Canning's court parodies on Mr. Southey's popular odes, are also an instance in point (I do not know which were the cleverest); and the best of the "Rejected Addresses" is the parody on Crabbe, though I do not certainly think that Crabbe is the most ridiculous poet now living.

Lear and the Fool are the sublimest instance I know of passion and wit united, or of imagination unfolding the most tremendous sufferings, and of burlesque on passion playing with it, aiding and relieving its intensity by the most pointed, but familiar and indif-ferent illustrations of the same thing in different objects, and on a meaner scale. The Fool's reproaching Lear with "making his daughters his mothers," his snatches of proverbs and old ballads, "The hedge-sparrow fed the cuckoo so long, that it had its head bit off by its young," and "Whoop jug, I know when the horse follows the cart," are a running commentary of trite truisms, pointing out the extreme folly of the infatuated old monarch, and in a manner reconciling us to its inevitable consequences.

Lastly, there is a wit of sense and observation, which consists in the acute illustration of good sense and practical wisdom, by means of some far-fetched conceit or quaint imagery. The matter is sense, but the form is wit. Thus the lines in Pope:

> Tis with our judgments as our watches, none
> Go just alike; yet each believes his own—

are witty, rather than poetical; because the truth they convey is a mere dry observation on human life, without elevation or enthusiasm, and the illustration of it is of that quaint and familiar kind that is merely curious and fanciful. Cowley is an instance of the same kind in almost all his writings. Many of the jests and witticisms in the best comedies are moral aphorisms and rules for the conduct of life, sparkling with wit and fancy in the mode of expression. The ancient philosophers also abounded in the same kind of wit, in telling home truths in the most unexpected manner. In this sense Æsop was the greatest wit and moralist that ever lived. Ape and slave, he looked askance at human nature, and beheld its weaknesses and errors transferred to another species. Vice and virtue were to him as plain as any objects of sense. He saw in man a talking, absurd, obstinate, proud, angry animal; and clothed these abstractions with wings, or a beak, or tail, or claws, or long ears, as they appeared embodied in these hieroglyphics in the brute creation. His moral philosophy is natural history. He makes an ass bray wisdom, and a frog croak humanity. The store of moral truth, and the fund of invention in exhibiting it in eternal forms, palpable and intelligible, and delightful to children and grown persons, and to all ages and nations, are almost miraculous. The invention of a fable is to me the most enviable exertion of human genius: it is the discovering a truth to which there is no clue, and which, when once found out, can never be forgotten. I would rather have been the author of "Æsop's Fables," than of "Euclid's Elements!" . . .

I will only add by way of general caution, that there is nothing more ridiculous than laughter without a cause, nor anything more troublesome than what are called laughing people. A professed laugher is as contemptible and tiresome a character as a professed wit: the one is always contriving something to laugh at, the other is always laughing at nothing. An excess of levity is as impertinent as an excess of gravity. A character of this sort is well personified by Spenser, in the "Damsel of the Idle Lake":

> . . . Who did assay
> To laugh at shaking of the leaves light.

Anyone must be mainly ignorant or thoughtless, who is surprised at everything he sees; or wonderfully conceited, who expects everything to conform to his standard of propriety. Clowns and idiots laugh on all occasions; and the common failing of wishing to be thought satirical often runs through whole families in country places, to the great annoyance of their neighbors. To be struck with incongruity in whatever comes before us, does not argue great comprehension or refinement of perception, but rather a looseness and flippancy of mind and temper, which prevents the individual from connecting any two ideas steadily or consistently together. It is owing to a natural crudity and precipitateness of the imagination, which assimilates nothing properly to itself. People who are always laughing, at length laugh on the wrong side of their faces, for they cannot get others to laugh with them. In like manner, an affectation of wit by degrees hardens the heart, and spoils good company and good manners. A perpetual succession of good things puts an end to common conversation. There is no answer to a jest, but another; and even where the ball can be kept up in this way without ceasing, it tires the patience of the bystanders, and runs the speakers out of breath. Wit is the salt of conversation, not the food.

Notes

1. A child that has hid itself out of the way in sport, is under a great temptation to laugh at the unconsciousness of others as to its situation. A person concealed from assassins is in no danger of betraying his situation by laughing.

2. His words are: "If in having our ideas in the memory ready at hand consists quickness of parts, in this of having them unconfused, and being able nicely to distinguish one thing from another, where there is but the least difference, consists in a great measure the exactness of judgment and clearness of reason, which is to be observed in one man above another. And hence, perhaps, may be given some reason of that common observa-

tion, that men who have a great deal of wit and prompt memories, have not always the clearest judgment or deepest reason. For wit lying mostly in the assemblage of ideas, and putting them together with quickness and variety, wherein can be found any resemblance or congruity, thereby to make up pleasant pictures and agreeable visions in the fancy: judgment, on the contrary, lies quite on the other side, in separating carefully one from another, ideas wherein can be found the least difference, thereby to avoid being misled by similitude, and by affinity to take one thing for another." ("Essay," vol i. p. 143.) This definition, such as it is, Mr. Locke took without acknowledgment from Hobbes, who said in his "Leviathan," "This difference of quickness is caused by the difference of men's passions that love and dislike some one thing, some another, and therefore some men's thoughts run one way, some another, and are held to, and observe differently the things that pass through their imagination. And whereas in this succession of men's thoughts there is nothing to observe in the things they think on, but either in what they be like one another, or in what they be unlike, . . . those that observe their similitudes, in case they be such as are but rarely observed by others, are said to have a good wit, by which on this occasion is meant a good fancy. But they that observe their differences and dissimilitudes, which is called distinguishing and discerning, and judging between thing and thing, in case such discerning be not easy, are said to have a good judgment; and particularly in matter of conversation and business; wherein times, places, and persons are to be discerned, this virtue is called discretion. The former, that is, fancy, without the help of judgment, is not commended for a virtue; but the latter, which is judgment or discretion, is commended for itself, without the help of fancy." "Leviathan" [Ed. 1651] p. 32.

11   Søren Kierkegaard (1813-1855)

In the passages below, from his *Concluding Unscientific Postcript*, Kierkegaard presents another version of the Incongruity Theory of humor, along with several illuminating examples. He analyzes humor in terms of "the comical," and holds that the primary element in the comical is "contradiction." From Kierkegaard's examples it is clear that what he has in mind is something weaker than logical or formal contradiction: he means incongruity. Kierkegaard is interested in humor and its close relative, irony, for their relations to the "three spheres of existence," or three existential stages of life — the aesthetic sphere, the ethical sphere, and the religious sphere. He claims that irony marks the boundary between the aesthetic and ethical spheres, while humor marks the boundary between the ethical and religious spheres. "Humor is the last stage of existential awareness before faith."[1] Kierkegaard also saw a strong connection between having a religious view of life and having a sense of humor. In his *Journals and Papers* he wrote that "the humorous is present throughout Christianity," indeed, that Christianity is the most humorous view of life in world-history.[2]

Concluding Unscientific Postcript, *translated by David F. Swenson (Princeton: Princeton University Press, 1941), pp. 459-468*

The matter is quite simple. The comical is present in every stage of life (only that the relative positions are different), for wherever there is life, there is contradiction, and wherever there is contradiction, the comical is present. The tragic and the comic are the same, in so far as both are based on contradiction; but *the tragic is the suffering contradiction, the comical, the painless contradiction.*[3] That something which the comic apprehension envisages as comical may entail imaginary suffering for the comical individual, is quite irrelevant. In that case, for example, it would be incorrect to apprehend the hero of Holberg's *The Busy Man* as comical. Satire also entails pain, but this pain has a dialectic which gives it a teleology in the direction of a cure. The difference between the tragic and the comic lies in the relationship between the contradiction and the controlling idea. The comic apprehension evokes the contradiction or makes it manifest by having in mind the way out, which is why the contradiction is painless. The tragic apprehension sees the contradiction and despairs of a way out. It is a matter of course that this must be understood so that the various nuances of the comic are again kept subject to the qualitative dialectic of the different spheres, which passes judgment upon all subjective arbitrariness. Thus if one proposed to make everything comical by means of nothing, it is clear at once that his comedy is nowhere at home, since it lacks a foothold in any sphere. The discoverer of this type of comedy would himself be open to comic apprehension from the standpoint of the ethical sphere, because as an existing individual he must himself in one way or another have a foothold in existence. . . .

One finds, frequently enough, examples of a misdirected effort to emphasize the pathetic and the serious in a ridiculous, superstitious sense, as if it were a bliss-bringing panacea, as if seriousness were a good in and for itself, something to be taken without directions, so that all is well if one is merely serious at all times, even if it happens that one is never serious in the right place. No, everything has its dialectic, not indeed such a dialectic as makes it sophistically relative (this is mediation), but a dialectic by which the absolute becomes manifest as the absolute by virtue of the dialectical. It is therefore quite as dubious, precisely quite as dubious, to be pathetic and serious in the wrong place, as it is to laugh in the wrong place. One-sidedly we say that a fool laughs all the time, one-sidedly, for it is indeed true that it is folly always to laugh; but it is nevertheless one-sided to stamp only the misuse of laughter as folly, since the folly is quite as great and quite as ruinous when it expresses itself by always being equally serious in stupidity.

Notes

1. *Kierkegaard's Concluding Unscientific Postcript*, tr. by David Swenson and Walter Lowrie (Princeton: Princeton University Press, 1941), pp. 448 and 259.

2. *Søren Kierkegaard's Journals and Papers*, ed. and trans. by Howard Hong and Edna Hong (Bloomington, Ind.: Indiana University Press, 1970), Entries 1681–1682. For more on the relation of humor to the spheres of life in Kierkegaard, see C. Stephen Evans, *Kierkegaard's "Fragments" and "Postscript": The Religious Philosophy of Johannes Climacus* (Atlantic Heights, N.J.: Humanities Press, 1983), ch. 10.

3. The Aristotelian definition (Chapter 5 of the *Poetics*): "The ridiculous is a mistake or unseemliness that is not painful or destructive" is such that it fails to leave entire families of the comical secure in their ludicrousness, and it becomes doubtful whether the definition, even in relation to the part of the comical that it covers, does not bring us into collision with the ethical. His example: that we laugh at an ugly and distorted countenance when this does not entail pain for the one who has it, is neither quite correct nor so happily chosen as to clear up at a single stroke the secret of the comical. The example lacks reflection, for even if the distorted countenance does not cause pain, it is nevertheless painful to be destined thus to arouse laughter as soon as one shows one's face. It is handsome and correct of Aristotle that he wishes to separate from the sphere of the ridiculous that which tends to arouse compassion, to which also belongs the wretched and the pitiful. Even in comic poets of high rank it is possible to find examples of the use of what is not purely ludicrous, but has an admixture of the pitiful: ("Trop," for example, is in several scenes more pitiful than ludicrous. The "Busy Man," on the contrary, exemplifies the ridiculous unmixed, precisely because he is in possession of every condition necessary to live carefree and happily). In this sense the Aristotelian example lacks reflection, but the definition also lacks it, in so far as it conceives the ludicrous as a something, instead of recognizing that the comical is a relation, the faulty relationship of contradiction, but free from pain.

I shall here tumultuously throw in a few examples, to show that the comical is present wherever there is a contradiction, and wherever one is justified in ignoring the pain, because it is non-essential.

Hamlet swears by the fire-tongs; the comical lies in the contradiction between the solemnity of an oath and the attribution which annuls the oath, whatever its object. If one were to say: "I would stake my life that there is fully four shillings worth of gold in the binding of this book," it would be comical. The contradiction is that between the highest pathos (to risk one's life) and the object; it is teasingly sharpened by the word *fully*, which keeps open the prospect of perhaps four and one-half shillings worth, as if that were less contradictory. Holophernes is said to be seven and one-fourth yards tall. The contradiction lies essentially in the fraction. The seven yards are fantastic, but the fantastic is not in the habit of speaking about quarter-fractions; the quarter of a yard as a measure is reminiscent of reality. Whoever laughs at the seven yards does not laugh correctly, but he who laughs as the seven yards and a quarter, knows what he laughs at. When the clergyman gesticulates most vigorously where the category is in a lower sphere, it is comical; it is as if one were to say calmly and indifferently, "I will sacrifice my life for my country," and then add with the highest pathos, with gestures and play of countenance, "Aye, I will do it for ten dollars." But when it happens in church I must not laugh, because I am not an aesthetic spectator but a religious auditor, whatever the clergyman may be. . . .

When a child of four turns to a child of three and a half years and says patronizingly: "Come now, my little lamb," it is comical; although because neither of the children is ridiculous *per se*, one smiles rather than laughs, and the smile is not without its emotion. But the comic lies in the relativity that the youngster seeks to establish against the other; the moving feature lies in the childlike manner in which it is done.

When a man seeks permission to establish himself as innkeeper and is refused, it is not comical; but if the refusal is based on the fact that there are so few innkeepers, then it is comical, because a reason for is used as a reason against. Thus there is a story about a baker who said to a poor person: "No, mother, I cannot give you anything; there was another here recently whom I had to send away without giving anything: we cannot give to everybody." The comical lies in the circumstances that he seems to reach the sum and result—all, by subtracting.

When a woman seeks permission to establish herself as a public prostitute, this is comical. We properly feel that it is difficult to become something respectable (so that when a man is refused permission to become master of the hounds, for example, this is not comical), but to be refused permission to become something despicable, is a contradiction. To be sure, if she receives permission, it is also comical, but the contradiction is different, namely, that the legal authority shows its impotence precisely when it shows its power: its power by giving permission, its impotence by not being able to make it permissible.

Errors are comical, and are all to be explained by the contradiction involved, however complicated the combinations.

When something that is in itself comical has become customary, and so belongs to the order of the day, it does not arouse attention, and we laugh only when it is manifested in some higher degree. When we know that a man suffers from distraction, we become familiar with it and do not reflect upon the contradiction, until it reduplicates itself upon occasion, when the contradiction is, that what is intended to conceal the first distraction reveals one still greater. As when an absent-minded person puts his fingers in a bowl of salad served by the waiter, and when he discovers his distraction, in order to conceal it, says: "Ah, I thought it was caviar"; for caviar is not eaten with the fingers either.

A discontinuity in speech may produce a comic effect because there is a contradiction between the discontinuity and the rational conception of human speech as something connected. If it is a madman who speaks thus, we do not laugh.

When a farmer knocks at the door of a man who speaks only German, and talks with him to find out whether there is not someone in the house, whose name the farmer has forgotten, but who has ordered a load of peat, and the German, in impatience at being unable to understand what the farmer is talking about, says: "Das ist doch wunderlich," to the great joy of the farmer who says: "That is right, Wunderlich was the man's name"; then the contradiction is that the German and the farmer cannot talk together because the language is in the way, and in spite of this, the farmer gets his information with the aid of the language.

Through being involved in a contradiction, that which is not in itself ridiculous may produce laughter. When a man goes dressed in a strange manner for everyday use, but then once in a while appears elegantly dressed, we laugh at this, because we remember the other.

When a soldier stands in the street and gazes at the glorious display in the window of a fancy goods shop, and he comes closer to see better, when he then with glowing countenance, and eyes fixed solely on the window display, fails to discover that the cellar comes dangerously far forward, so that just as he is about to see best, he pitches into the cellar—the contradiction is in his movement, the head and the eyes directed upward, and then the subterranean movement down into the cellar. If he had not been looking upward, it would not have been so ludicrous. Therefore it is also more comical when a man who walks about gazing at the stars falls into a hole in the ground, than when it happens to one who is not so uplifted above the earthly sphere.

It is for this reason that an intoxicated man can produce so comical an impression, because he expresses a contradiction in his movements. The eye requires steadiness of gait; the more there still remains some sort of reason to require it, the more comical is the contradiction (a completely intoxicated man is therefore less comical). Now if a purposeful man, for example, comes by, and the intoxicated individual, his attention drawn to him, gathers himself together and tries to steady his gait, then the comical becomes more evident; because the contradiction is clearer. He succeeds entirely while passing the purposeful man, the first contradiction becomes another: that we know him to be intoxicated, and that this is, nevertheless, not apparent. In the one case we laugh at him while he sways, because the eye requires steadiness of him; in the second case we laugh at him because he holds himself steady when our knowledge of his condition requires that we should see him sway. So it also produces a comic effect when a sober man engages in sympathetic and confidential conversation with one whom he does not know is intoxicated, while the observer knows of the condition. The contradiction lies in the mutuality presupposed by the conversation, that it is not there, and that the sober man has not noticed its absence.

It is comical when in ordinary conversation a man uses the rhetorical question of the sermon (which does not demand an answer, but only forms a transition for the speaker's answering it himself); it is comical when the man he speaks to misunderstands it, and interjects the answer. The comic lies in the contradiction involved in attempting to be an orator and a conversationalist at the same time, or wishing to be an orator in a conversation; the other's error reveals this, and is a righteous nemesis; for anyone who uses such forms in talking with another says indirectly—"We do not converse with one another, but it is I who am the speaker."

A caricature is comical, and why? Because of the contradiction between likeness and unlikeness; the caricature must resemble a human being, an actual, particular person; if it resembles no one at all, it is not comical, but is a straightforward essay in the sphere of the unmeaning fantastic.

The shadow of a man on the wall, while you sit and talk with him, can produce a comic effect because it is the shadow of the man you are talking with (the contradiction is that you see at the same time that it is not he). If you were to see the same shadow on the wall, but no man was present, or if you saw the shadow and not the man, it would not be comical. The more the man's reality is accentuated, the more comical the shadow becomes. If one is impressed by the expression of the face, for example, the tone of voice, and the correctness of the remarks—and at the same moment sees the caricaturing shadow, then the comic effect is greatest, unless it wounds the sensibilities. If it is a scatterbrain who talks, the shadow does not so much impress itself as comical, but it rather satisfies one that the shadow resembles him ideally.

Contrast produces a comic effect by means of the contradiction, whether the relationship is that the in and for itself non-ridiculous is used to make ridiculous the ridiculous, or the ridiculous makes that ridiculous which is in itself non-ridiculous, or the ridiculous and the ridiculous make each other mutually ridiculous, or the in and for itself non-ridiculous and the in and for itself non-ridiculous becomes ridiculous through the relationship.

When a German-Danish clergyman says from the pulpit: "The word became pork (*Flaesk, Fleisch*) that is comical. The comical lies not merely in the general contradiction which arises when a man speaks in a foreign language with which he is unfamiliar, and produces on the mind an entirely different impression from the one he intends; but the contradiction is made sharper by the fact that he is a clergyman, and that he is preaching, since speaking in connection with a clergyman's address is used in a very specific sense, and the least that can be assumed is that he can speak the language. Besides, the contradiction tends to wander in upon the ethical sphere: that a man may innocently come to make himself guilty of blasphemy. . . .

Let these examples be sufficient, and let everyone whom the note disturbs leave it unread. It is easy to see that the examples are not carefully collected, but also that they are not odds and ends from aestheticians. Of the comical there is certainly enough everywhere, and at every time, if a man only has an eye for it; one could continue indefinitely, unless through being clear about where to laugh, one also understood where not to laugh. Let the comic be brought to consciousness; it is no more immoral to laugh than it is immoral to weep. But just as it is immoral to go around whining at all times, so it is also immoral to give oneself up to the indefinite excitement which lies in laughing when one does not really know whether to laugh or not, so that one does not enjoy the laughter, and makes it impossible to repent if one has laughed in the wrong place. Hence the comical has become the tempter in our time, because it is almost as if it desires the appearance of illegitimacy in order to acquire the enchantment of the forbidden, and again as the forbidden intimates that laughter can destroy everything. But though I do not have much to be proud of *qua* author, I am nevertheless proud in the consciousness that I can scarcely be accused of having exercised my pen in connection with the comical, that I have never permitted my pen to serve the interest of the moment, that I have never applied the comic point of view to anyone or anything, without first, by putting the categories together, inquired from what sphere the comic came, and how it would be related to the same thing or the same person if pathetically apprehended. Really to acquire a clear consciousness of where the comic lies is also satisfying, and there are perhaps many who would lose their laughter if they understood it, but such a man has really never had a sense for the comic, and yet it is on the laughter of such people that all those reckon who muddle around with the comical. There are also perhaps some who can be comically productive only in recklessness and abandon, who, if it were said to them: "Remember you are ethically responsible for the way in which you use your comic powers," would lose their *vis comica.* And yet in relation to the comical it is precisely the opposition which gives it its vigor, and prevents a man from capsizing. Recklessness and frivolity as productive energies produce the loud laughter of indeterminancy and sensuous irritability, which is extremely different from the laughter that accompanies the great translucency of the comical. If one desires to learn in a good school, one should for a time renounce laughing at what arouses antipathetic passion, where turgid forces may easily carry a man away; exercising oneself rather in perceiving the comical in this or that for which one has partiality, where the sympathy and the interest, aye, the partiality, create the disciplinary opposition against inconsiderateness.

12   George Santayana (1863–1952)

In this section from his early work on asthetics, *The Sense of Beauty*, Santayana challenges both the Incongruity and Superiority Theories. Amusement, which is what Santayana calls the feeling prompting laughter, is more directly a physical thing than these theories claim, he argues; it depends on some nervous excitement. We can be amused merely by being tickled, for example, or by hearing other people laughing. Santayana does not totally reject the Incongruity and Superiority Theories, however, for he agrees that we often laugh in situations involving incongruity and degradation. But he does want us to understand just what it is that produces our enjoyment in such situations. When we react to a comic incongruity or degradation, he claims, it is never the incongruity or the degradation itself that gives us pleasure; it is rather the stimulation and excitement caused by our perception of those things. "The shock which they bring may sometimes be the occasion of a subsequent pleasure . . . but the incongruity and degradation, as such, always remain unpleasant." Santayana seems especially bothered by the idea found in some versions of the Incongruity Theory, that we could enjoy incongruity itself. He insists that this is impossible since, as rational animals, we are constitutionally averse to incongruity, absurdity, or nonsense in any form. We endure such things only for the pleasure of stimulation. Santayana would agree with Plato that amusement is a pleasure mixed with pain. That is why, he says, we prefer to get our mental stimulation with no incongruity, as in wit, rather than with incongruity, as in humor.

The Sense of Beauty *(New York: Scribner's, 1896), pp. 245-258*

The Comic

Something analogous takes place in the other spheres where an aesthetic value seems to arise out of suggestions of evil, in the comic, namely, and the grotesque. But here the translation of our sympathies is partial, and we are carried away from ourselves only to become smaller. The larger humanity, which cannot be absorbed, remains ready to contradict the absurdity of our fiction. The excellence of comedy lies in the invitation to wander along some by-

90

path of the fancy, among scenes not essentially impossible, but not to be actually enacted by us on account of the fixed circumstances of our lives. If the picture is agreeable, we allow ourselves to dream it true. We forget its relations; we forbid the eye to wander beyond the frame of the stage, or the conventions of the fiction. We indulge an illusion which deepens our sense of the essential pleasantness of things.

So far, there is nothing in comedy that is not delightful, except, perhaps, the moment when it is over. But fiction, like all error or abstraction, is necessarily unstable; and the awakening is not always reserved for the disheartening moment at the end. Everywhere, when we are dealing with pretension or mistake, we come upon sudden and vivid contradictions; changes of view, transformations of apperception which are extremely stimulating to the imagination. We have spoken of one of these: when the sudden dissolution of our common habits of thought lifts us into a mystical contemplation, filled with the sense of the sublime; when the transformation is back to common sense and reality, and away from some fiction, we have a very different emotion. We feel cheated, relieved, abashed, or amused, in proportion as our sympathy attaches more to the point of view surrendered or to that attained.

The disintegration of mental forms and their redintegration is the life of the imagination. It is a spiritual process of birth and death, nutrition and generation. The strongest emotions accompany these changes, and vary infinitely with their variations. All the qualities of discourse, wit, eloquence, cogency, absurdity, are feelings incidental to this process, and involved in the juxtapositions, tensions, and resolutions of our ideas. Doubtless the last explanation of these things would be cerebral; but we are as yet confined to verbal descriptions and classifications of them, which are always more or less arbitrary.

The most conspicuous headings under which comic effects are gathered are perhaps incongruity and degradation. But clearly it cannot be the logical essence of incongruity or degradation that constitutes the comic; for then contradiction and deterioration would always amuse. Amusement is a much more directly physical thing. We may be amused without any idea at all, as when we are tickled, or laugh in sympathy with others by a contagious imitation of their gestures. We may be amused by the mere repetition of a thing at first not amusing. There must therefore be some nervous excitement on which the feeling of amusement directly depends, although this excitement may most often coincide with a sudden transition to an incongruous or meaner image. Nor can we suppose that particular ideational excitement to be entirely dissimilar to all others; wit is often hardly distinguishable from brilliancy, as humor from pathos. We must, therefore, be satisfied with saying vaguely that the process of ideation involves various feelings of movement and relation—feelings capable of infinite gradation and complexity, and ranging from sublimity to tedium and from pathos to uncontrollable merriment.

Certain crude and obvious cases of the comic seem to consist of little more than a shock of surprise: a pun is a sort of jack-in-the-box, popping from nowhere into our plodding thoughts. The liveliness of the interruption, and its futility, often please; *dulce est desipere in loco;* and yet those who must endure the society of inveterate jokers know how intolerable this sort of scintillation can become. There is something inherently vulgar about it; perhaps because our train of thought cannot be very entertaining in itself when we are so glad to break in upon it with irrelevant nullities. The same undertone of disgust mingles with other amusing surprises, as when a dignified personage slips and falls, or some disguise is thrown off, or those things are mentioned and described which convention ignores. The novelty and the freedom please, yet the shock often outlasts the pleasure, and we have cause to wish we had been stimulated by something which did not involve this degradation. So, also, the impossibility in plausibility which tickles the fancy in Irish bulls, and in wild exaggerations, leaves an uncomfortable impression, a certain aftertaste of foolishness.

The reason will be apparent if we stop to analyze the situation. We have a prosaic background of common sense and everyday reality; upon this background an unexpected idea suddenly impinges. But the thing is a futility. The comic accident falsifies the nature before us, starts a wrong analogy in the mind, a suggestion that cannot be carried out. In a word, we are in the presence of an absurdity; and man, being a rational animal, can like absurdity no better than he can like hunger or cold. A pinch of either may not be so bad, and he will endure it merrily enough if you repay him with abundance of warm victuals; so, too, he will play with all kinds of nonsense for the sake of laughter and good fellowship and the tickling of his fancy with a sort of caricature of thought. But the qualm remains, and the pleasure is never perfect. The same exhilaration might have come without the falsification, just as repose follows more swiftly after pleasant than after painful exertions.

Fun is a good thing, but only when it spoils nothing better. The best place for absurdity is in the midst of what is already absurd — then we have the play of fancy without the sense of ineptitude. Things amuse us in the mouth of a fool that would not amuse us in that of a gentleman; a fact which shows how little incongruity and degradation have to do with our pleasure in the comic. In fact, there is a kind of congruity and method even in fooling. The incongruous and the degraded displease us even there, as by their nature they must at all times. The shock which they bring may sometimes be the occasion of a subsequent pleasure, by attracting our attention, or by stimulating passions, such as scorn, or cruelty, or self-satisfaction (for there is a good deal of malice in our love of fun); but the incongruity and degradation, as such, always remain unpleasant. The pleasure comes from the inward rationality and movement of the fiction, not from its inconsistency with anything else. There are a great many topsy-turvy worlds possible to our fancy, into which we like to drop at times. We enjoy the stimulation and the shaking up of our wits. It is like getting into a new posture, or hearing a new song.

Nonsense is good only because common sense is so limited. For reason, after all, is one convention picked out of a thousand. We love expansion, not disorder, and when we attain freedom without incongruity we have a much greater and a much purer delight. The excellence of wit can dispense with absurdity. For on the same prosaic background of common sense, a novelty might have appeared that was not absurd, that stimulated the attention quite as much as the ridiculous, without so baffling the intelligence. This purer and more thoroughly delightful amusement comes from what we call wit.

Wit

Wit also depends upon transformation and substitution of ideas. It has been said to consist in quick association by similarity. The substitution must here be valid, however, and the similarity real, though unforeseen. Unexpected justness makes wit, as sudden incongruity makes pleasant foolishness. It is characteristic of wit to penetrate into hidden depths of things, to pick out there some telling circumstance or relation, by noting which the whole object appears in a new and clearer light. Wit often seems malicious because analysis in discovering common traits and universal principles assimilates things at the poles of being; it can apply to cookery the formulas of theology, and find in the human heart a case of the fulcrum and lever. We commonly keep the departments of experience distinct; we think that different principles hold in each and that the dignity of spirit is inconsistent with the explanation of it by physical analogy, and the meanness of matter unworthy of being an illustration of moral truths. Love must not be classed under physical cravings, nor faith under hypnotization. When, therefore, an original mind overleaps these boundaries, and recasts its categories, mixing up our old classifications, we feel that the values of things are also confused. But these depended upon a deeper relation, upon their response to human needs and aspirations. All that can be changed by the exercise of intelligence is our sense of the unity and homogeneity of the world. We may come to hold an object of thought in less isolated respect, and another in less hasty derision; but the pleasures we derive from all, or our total happiness and wonder, will hardly be diminished. For this reason the malicious or destructive character of intelligence must not be regarded as fundamental. Wit belittles one thing and dignifies another; and its comparisons are as often flattering as ironical.

The same process of mind that we observed in wit gives rise to those effects we call charming, brilliant, or inspired. When Shakespeare says,

> come and kiss me, *sweet and twenty*,
> Youth's a stuff will not endure,

the fancy of the phrase consists in a happy substitution, a merry way of saying something both true and tender. And where could we find a more exquisite charm? So, to take a weightier example, when St. Augustine is made to say that pagan virtues were *splendid vices*, we have — at least if we catch the full meaning — a pungent assimilation of contrary things, by force of a powerful principle; a triumph of theory, the boldness of which can only be matched by its consistency. In fact, a phrase could not be more brilliant, or better condense one theology and two civilizations. The Latin mind is particularly capable of this sort of excellence. Tacitus alone could furnish a hundred examples. It goes with the power of satirical and bitter eloquence, a sort of scornful rudeness of intelligence, that makes for the core of a passion or of a character, and affixes to it a more or less scandalous label. For in our analytical zeal it is often possible to condense and abstract too much. Reality is more fluid and elusive than reason, and has, as it were, more dimensions than are known even to the latest geometry. Hence the understanding, when not suffused with some glow of sympathetic emotion or some touch of mysticism, gives but a dry, crude image of the world. The quality of wit inspires more admiration than confidence. It is a merit we should miss little in any one we love.

The same principle, however, can have more sentimental embodiments. When our substitutions are brought on by the excitement of generous emotion, we call wit inspiration. There is the same finding of new analogies, and likening of disparate things; there is the same transformation of our apperception. but the brilliancy is here not only penetrating, but also exalting. For instance:

> Peace, peace, he is not dead, he doth not sleep,
>> He hath awakened from the dream of life:
> 'Tis we that wrapped in stormy visions keep
>> With phantoms an unprofitable strife.

There is here paradox, and paradox justified by reflection. The poet analyzes, and analyzes without reserve. The dream, the storm, the phantoms, and the unprofitableness could easily make a satirical picture. But the mood is transmuted; the mind takes an upward flight, with a sense of liberation from the convention it dissolves, and of freer motion in the vagueness beyond. The disintegration of our ideal here leads to mysticism, and because of this effort towards transcendence, the brilliancy becomes sublime.

Humor

A different mood can give a different direction to the same processes. The sympathy by which we reproduce the feeling of another, is always very much opposed to the aesthetic attitude to which the whole world is merely a stimulus to our sensibility. In the tragic, we have seen how the sympathetic feeling, by which suffering is appreciated and shared, has to be overlaid by many incidental aesthetic pleasures, if the resulting effect is to be on the whole good. We have also seen how the only way in which the ridiculous can be kept within the sphere of the aesthetically good is abstracting it from its relations, and treating it as an independent and curious stimulus; we should stop laughing and begin to be annoyed if we tried to make sense out of our absurdity. The less sympathy we have with men the more exquisite is our enjoyment of their folly: satirical delight is closely akin to cruelty. Defect and mishap stimulate our fancy, as blood and tortures excite in us the passions of the beast of prey. The more this inhuman attitude yields to sympathy and reason, the less are folly and error capable of amusing us. It would therefore seem impossible that we should be pleased by the foibles or absurdities of those we love. And in fact we never enjoy seeing our own persons in a satirical light, or any one else for whom we really feel affection. Even in farces, the hero and heroine are seldom made ridiculous, because that would jar upon the sympathy with which we are expected to regard them. Nevertheless, the essence of what we call humor is that amusing weaknesses should be combined with an amicable humanity. Whether it be in the way of ingenuity, or oddity, or drollery, the humorous person must have an absurd side, or be placed in an absurd situation. Yet this comic aspect, at which we ought to wince, seems to endear the character all the more. This is a parallel case to that of tragedy, where the depth of the woe we sympathize with seems to add to our satisfaction. And the explanation of the paradox is the same. We do not enjoy the expression of evil, but only the pleasant excitements that come with it; namely, the physical stimulus and the expression of good. In tragedy, the misfortunes help to give the impression of truth, and to bring out the noble qualities of the hero, but are in themselves depressing, so much so that over-sensitive people cannot enjoy the beauty of the representation. So also in humor, the painful suggestions are felt as such, and need to be overbalanced by agreeable elements. These come from both directions, from the aesthetic and the sympathetic reaction. On the one hand there is the sensuous and merely perceptive stimulation, the novelty, the movement, the vivacity of the spectacle. On the other hand, there is the luxury of imaginative sympathy, the mental assimilation of another congenial experience, the expansion into another life.

The juxtaposition of these two pleasures produces just that tension and complication in which the humorous consists. We are satirical, and we are friendly at the same time. The consciousness of the friendship gives a regretful and tender touch to the satire, and the sting of the satire makes the friendship a trifle humble and sad. Don Quixote is mad; he is old, useless, and ridiculous, but he is the soul of honor, and in all his laughable adventures we follow him like the ghost of our better selves. We enjoy his discomfitures too much to wish he had been a perfect Amadis; and we have besides a shrewd suspicion that he is the only kind of Amadis there can ever be in this world. At the same time it does us good to see the courage of his idealism, the ingenuity of his wit, and the simplicity of his goodness. But how shall we reconcile our sympathy with his dream and our perception of its absurdity? The situation is contradictory. We are drawn to some different point of view, from which the comedy may no longer seem so amusing. As humor becomes deep and really different from satire, it changes into pathos, and passes out of the sphere of the comic altogether. The mischances that were to amuse us as scoffers now grieve us as men, and the value of the representation depends on the touches of beauty and seriousness with which it is adorned.

The Grotesque

Something analogous to humor can appear in plastic forms, when we call it the grotesque. This is an interesting effect produced by such a transformation of an ideal type as exaggerates one of its elements or combines it with other types. The real excellence of this, like that of all fiction, consists in re-creation; in the formation of a thing which nature has not, but might conceivably have offered. We call these inventions comic and grotesque when we are considering their divergence from the natural rather than their inward possibility. But the latter constitutes their real charm; and the more we study and develop them, the better we understand it. The incongruity with the conventional type then disappears, and what was impossible and ridiculous at first takes its place among recognized ideals. The centaur and the satyr are no longer grotesque; the type is accepted. And the grotesqueness of an individual has essentially the same nature. If we like the inward harmony, the characteristic balance of his features, we are able to disengage this individual from the class into which we were trying to force him; we can forget the expectation which he was going to disappoint. The ugliness then disappears, and only the reassertion of the old habit and demand can make us regard him as in any way extravagant.

What appears as grotesque may be intrinsically inferior or superior to the normal. That is a question of its abstract material and form. But until the new object impresses its form on our imagination, so that we can grasp its unity and proportion, it appears to us as a jumble and distortion of other forms. If this confusion is absolute, the object is simply null; it does not exist aesthetically, except by virtue of materials. But if the confusion is not absolute, and we have an inkling of the unity and character in the midst of the strangeness of the form, then we have the grotesque. It is the half-formed, the perplexed, and the suggestively monstrous.

The analogy to the comic is very close, as we can readily conceive that it should be. In the comic we have this same juxtaposition of a new and an old idea, and if the new is not futile and really inconceivable, it may in time establish itself in the mind, and cease to be ludicrous. Good wit is a novel truth, as the good grotesque is novel beauty. But there are natural conditions of organization, and we must not mistake every mutilation for the creation of a new form. The tendency of nature to establish well-marked species of animals shows what various combinations are most stable in the face of physical forces, and there is a fitness also for survival in the mind, which is determined by the relation of any form to our fixed method of perception. New things are therefore generally bad because, as has been well said, they are incapable of becoming old. A thousand originalities are produced by defect of faculty, for one that is produced by genius. For in the pursuit of beauty, as in that of truth, an infinite number of paths lead to failure, and only one to success.

13   Herbert Spencer (1820-1903)

In his philosophy Spencer relied heavily on nineteenth-century science, especially biology. His aim was not just to make philosophy more responsive to newly discovered facts, but to incorporate scientific methodology into philosophical thinking. The influence of science of Spencer's thought is best seen in his application of the new theory of evolution to psychology, sociology, ethics, politics, and education. When Spencer looked at the phenomenon of laughter, he was strongly influenced by the current "hydraulic" theory of nervous energy, in which nervous energy builds up within our bodies and requires release through muscular movement. Laughter, in Spencer's view, is a specialized channel of such release. This Relief Theory of laughter was further developed by Freud and it has also influenced many in contemporary psychology, most notably Daniel Berlyne, for whom laughter involves an "arousal jag."

The Physiology of Laughter, from Essays on Education, Etc. *(London: Dent, 1911)*

Why do we smile when a child puts on a man's hat? Or what induces us to laugh on reading that the corpulent Gibbon was unable to rise from his knees after making a tender declaration? The usual reply to such questions is, that laughter results from a perception of incongruity. Even were there not, on this reply, the obvious criticism that laughter often occurs from extreme pleasure or from mere vivacity, there would still remain the real problem: How comes a sense of the incongruous to be followed by these peculiar bodily actions? Some have alleged that laughter is due to the pleasure of a relative self-elevation, which we feel on seeing the humiliation of others. But this theory, whatever portion of truth it may contain, is, in the first place, open to the fatal objection that there are various humiliations to others which produce in us anything but laughter; and, in the second place, it does not apply to the many instances in which no one's dignity is implicated: as when we laugh at a good pun. Moreover, like the other, it is merely a generalization of certain conditions to laughter; and not an explanation of the odd movements which occur under these conditions. Why, when greatly delighted, or impressed with certain unexpected contrasts of ideas, should there be a contraction of particular facial muscles and particular muscles of the chest and abdomen? Such answer to this question as may be possible, can be rendered only by physiology.

Every child has made the attempt to hold the foot still while it is tickled, and has failed; and there is scarcely anyone who has not vainly tried to avoid winking when a hand has been suddenly passed before the eyes. These examples of muscular movements which occur independently of the will, or in spite of it, illustrate what physiologists call reflex action; as likewise do sneezing and coughing. To this class of cases, in which involuntary motions are accompanied by sensations, has to be added another class of cases, in which involuntary motions are unaccompanied by sensations: instance the pulsations of the heart; the contractions of the stomach during digestion. Further, the majority of seemingly voluntary acts in such creatures as insects, worms, molluscs, are considered by physiologists to be as purely automatic as is the dilation or closure of the iris under variations in the quantity of light; and similarly exemplify the law, that an impression on the end of an afferent nerve is conveyed to some ganglionic center, and is thence usually reflected along an efferent nerve to one or more muscles which it causes to contract.

In a modified form this principle holds with voluntary acts. Nervous excitation always *tends* to beget muscular motion; and when it rises to a certain intensity always does beget it. Not only in reflex actions, whether with or without sensation, do we see that special nerves, when raised to states of tension, discharge themselves on special muscles with which they are indirectly connected; but those external actions through which we read the feelings of others, show us that, under any considerable tension, the nervous system in general discharges itself on the muscular system in general: either with or without the guidance of the will. The shivering produced by cold implies irregular muscular contractions, which, though at first only partly involuntary, become, when the cold is extreme, almost wholly involuntary. When you have severely burnt your finger it is very difficult to preserve a dignified composure: contortion of face, or movement of limb, is pretty sure to follow. If a man receives good news with neither facial change nor bodily motion, it is inferred that he is not much pleased, or that he has extraordinary self-control: either inference implying that joy almost universally produces contraction of the muscles, and so, alters the expression, or attitude, or both. And when we hear of the feats of strength which men have performed when their lives were at stake — when we read how, in the energy of despair, even paralyzed patients have regained for a time the use of their limbs; we see still more clearly the relation between nervous and muscular excitements. It becomes manifest both that emotions and sensations tend to generate bodily movements, and that the movements are violent in proportion as the emotions or sensations are intense.

This, however, is not the sole direction in which nervous excitement expends itself. Viscera as well as muscles may receive the discharge. That the heart and blood vessels (which, indeed, being all contractile, may in a restricted sense be classed with the muscular system) are quickly affected by pleasures and pains, we have daily proved to us. Every sensation of any acuteness accelerates the pulse; and how sensitive the heart is to emotions, is testified by the familiar expressions which use heart and feeling as convertible terms. Similarly with the digestive organs. Without detailing the various ways in which these may be influenced by our mental states, it suffices to mention the marked benefits derived by dyspeptics, as well as other invalids, from cheerful society, welcome news, change of scene, to show how pleasurable feeling stimulates the viscera in general into greater activity.

There is still another direction in which any excited portion of the nervous system may discharge itself; and a direction in which it usually does discharge itself when the excitement is not strong. It may pass on the stimulus to some other portion of the nervous system. This is what occurs in quiet thinking and feeling. The successive states which constitute consciousness, result from this. Sensations excite ideas and emotions; these in their turns arouse other ideas and emotions; and so on continuously. That is to say, the tension existing in particular nerve centers, or groups of nerve centers, when they yield us certain sensations, ideas, or emotions, generates an equivalent tension in some other nervous structures, with which there is a connection: the flow of energy passing on, the one idea or feeling dies in producing the next.

Thus, then, while we are totally unable to comprehend how the excitement of certain nerve centers should generate feeling; while, in the production of consciousness by physical agents acting on physical structures, we come to a mystery never to be solved; it is yet quite possible for us to know by observation what are the successive forms which this mystery may take. We see that there are three channels along which nerve centers in a state of tension may discharge themselves; or rather, I should say, three classes of channels. They may pass on the excitement to other nerve centers that have no direct connections with the bodily members, and may so cause other feelings and ideas; or they may pass on the excitement to one or more motor nerves, and so cause muscular contractions; or they may pass on the excitement to nerves which supply the viscera, and may so stimulate one or more of these.

For simplicity's sake I have described these as alternative routes, one or other of which any current of nerve force must take; thereby, as it may be thought, implying that such current will be exclusively confined to some one of them. But this is by no means the case. Rarely, if ever, does it happen that a state of nervous tension, present to consciousness as a feeling, expends itself in one direction only. Very generally it may be observed to expend itself in two; and it is probable that the discharge is never absolutely absent from any one of the three. There is, however, variety in the *proportions* in which the discharge is divided among these different channels under different circumstances. In a man whose fear impels him to run, the mental tension generated is only in part transformed into a muscular stimulus: there is a surplus which causes a rapid current of ideas. An agreeable state of feeling produced, say by praise, is not wholly used up in arousing the succeeding phase of the feeling and the new ideas appropriate to it; but a certain portion overflows into the visceral nervous system, increasing the action of the heart and facilitating digestion. And here we come upon a class of considerations and facts which open the way to a solution of our special problem.

For, starting with the truth that at any moment the existing quantity of liberated nerve force which in an inscrutable way produces in us the state we call feeling, *must* expend itself in some direction, it follows that, if of the several channels it may take, one is wholly or partially closed, more must be taken by the others; or that if two are closed, the discharge along the remaining one must be more intense; and that, conversely, should anything determine an unusual efflux in one direction, there will be a diminished efflux in other directions.

Daily experience illustrates these conclusions. It is commonly remarked that the suppression of external signs of feeling, makes feeling more intense. The deepest grief is silent grief. Why? Because the nervous excitement not discharged in muscular action, discharges itself in other nervous excitements — arouses more numerous and more remote associations of melancholy ideas, and so increases the mass of feelings. People who conceal their anger are habitually found to be more revengeful than those who explode in loud speech and vehement action. Why? Because, as before, the emotion is reflected back, accumulates, and intensifies. Similarly, men who, as proved by their powers of representaion, have the keenest appreciation of the comic, are usually able to do and say the most ludicrous things with perfect gravity.

On the other hand, all are familiar with the truth that bodily activity deadens emotion. Under great irritation we get relief by walking about rapidly. Extreme effort in the bootless attempt to achieve a desired end, greatly diminishes the intensity of the desire. Those who are forced to exert themselves after misfortunes, do not suffer nearly so much as those who remain quiescent. If any one wishes to check intellectual excitement, he cannot choose a more efficient method than running till he is exhausted. Moreover, these cases, in which the production of feeling and thought is hindered by determining the nervous energy towards bodily movements, have their counterparts in the cases in which bodily movements are hindered by extra absorption of nervous energy in sudden thoughts and feelings. If, when walking, there flashes on you an idea that creates great surprise, hope, or alarm, you stop; or if sitting cross-legged, swinging your pendent foot, the movement is at once arrested. From the viscera, too, intense mental action abstracts energy. Joy, disappointment, anxiety, or any moral perturbation rising to a great height, destroys appetite; or, if food has been taken, arrests digestion; and even a purely intellectual activity, when extreme, does the like.

Facts, then, bear out these *a priori* inferences, that the nervous excitement at any moment present to consciousness as feeling, must expend itself in some way or other: that of the three classes of channels open to it, it must take one, two, or more, according to circumstances; that the closure or obstruction of one, must increase the discharge through the others; and, conversely, that if, to answer some demand, the efflux of nervous energy in one direction is unusually great, there must be a corresponding decrease of the efflux in other directions. Setting out from these premises, let us now see what intepretation is to be put on the phenomena of laughter.

That laughter is a form of muscular excitement, and so illustrates the general law that feeling passing a certain pitch habitually vents itself in bodily action, scarcely needs pointing out. It perhaps needs pointing out, however, that strong feeling of almost any kind produces this result. It is not a sense of the ludicrous, only, which does it; nor are the various forms of joyous emotion the sole additional causes. We have, besides, the sardonic laughter and the hysterical laughter which result from mental distress; to which must be added certain sensations, as tickling, and, according to Mr. Bain, cold, and some kinds of acute pain.

Strong feeling, mental or physical, being, then, the general cause of laughter, we have to note that the muscular actions constituting it are distinguished from most others by this, that they are purposeless. In general, bodily motions that are prompted by feelings are directed to special ends; as when we try to escape a danger, or struggle to secure a gratification. But the movements of chest and limbs which we make when laughing have no object. And now remark that these quasi-convulsive contractions of the muscles, having no object, but being results of an uncontrolled discharge of energy, we may see whence arise their special characters — how it happens that certain classes of muscles are affected first, and then certain other classes. For an overflow of nerve force undirected by any motive, will manifestly take first the most habitual routes; and if these do not suffice, will next overflow into the less habitual ones. Well, it is through the organs of speech that feeling passes into movement with the greatest frequency. The jaws, tongue, and lips are used not only to express strong irritation or gratification, but that very moderate flow of mental energy which accompanies ordinary conversation, finds its chief vent through this channel. Hence it happens that certain muscles round the mouth, small and easy to move, are the first to contract under pleasurable emotion. The class of muscles which, next after those of articulation, are most constantly set in action (or extra action, let us say) by feelings of all kinds, are those of respiration. Under pleasurable or painful sensations we breathe more rapidly: possibly as a consequence of the increased demand for oxygenated blood. The sensations that accompany exertion also bring on hard breathing; which here more evidently responds to the physiological needs. And emotions, too, agreeable and disagreeable, both, at first, excite respiration; though the last subsequently depress it. That is to say, of the bodily muscles, the respiratory are more constantly implicated than any others in those various acts which our feelings impel us to; and, hence, when there occurs an undirected discharge of nervous energy into the muscular system, it happens that, if the quantity be considerable, it convulses not only certain of the articulatory and vocal muscles, but also those which expel air from the lungs. Should the feeling to be expended be still greater in amount — too great to find vent in these classes of muscles — another class comes into play. The upper limbs are set in motion. Children frequently clap their hands in glee; by some adults the hands are rubbed together; and others, under still greater intensity of delight, slap their knees and sway their bodies backwards and forwards. Last of all, when the other channels for the escape of the surplus nerve force have been filled to overflowing, a yet further and less used group of muscles is spasmodically affected: the head is thrown back and the spine bent inwards — there is a slight degree of what medical men call opisthotonos. Thus, then, without contending that the phenomena of laughter in all their details are to be so accounted for, we see that in their *ensemble* they conform to these general principles: that feeling excites to muscular action; that when the muscular action is unguided by a purpose the muscles first affected are those which feeling most habitually stimulates; and that as the feeling to be expended increases in quantity it excites an increasing number of muscles, in a succession determined by the relative frequency with which they respond to the regulated dictates of feeling. To which as a qualifying and complicating factor must be added the relative sizes of the muscles; since, other things equal, the smaller muscles will be moved more readily than the larger.

There still, however, remains the question with which we set out. The explanation here given applies only to the laughter produced by acute pleasure or pain: it does not apply to the laughter which follows certain perceptions of incongruity. It is an insufficient explanation that in these cases, laughter is a result of the pleasure we take in escaping from the restraint of grave feelings. That this is a part-cause is true. Doubtless very often, as Mr. Bain says, "it is the coerced form of seriousness and solemnity without the reality that gives us that stiff position from which a contact with triviality or vulgarity relieves us, to our uproarious delight." And insofar as mirth is caused by the gush of agreeable feeling which follows the cessation of unpleasant mental strain, it further illustrates the general principle above set forth. But no explanation is thus afforded of the mirth which ensues when the short silence between the *andante* and *allegro* in one of Beethoven's symphonies, is broken by a loud sneeze. In this, and a host of like cases, the mental tension is not coerced by spontaneous, not disagreeable but agreeable; and the coming impressions to which attention is directed, promise a gratification which few, if any, desire to escape. Hence, when the unlucky sneeze occurs, it cannot be that the laughter of the audience is due simply to the release from an irksome attitude of mind: some other cause must be sought.

This cause we shall arrive at by carrying our analysis a step further. We have but to consider the quantity of feeling which exists under such circumstances, and then to ask what are the conditions determining the direction of its discharge, to reach a solution. Take a case. You are sitting in a theatre, absorbed in the progress of an interesting drama. some climax has been reached which has aroused your sympathies — say, a reconciliation between the hero and heroine, after long and painful misunderstanding. The feelings excited by this scene are not of a kind from which you seek relief; but are, on the contrary, a grateful relief from the painful feelings with which you have witnessed the previous estrangement. Moreover, the sentiments these fictitious personages have for the moment inspired you with, are not such as would lead you to rejoice in any indignity offered to them; but rather, such as would make you resent the indignity. And now, while you are contemplating the reconciliation with a pleasurable sympathy, there appears from behind the scenes a tame kid, which, having stared round at the audience, walks up to the lovers and sniffs at them. You cannot help joining in the roar which greets this *contretemps*. Inexplicable as is this irresistible burst on the hypothesis of a pleasure in escaping from mental restraint; or on the hypothesis of a pleasure from relative increase of self-importance, when witnessing the humiliation of others; it is readily explicable if we consider what, in such a case, must become of the feeling that existed at the moment the incongruity arose. A large mass of emotion had been produced; or, to speak in physiological language, a large portion of the nervous system was in a state of tension. There was also great expectation with respect to the further evolution of the scene — a quantity of vague, nascent thought and emotion, into which the existing quantity of thought and emotion was about to pass. Had there been no interruption, the body of new ideas and feelings next excited, would have sufficed to absorb the whole of the liberated nervous energy. But now, this large amount of nervous energy, instead of being allowed to expend itself in producing an equivalent amount of the new thoughts and emotions which were nascent, is suddenly checked in its flow. The channels along which the discharge was about to take place, are closed. The new channel opened — that afforded by the appearance and proceedings of the kid — is a small one; the ideas and feelings suggested are not numerous and massive enough to carry off the nervous energy to be expended. The excess must therefore discharge itself in some other direction; and in the way already explained, there results an efflux through the motor nerves to various classes of the muscles, producing the half-convulsive actions we term laughter.

This explanation is in harmony with the fact that when, among several persons who witness the same ludicrous occurrence, there are some who do not laugh, it is because there has arisen in them an emotion not participated in by the rest, and which is sufficiently massive to absorb all the nascent excitement. Among the spectators of an awkward tumble, those who preserve their gravity are those in whom there is excited a degree of sympathy with the sufferer, sufficiently great to serve as an outlet for the feeling which the occurrence had turned out of its previous course. Sometimes anger carries off the arrested current; and so prevents laughter. An instance of this was lately furnished me by a friend who had been witnessing the feats at Franconi's. A tremendous leap had just been made by an acrobat over a number of horses. The clown, seemingly envious of this success, made ostentatious preparation for doing the like; and then, taking the preliminary run with immense energy, stopped short on reaching the first horse, and pretended to wipe some dust from its haunches. In most of the spectators, merriment was excited; but in my friend, wound up by the expectation of the coming leap to a state of great nervous tension, the effect of the balk was to produce indignation. Experience thus proves what the theory implies, namely, that the discharge of arrested feelings into the muscular system takes place only in the absence of other adequate channels, does not take place if there arise other feelings equal in amount to those arrested.

Evidence still more conclusive is at hand. If we contrast the incongruities which produce laughter with those which do not, we see that in the non-ludicrous ones the unexpected feeling aroused, though wholly different in kind, is not less in quantity or intensity. Among incongruities which may excite anything but a laugh, Mr. Bain instances "A decrepit man under a heavy burden, five loaves and two fishes among a multitude, and all unfitness and gross disproportion; an instrument out of tune, a fly in ointment, snow in May, Archimedes studying geometry in a siege, and all discordant things; a wolf in sheep's clothing, a breach of bargain, and falsehood in general; the multitude taking the law in their own hands, and everything of the nature of disorder; a corpse at a feast, parental cruelty, filial ingratitude, and whatever is unnatural; the entire catalogue of the vanities given by Solomon, are all incongruous, but they cause feelings of pain, anger, sadness, loathing, rather than mirth." Now in these cases, where the totally unlike state of consciousness suddenly produced is not inferior in mass to the preceding one, the conditions to laughter are not fulfilled. As above shown, laughter naturally results only when consciousness is unawares transferred from great things to small—only when there is what we may call a *descending* incongruity.

And now observe, finally, the fact, alike inferable *a priori* and illustrated in experience, that an *ascending* incongruity not only fails to cause laughter, but works on the muscular system an effect of the reverse kind. When after something very insignificant there arises without anticipation something very great, the emotion we call wonder results; and this emotion is accompanied not by contraction of the muscles, but by relaxation of them. In children and country people, that falling of the jaw which occurs on witnessing an imposing and unexpected change, exemplifies this effect. Persons wonder-struck at the production of a striking result by a seemingly inadequate cause, are frequently described as unconsciously dropping the things they held in their hands. Such are just the effects to be anticipated. After an average state of consciousness, absorbing but a small quantity of nervous energy, is aroused without notice, a strong emotion of awe, terror, or admiration; joined with the astonishment due to an apparent want of adequate causation. This new state of consciousness demands far more nervous energy than that which it has suddenly replaced; and this increased absorption of nervous energy in mental changes, involves a temporary diminution of the outflow in other directions: whence the pendent jaw and the relaxing grasp.

One further observation is worth making. Among the several sets of channels into which surplus feeling might be discharged, was named the nervous system of the viscera. The sudden overflow of an arrested mental excitement, which, as we have seen, results from a descending incongruity, must doubtless stimulate not only the muscular system, as we see it does, but also the internal organs: the heart and stomach must come in for a share of the discharge. And thus there seems to be a good physiological basis for the popular notion that mirth-creating excitement facilitates digestion.

Though, in doing so, I go beyond the boundaries of the immediate topic, I may fitly point out that the method of inquiry here followed, opens the way to interpretation of various phenomena besides those of laughter. To show the importance of pursuing it, I will indicate the explanation it furnishes of another familiar class of facts.

All know how generally a large amount of emotion disturbs the action of the intellect, and interferes with the power of expression. A speech delivered with great facility to tables and chairs, is by no means so easily delivered to an audience. Every schoolboy can testify that his trepidation, when standing before a master, has often disabled him from repeating a lesson which he had duly learnt. In explanation of this we commonly say that the attention is distracted, that the proper train of ideas is broken by the intrusion of ideas that are irrelevant. But the question is, in what manner does unusual emotion produce this effect; and we are here supplied with a tolerably obvious answer. The repetition of a lesson, or set speech previously thought out, implies the flow of a very moderate amount of nervous excitement through a comparatively narrow channel. The thing to be done is simply to call up in succession certain previously-arranged ideas — a process in which no great amount of mental energy is expended. Hence, when there is a large quantity of emotion, which must be discharged in some direction or other; and when, as usually happens, the restricted series of intellectual actions to be gone through, does not suffice to carry it off; there result discharges along other channels besides the one prescribed: there are aroused various ideas foreign to the train of thought to be pursued; and these tend to exclude from consciousness those which should occupy it.

And now observe the meaning of those bodily actions spontaneously set up under these circumstances. The schoolboy saying his lesson, commonly has his fingers actively engaged, perhaps in twisting about a broken pen, or perhaps in squeezing the angle of his jacket; and if told to keep his hands still, he soon again falls into the same or a similar trick. Many anecdotes are current of public speakers having incurable automatic actions of this class: barristers who perpetually wound and unwound pieces of tape; members of parliament ever putting on and taking off their spectacles. So long as such movements are unconscious, they facilitate the mental actions. At least this seems a fair inference from the fact that confusion frequently results from putting a stop to them: witness the case narrated by Sir Walter Scott of his school-fellow, who became unable to say his lesson after the removal of the waistcoat button which he habitually fingered while in class. But why do they facilitate the mental actions? Clearly because they draw off a portion of the surplus nervous excitement. If, as above explained, the quantity of mental energy generated is greater than can find vent along the narrow channel of thought that is open to it; and if, in consequence, it is apt to produce confusion by rushing into other channels of thought; then, by allowing it an exit through the motor nerves into the muscular system, the pressure is diminished, and irrelevant ideas are less likely to intrude on consciousness.

This further illustration will, I think, justify the position that something may be achieved by pursuing in other cases this kind of psychological inquiry. A complete explanation of the phenomena requires us to trace out *all* the consequences of any given state of consciousness; and we cannot do this without studying the effects, bodily and mental, as varying in quantity at one another's expense. We should probably learn much if in every case we asked: Where is all the nervous energy gone?

14   Sigmund Freud (1856-1939)

Freud's theory of laughter and humor is based on the "hydraulic" theory of psychic energy popular in the nineteenth century. Like Spencer, Freud saw laughter as an outlet for psychic or nervous energy, and his theory is classified as a Relief Theory. But Freud's theory is more complicated than previous Relief Theories. In his early book, *Jokes and Their Relation to the Unconscious*, Freud distinguished three kinds of laughter situations: joking or wit (*der Witz*), the comic, and humor. In each there is a saving of psychic energy which is summoned for a particular task but is then seen not to be needed for that purpose. This superfluous energy is what is discharged in the muscular movements of laughter. In joking, Freud claimed, the energy saved is that which would ordinarily be used to repress hostile or sexual feelings and thoughts. Joking (like dreaming) serves as a safety valve for forbidden feelings and thoughts, and when we express what is usually inhibited, the energy of repression is released in laughter. In the comic, the energy saved is energy of thought: we are spared some cognitive processing that we have summoned the energy to perform, and we discharge this surplus energy in laughter. In humor, the energy saved is energy of emotion. We prepare ourselves for feeling fear, pity, or some other negative emotion; but then we realize that we need not be concerned, so that the energy summoned for the emotion is suddenly superfluous and available for discharge in laughter. Freud's use of the term "humor," needless to say, is narrower than the contemporary term, which would include joking and the comic. The following essay, written more than twenty years after *Jokes and Their Relation to the Unconscious*, extends Freud's account of humor in his narrow sense. His idea here that humor involves a repudiation of suffering is reminiscent of Kierkegaard, who said that the humorist recognizes the suffering in life, but "turns deceptively aside and revokes the suffering in the form of the jest" (*Concluding Unscientific Postscript*, p. 400).

Humor

In my work on *Jokes and Their Relation to the Unconscious*, I considered humor really from the economic point of view alone. My object was to discover the source of the pleasure derived from humor, and I think I was able to show that that pleasure proceeds from a saving in expenditure of affect.

There are two ways in which the process at work in humor may take place. Either one person may himself adopt a humorous attitude, while a second person acts as spectator, and derives enjoyment from the attitude of the first; or there may be two people concerned, one of whom does not himself take any active share in producing the humorous effect, but is regarded by the other in a humorous light. To take a very crude example: when a criminal who is being led to the gallows on a Monday observes, "Well, this is a good beginning to the week," he himself is creating the humor; the process works itself out in relation to himself and evidently it affords him a certain satisfaction. I am merely a listener who has not assisted in this functioning of his sense of humor, but I feel its effect, as it were from a distance. I detect in myself a certain humorous satisfaction, possibly much as he does.

We have an instance of the second type of humor when a writer or a narrator depicts the behavior of real or imaginary people in a humorous fashion. There is no need for the people described to display any humor; the humorous attitude only concerns the person who makes them the object of it, and the reader or hearer shares his enjoyment of the humor, as in the former instance. To sum up, then, we may say that the humorous attitude — in whatever it consists — may have reference to the subject's self or to other people; further, we may assume that it is a source of enjoyment to the person who adopts it, and, finally, a similar pleasure is experienced by observers who take no actual part in it.

We shall best understand the origin of the pleasure derived from humor if we consider the process which takes place in the mind of anyone listening to another man's jest. He sees this other person in a situation which leads him to anticipate that the victim will show signs of some affect; he will get angry, complain, manifest pain, fear, horror, possibly even despair. The person who is watching or listening is prepared to follow his lead, and to call up the same emotions. But his anticipations are deceived; the other man does not display any affect — he makes a joke. It is from the saving of expenditure in feeling that the hearer derives the humorous satisfaction.

It is easy to get so far, but we soon say to ourselves that it is the process in the other man, the "humorist," which calls for the greater attention. There is no doubt that the essence of humor is that one spares oneself the affects to which the situation would naturally give rise and overrides with a jest the possibility of such an emotional display. Thus far, the process must be the same in the humorist and his hearer. Or, to put it more accurately, the hearer must have copied the process in the mind of the humorist. But how does the latter arrive at that mental attitude, which makes the discharge of affect superfluous? What is the dynamic process underlying the "humorous attitude"? Clearly, the solution of this problem is to be found in the humorist himself; in the listener we may suppose there is only an echo, a copy of this unknown process.

It is now time to acquaint ourselves with some of the characteristics of humor. Like wit and the comic, humor has in it a *liberating* element. But it has also something fine and elevating, which is lacking in the other two ways of deriving pleasure from intellectual activity. Obviously, what is fine about it is the triumph of narcissism, the ego's victorious assertion of its own invulnerability. It refuses to be hurt by the arrows of reality or to be compelled to suffer. It insists that it is impervious to wounds dealt by the outside world, in fact, that these are merely occasions for affording it pleasure. This last trait is a fundamental characteristic of humor. Suppose the criminal being led to execution on a Monday had said: "It doesn't worry me. What does it matter, after all, if a fellow like me is hanged? The world won't come to an end." We should have to admit that this speech of his displays the same magnificent rising superior to the real situation; what he says is wise and true, but it does not betray a trace of humor. Indeed, it is based on an appraisal of reality which runs directly counter to that of humor. Humor is not resigned; it is rebellious. It signifies the triumph not only of the ego, but also of the pleasure principle, which is strong enough to assert itself here in the face of the adverse real circumstances.

These last two characteristics, the denial of the claim of reality and the triumph of the pleasure principle, cause humor to approximate to the regressive or reactionary processes which engage our attention so largely in psychopathology. By its repudiaton of the possibility of suffering, it takes its place in the great series of methods devised by the mind of man for evading the compulsion to suffer—a series which begins with neurosis and culminates in delusions, and includes intoxication, self-induced states of abstraction and ecstasy. Owing to this connection, humor possesses a dignity which is wholly lacking, for instance, in wit, for the aim of wit is either simply to afford gratification, or, in so doing, to provide an outlet for aggressive tendencies. Now in what does this humorous attitude consist, by means of which one refuses to undergo suffering, asseverates the invincibility of one's ego against the real world and victoriously upholds the pleasure principle, yet all without quitting the ground of mental sanity, as happens when other means to the same end are adopted? Surely it seems impossible to reconcile the two achievements.

If we turn to consider the situation in which one person adopts a humorous attitude towards others, one view which I have already tentatively suggested in my book on wit will seem very evident. It is this: that the one is adopting towards the other the attitude of an adult towards a child, recognizing and smiling at the triviality of the interests and sufferings which seem to the child so big. Thus the humorist acquires his superiority by assuming the role of the grown-up, identifying himself to some extent with the father, while he reduces the other people to the position of children. This supposition is probably true to fact, but it does not seem to take us very far. We ask ourselves what makes the humorist arrogate to himself this role?

Here we must recall the other, perhaps the original and more important, situation in humor, in which a man adopts a humorous attitude towards himself in order to ward off possible suffering. Is there any sense in saying that someone is treating himself like a child and is at the same time playing the part of the superior adult in relation to this child?

This idea does not seem very plausible, but I think that if we consider what we have learnt from pathological observations of the structure of our ego, we shall find a strong confirmation of it. This ego is not a simple entity; it harbors within it, as its innermost core, a special agency: the super-ego. Sometimes it is amalgamated with this, so that we cannot distinguish the one from the other, while in other circumstances the two can be sharply differentiated. Genetically the super-ego inherits the parental function; it often holds the ego in strict subordination, and still actually treats it as the parents (or the father) treated the child in his early years. We obtain a dynamic explanation of the humorous attitude, therefore, if we conclude that it consists in the subject's removing the accent from his own ego and transferring it on to his super-ego. To the super-ego, thus inflated, the ego can appear tiny and all its interests trivial, and with this fresh distribution of energy it may be an easy matter for it to suppress the potential reactions of the ego.

To preserve our customary phraseology, let us not speak of transferring the accent, but rather of displacing large quantities of cathexis. We shall then ask whether we are justified in imagining such extensive displacements from one agency in the mental apparatus to another. It looks like a new hypothesis, conceived *ad hoc*; yet we may recollect that repeatedly, even if not often enough, we have taken such a factor into account when endeavoring to form some metapsychological conception of the mental processes. For instance, we assumed that the difference between ordinary erotic object-cathexis and the state of being in love was that in the latter case incomparably more cathexis passes over to the object, the ego as it were emptying itself into the object. The study of some cases of paranoia proved to me that ideas of persecution are formed early, and exist for a long time without any perceptible effect, until as the result of some definite occasion they receive a sufficient amount of cathexis to cause them to become dominant. The cure of paranoiac attacks of this sort, too, would lie not so much in resolving and correcting the delusional ideas as in withdrawing from them the cathexis they have attracted. The alternation between melancholia and mania, between a cruel suppressing of the ego by the super-ego and the liberation of the ego after this oppression, suggests some such shifting of cathexis; and this conception would, moreover, explain a number of phenomena in normal mental life. If, hitherto, we have but seldom had recourse to this explanation, it has been on account of our customary caution, which is surely rather praiseworthy than otherwise. The ground on which we feel ourselves secure is that of mental pathology; it is here that we make our observations and win our convictions. For the present we commit ourselves to an opinion concerning the normal only insofar as we detect it amongst the isolated and distorted features of the morbid. When once this hesitation is overcome, we shall recognize how greatly the static conditions as well as the dynamic alteration in the quantity of the energic cathexis contribute to our understanding of mental processes.

I think, therefore, that the possibility I have suggested, namely, that in a given situation the subject suddenly effects a hyper-cathexis of the super-ego, which in its turn alters the reactions of the ego, is one which deserves to be retained. Moreover, we find a striking analogy to this hypothesis of mine about humor in the kindred field of wit. I was led to assume that wit originates in the momentary abandoning of a conscious thought to unconscious elaboration, wit being therefore the contribution of the unconscious to the comic. In just the same way humor would be a contribution to the comic made through the agency of the super-ego.

In other respects we know that the super-ego is a stern master. It may be said that it accords ill with its character that it should wink at affording the ego a little gratification. It is true that the pleasure derived from humor is never so intense as that produced by the comic or by wit and never finds a vent in hearty laughter. It is also true that, in bringing about the humorous attitude, the super-ego is in fact repudiating reality and serving an illusion. But (without quite knowing why) we attribute to this less intensive pleasure a high value: we feel it to have a peculiarly liberating and elevating effect. Besides, the jest made in humor is not the essential; it has only the value of a demonstration. The principal thing is the intention which humor fulfils, whether it concerns the subject's self or other people. Its meaning is: "Look here! This is all that this seemingly dangerous world amounts to. Child's play—the very thing to jest about!"

If it is really the super-ego which, in humor, speaks such kindly words of comfort to the intimidated ego, this teaches us that we have still very much to learn about the nature of that agency. Further, we note that it is not everyone who is capable of the humorous attitude: it is a rare and precious gift, and there are many people who have not even the capacity for deriving pleasure from humor when it is presented to them by others. Finally, if the super-ego does try to comfort the ego by humor and to protect it from suffering, this does not conflict with its derivation from the parental function.

15   Henri Bergson (1859-1941)

Some philosophers have developed theories of laughter and humor which had little connection with the rest of their philosophy. This is not the case with Bergson, whose account of humor is an extension of his metaphysics and ethics. Much of Bergson's thought springs from his opposition to materialism and mechanism, especially as found in the theories of evolution of his day. His own theory of "creative evolution" posited a non-material "vital force" (*élan vital*) which drives biological and social evolution. We know this vital force best as it is found in ourselves, and we know it not through conceptual thought but by intuition. By intuition of ourselves, too, we know that our life is not a succession of discrete states, as our rational intellect usually pictures it; it is rather a continuous process of becoming. Real duration, lived time, as opposed to the static abstractions of time invented by our rational intellect, is an irreversible flow of experience. Rational thought also has practical disadvantages: when dominated by it, Bergson says, we tend to handle our experience in a rigid, repetitious way, much as a machine might, treating what are actually new things and events as repetitions of familiar concepts. Now this approach, so common in science and daily life, is often successful, but it can be harmful when what is called for is an open attitude sensitive to the uniqueness of things and events, and to the irreversibility of time. And this is where laughter is useful, for it is a social gesture of mockery toward those who are not behaving in a flexible, context-sensitive way. The ridiculous, according to Bergson, is something mechanical encrusted on the living; the purpose of laughter is to remove that encrustation through humiliation, and thus promote free, well-adapted behavior. Bergson's theory, then, is in the tradition of Superiority Theories (although he does not treat amusement as an emotion, as most Superiority Theories do). What Bergson adds to the Superiority Theory is a view about the object of the mockery—mechanical inelasticity—and the social function of laughter.

From Laughter: An Essay on the Meaning of the Comic, *translated by Cloudesley Brereton and Fred Rothwell (New York: Macmillan, 1911)*

I

The first point to which attention should be called is that the comic does not exist outside the pale of what is strictly *human*. A

117

landscape may be beautiful, charming and sublime, or insignificant and ugly; it will never be laughable. You may laugh at an animal, but only because you have detected in it some human attitude or expression. You may laugh at a hat, but what you are making fun of, in this case, is not the piece of felt or straw, but the shape that men have given it — the human caprice whose mold it has assumed. It is strange that so important a fact, and such a simple one too, has not attracted to a greater degree the attention of philosophers. Several have defined man as "an animal which laughs." They might equally well have defined him as an animal which is laughed at; for if any other animal, or some lifeless object, produces the same effect, it is always because of some resemblance to man, of the stamp he gives it or the use he puts it to.

Here I would point out, as a symptom equally worthy of notice, the *absence of feeling* which usually accompanies laughter. It seems as though the comic could not produce its disturbing effect unless it fell, so to say, on the surface of a soul that is thoroughly calm and unruffled. Indifference is its natural environment, for laughter has no greater foe than emotion. I do not mean that we could not laugh at a person who inspires us with pity, for instance, or even with affection, but in such a case we must, for the moment, put our affection out of court and impose silence upon our pity. In a society composed of pure intelligences there would probably be no more tears, though perhaps there would still be laughter; whereas highly emotional souls, in tune and unison with life, in whom every event would be sentimentally prolonged and re-echoed, would neither know nor understand laughter. Try, for a moment, to become interested in everything that is being said and done; act, in imagination, with those who act, and feel with those who feel; in a word, give your sympathy its widest expansion: as though at the touch of a fairy wand you will see the flimsiest of objects assume importance, and a gloomy hue spread over everything. Now step aside, look upon life as a disinterested spectator: many a drama will turn into a comedy. It is enough for us to stop our ears to the sound of music in a room, where dancing is going on, for the dancers at once to appear ridiculous. How many human actions would stand a similar test? Should we not see many of them suddenly pass from grave to gay, on isolating them from the accompanying music of sentiment? To produce the whole of its effect, then, the comic demands something like a momentary anesthesia of the heart. Its appeal is to intelligence, pure and simple.

This intelligence, however, must always remain in touch with other intelligences. And here is the third fact to which attention should be drawn. You would hardly appreciate the comic if you felt yourself isolated from others. Laughter appears to stand in need of an echo. Listen to it carefully: it is not an articulate, clear, well-defined sound; it is something which would be prolonged by reverberating from one to another, something beginning with a crash, to continue in successive rumblings, like thunder in a mountain. Still, this reverberation cannot go on forever. It can travel within as wide a circle as you please: the circle remains, nonetheless, a closed one. Our laughter is always the laughter of a group. It may, perchance, have happened to you, when seated in a railway carriage or at *table d'hôte*, to hear travellers relating to one another stories which must have been comic to them, for they laughed heartily. Had you been one of their company, you would have laughed like them, but, as you were not, you had no desire whatever to do so. A man who was once asked why he did not weep at a sermon when everybody else was shedding tears replied: "I don't belong to the parish!" What that man thought of tears would be still more true of laughter. However spontaneous it seems, laughter always implies a kind of secret freemasonry, or even complicity, with other laughers, real or imaginary. How often has it been said that the fuller the theatre, the more uncontrolled the laughter of the audience! On the other hand, how often has the remark been made that many comic effects are incapable of translation from one language to another, because they refer to the customs and ideas of a particular social group! It is through not understanding the importance of this double fact that the comic has been looked upon as a mere curiosity in which the mind finds amusement, and laughter itself as a strange, isolated phenomenon, without any bearing on the rest of human activity. Hence those definitions which tend to make the comic into an abstract relation between ideas: "an intellectual contrast," "a patent absurdity," etc., definitions which, even were they really suitable to every form of the comic, would not in the least explain why the comic makes us laugh. How, indeed, should it come about that this particular logical relation, as soon as it is perceived, contracts, expands and shakes our limbs, while all other relations leave the body unaffected? It is not from this point of view that we shall approach the problem. To understand laughter, we must put it back into its natural environment, which is society, and above all must we determine the utility of its function, which is a social one. Such, let us say at once, will be the leading idea of all our investigations. Laughter must answer to certain requirements of life in common. It must have a *social* signification.

Let us clearly mark the point towards which our three preliminary observations are converging. The comic will come into being, it appears, whenever a group of men concentrate their attention on one of their number, imposing silence on their emotions and calling into play nothing but their intelligence. What, now, is the particular point on which their attention will have to be concentrated, and what will here be the function of intelligence? To reply to these questions will be at once to come to closer grips with the problem. But here a few examples have become indispensable.

II

A man, running along the street, stumbles and falls; the passers-by burst out laughing. They would not laugh at him, I imagine, could they suppose that the whim had suddenly seized him to sit down on the ground. They laugh because his sitting down is involuntary. Consequently, it is not his sudden change of attitude that raises a laugh, but rather the involuntary element in this change, — his clumsiness, in fact. Perhaps there was a stone on the road. He should have altered his pace or avoided the obstacle. Instead of that, through lack of elasticity, through absentmindedness and a kind of physical obstinacy, *as a result, in fact, of rigidity or of momentum*, the muscles continued to perform the same movement when the circumstances of the case called for something else. That is the reason of the man's fall, and also of the people's laughter.

Now, take the case of a person who attends to the petty occupations of his everyday life with mathematical precision. The objects around him, however, have all been tampered with by a mischievous wag, the result being that when he dips his pen into the inkstand he draws it out all covered with mud, when he fancies he is sitting down on a solid chair he finds himself sprawling on the floor, in a word his actions are all topsy-turvy or mere beating the air, while in every case the effect is invariably one of momentum. Habit has given the impulse: what was wanted was to check the movement or deflect it. He did nothing of the sort, but continued like a machine in the same straight line. The victim, then, of a practical joke is in a position similar to that of a runner who falls; he is comic for the same reason. The laughable element in both cases consists of a certain *mechanical inelasticity*, just where one would expect to find the wide-awake adaptability and the living pliableness of a human being. The only difference in the two cases is that the former happened of itself, while the latter was obtained artifically. In the first instance, the passer-by does nothing but look on, but in the second the mischievous wag intervenes.

All the same, in both cases the result has been brought about by an external circumstance. The comic is therefore accidental: it remains, so to speak, in superficial contact with the person. How is it to penetrate within? The necessary conditions will be fulfilled when mechanical rigidity no longer requires for its manifestation a stumbling-block which either the hazard of circumstance or human knavery has set in its way, but extracts by natural processes, from its own store, an inexhaustible series of opportunities for externally revealing its presence. Suppose, then, we imagine a mind always thinking of what it has just done and never of what it is doing, like a song which lags behind its accompaniment. Let us try to picture to ourselves a certain inborn lack of elasticity of both senses and intelligence, which brings it to pass that we continue to see what is no longer visible, to hear what is no longer audible, to say what is no longer to the point: in short, to adapt ourselves to a past and therefore imaginary situation, when we ought to be shaping our conduct in accordance with the reality which is present. This time the comic will take up its abode in the person himself; it is the person who will supply it with everything — matter and form, cause and opportunity. Is it then surprising that the absent-minded individual — for this is the character we have just been describing — has usually fired the imagination of comic authors? When La Bruyère came across this particular type, he realized, on analyzing it, that he had got hold of a recipe for the wholesale manufacture of comic effects. As a matter of fact he overdid it, and gave us far too lengthy and detailed a description of *Ménalque*, coming back to his subject, dwelling and expatiating on it beyond all bounds. The very facility of the subject fascinated him. Absentmindedness, indeed, is not perhaps the actual fountainhead of the comic, but surely it is contiguous to a certain stream of facts and fancies which flows straight from the fountainhead. It is situated, so to say, on one of the great natural watersheds of laughter.

Now, the effect of absentmindedness may gather strength in its turn. There is a general law, the first example of which we have just encountered, and which we will formulate in the following terms:

when a certain comic effect has its origin in a certain cause, the more natural we regard the cause to be, the more comic shall we find the effect. Even now we laugh at absentmindedness when presented to us as a simple fact. Still more laughable will be the absentmindedness we have seen springing up and growing before our very eyes, with whose origin we are acquainted and whose life-history we can reconstruct. To choose a definite example: suppose a man has taken to reading nothing but romances of love and chivalry. Attracted and fascinated by his heroes, his thoughts and intentions gradually turn more and more towards them, till one fine day we find him walking among us like a somnambulist. His actions are distractions. But then his distractions can be traced back to a definite, positive cause. They are no longer cases of *absence* of mind, pure and simple; they find their explanation in the *presence* of the individual in quite definite, though imaginary, surroundings. Doubtless a fall is always a fall, but it is one thing to tumble into a well because you were looking anywhere but in front of you, it is quite another thing to fall into it because you were intent upon a star. It was certainly a star at which Don Quixote was gazing. How profound is the comic element in the over-romantic, Utopian bent of mind! And yet, if you reintroduce the idea of absentmindedness, which acts as a go-between, you will see this profound comic element uniting with the most superficial type. Yes, indeed, these whimsical wild enthusiasts, these madmen who are yet so strangely reasonable, excite us to laughter by playing on the same chords within ourselves, by setting in motion the same inner mechanism, as does the victim of a practical joke or the passer-by who slips down in the street. They, too, are runners who fall and simple souls who are being hoaxed—runners after the ideal who stumble over realities, childlike dreamers for whom life delights to lie in wait. But, above all, they are past-masters in absentmindedness, with this superiority over their fellows that their absentmindedness is systematic and organized around one central idea, and that their mishaps are also quite coherent, thanks to the inexorable logic which reality applies to the correction of dreams, so that they kindle in those around them, by a series of cumulative effects, a hilarity capable of unlimited expansion.

Now, let us go a little further. Might not certain vices have the same relation to character that the rigidity of a fixed idea has to intellect? Whether as a moral kink or a crooked twist given to the will, vice has often the appearance of a curvature of the soul. Doubtless there are vices into which the soul plunges deeply with all its pregnant potency, which it rejuvenates and drags along with it into a moving circle of reincarnations. Those are tragic vices. But the vice capable of making us comic is, on the contrary, that which is brought from without, like a ready-made frame into which we are to step. It lends us its own rigidity instead of borrowing from us our flexibility. We do not render it more complicated; on the contrary, it simplifies us. Here, as we shall see later on in the concluding section of this study, lies the essential difference between comedy and drama. A drama, even when portraying passions or vices that bear a name, so completely incorporates them in the person that their names are forgotten, their general characteristics effaced, and we no longer think of them at all, but rather of the person in whom they are assimilated; hence, the title of a drama can seldom be anything else than a proper noun. On the other hand, many comedies have a common noun as their title: *l'Avare, le Joueur*, etc. Were you asked to think of a play capable of being called *le Jaloux*, for instance, you would find that *Sganarelle* or *George Dandin* would occur to your mind, but not *Othello*: *le Jaloux* could only be the title of a comedy. The reason is that, however intimately vice, when comic, is associated with persons, it nonetheless retains its simple, independent existence, it remains the central character, present though invisible, to which the characters in flesh and blood on the stage are attached. At times it delights in dragging them down with its own weight and making them share in its tumbles. More frequently, however, it plays on them as on an instrument or pulls the strings as though they were puppets. Look closely: you will find that the art of the comic poet consists in making us so well acquainted with the particular vice, in introducing us, the spectators, to such a degree of intimacy with it, that in the end we get hold of some of the strings of the marionette with which he is playing, and actually work them ourselves; this it is that explains part of the pleasure we feel. Here, too, it is really a kind of automatism that makes us laugh — an automatism, as we have already remarked, closely akin to mere absentmindedness. To realize this more fully, it need only be noted that a comic character is generally comic in proportion to his ignorance of himself. The comic person is unconscious. As though wearing the ring of Gyges with reverse effect, he becomes invisible to himself while remaining visible to all the world. A character in a tragedy will make no change in his conduct because he will know how it is judged by us; he may continue therein even though fully conscious of what he is and feeling keenly the horror he inspires in us. But a defect that is ridiculous, as soon as it feel itself to be so, endeavors to modify itself or at least to appear as though it did. Were Harpagon to see us laugh at his miserliness, I do not say that he would get rid of it, but he would either show it less or show it differently. Indeed, it is in this sense only that laughter "corrects men's manners." It makes us at once endeavor to appear what we ought to be, what some day we shall perhaps end in being.

It is unnecessary to carry this analysis any further. From the runner who falls to the simpleton who is hoaxed, from a state of being hoaxed to one of absentmindedness, from absentmindedness to wild enthusiasm, from wild enthusiasm to various distortions of character and will, we have followed the line of progress along which the comic becomes more and more deeply imbedded in the person, yet without ceasing, in its subtler manifestations, to recall to us some trace of what we noticed in its grosser forms, and effect of automatism and of inelasticity. Now we can obtain a first glimpse — a distant one, it is true, and still hazy and confused — of the laughable side of human nature and of the ordinary function of laughter.

What life and society require of each of us is a constantly alert attention that discerns the outlines of the present situation, together with a certain elasticity of mind and body to enable us to adapt ourselves in consequence. *Tension* and *elasticity* are two forces, mutually complementary, which life brings into play. If these two forces are lacking in the body to any considerable extent, we have sickness and infirmity and accidents of every kind. If they are lacking in the mind, we find every degree of mental deficiency, every variety of insanity. Finally, if they are lacking in the character, we have cases of the gravest inadaptability to social life, which are the sources of misery and at times the causes of crime. Once these elements of inferiority that affect the serious side of existence are removed — and they tend to eliminate themselves in what has been called the struggle for life — the person can live, and that in common with other persons. But society asks for something more; it is not satisfied with simply living, it insists on living well. What it now has to dread is that each one of us, content with paying attention to what affects the essentials of life, will, so far as the rest is concerned, give way to the easy automatism of acquired habits. Another thing it must fear is that the members of whom it is made up, instead of aiming after an increasingly delicate adjustment of wills which will fit more and more perfectly into one another, will confine themselves to respecting simply the fundamental conditions of this adjustment: a cut-and-dried agreement among the persons will not satisfy it, it insists on a constant driving after reciprocal adaptation. Society will therefore be suspicious of all *inelasticity* of character, of mind and even of body, because it is the possible sign of a slumbering activity as well as of an activity with separatist tendencies, that inclines to swerve from the common center around which society gravitates: in short, because it is the sign of an eccentricity. And yet, society cannot intervene at this stage by material repression, since it is not affected in a material fashion. It is confronted with something that makes it uneasy, but only as a symptom—scarcely a threat, at the very most a gesture. A gesture, therefore, will be its reply. Laughter must be something of this kind, a sort of *social gesture*. By the fear which it inspires, it restrains eccentricity, keeps constantly awake and in mutual contact certain activities of a secondary order which might retire into their shell and go to sleep, and in short, softens down whatever the surface of the social body may retain of mechanical inelasticity. Laughter, then, does not belong to the province of esthetics alone, since unconsciously (and even immorally in many particular instances) it pursues a utilitarian aim of general improvement. And yet there is something esthetic about it, since the comic comes into being just when society and the individual, freed from the worry of self-preservation, begin to regard themselves as works of art. In a word, if a circle be drawn round those actions and dispositions—implied in individual or social life—to which their natural consequences bring their own penalties, there remains outside this sphere of emotion and struggle—and within a neutral zone in which man simply exposes himself to man's curiosity—a certain rigidity of body, mind and character that society would still like to get rid of in order to obtain from its members the greatest possible degree of elasticity and sociability. This rigidity is the comic, and laughter is its corrective.

Still, we must not accept this formula as a definition of the comic. It is suitable only for cases that are elementary, theoretical and perfect, in which the comic is free from all adulteration. Nor do we offer it, either, as an explanation. We prefer to make it, if you will, the *leitmotiv* which is to accompany all our explanations. We must ever keep it in mind, though without dwelling on it too much, somewhat as a skilful fencer must think of the discontinuous movements of the lesson while his body is given up to the continuity of the fencing-match.

II. Contemporary Theories of Laughter and Humor

16   John Morreall

This essay is a condensed version of Part I of Morreall's Taking Laughter
Seriously. *He examines the three traditional theories of laughter and shows that
none explains all cases of laughter. But by drawing on features shared by the
three theories, he creates a new formula—that laughter results from a pleasant
psychological shift (sudden change). This formula, he argues, does account for
all cases of laughter.*

A New Theory of Laughter

In the first century the Roman Quintilian complained that no
one had yet explained what laughter is, though many had tried.
And even with all the philosophers and psychologists who have
tackled the problem in the intervening centuries, the story is pretty
much the same today—we are still without an adequate general
theory of laughter. The major difficulty in constructing a comprehensive theory is that we laugh in situations which are so diverse
that they seem to have nothing in common but our laughter. We
laugh not only at humor, but also when we are tickled, when a
magician makes an object appear or disappear, when we regain our
safety after being in danger, solve a puzzle or win a game, run into
an old friend on the street, anticipate some enjoyable activity, and
feel embarrassed, to name a few representative cases.

In the face of this diversity, many have suggested that there
could not be a single formula which covered all laughter situations.
The correct approach, they say, is not to look for an essence of
laughter, but to treat laughter situations in the way Wittgenstein
treated games, as a set whose members show only family
resemblances. Most of the work currently being done by
psychologists on laughter and humor takes this approach, and simply catalogs different kinds of laughter along with their more interesting features.

Now while I heartily agree with Wittgenstein's complaint that
bad philosophy often springs from an aversion to dirtying one's
hands with empirical details, I think that when we examine the
details of laughter situations, we can find an essence to laughter.

And a good way to gain the insights necessary for constructing a comprehensive theory of laughter is to examine the three traditional theories; though none of them is adequate as a general theory, they each have features which belong in a general theory.

The oldest, and probably still the most widespread theory of laughter is that laughter is an expression of a person's feelings of superiority over others. This theory goes back at least as far as Plato and Aristotle,[1] and was given its classic statement in Hobbes, who said that laughter expresses "a sudden glory arising from some conception of some eminency in ourselves, by comparison with the infirmity of others, or with our own formerly."[2] In our century many have adopted versions of the Superiority Theory. Albert Rapp, for example, claims that all laughter developed from one primitive behavior in early man, "the roar of triumph in an ancient jungle duel."[3] Konrad Lorenz and others treat laughter as a controlled form of aggression; for them the baring of the teeth in laughing is a way of asserting one's prowess.

Now some have responded to the Superiority Theory by denying the reality of hostile and derisive laughter. Voltaire, for instance, wrote that "laughter always arises from a gaiety of disposition, absolutely incompatible with contempt and indignation."[4] But this response is naive. Clearly people do laugh in scorn at other people, and have done so throughout recorded history. Even in Voltaire's day it was common for the rich to amuse themselves by taking a coach to an insane asylum to taunt the inmates. We may feel that people *should* not laugh in derision, but that is another matter.

The proper way to criticize the Hobbesian theory, I think, is to show that not all cases of laughter involve feelings of superiority, and hence that the expression of "sudden glory" cannot be the essence of laughter. The laughter of the baby at being tickled or at peekaboo, for example, cannot be attributed to a sense of superiority in the baby, because these kinds of laughter occur before the baby is capable of self-evaluation, indeed before the baby even distinguishes himself or herself as a being separate from the surroundings. There are many situations in which adults laugh, too, where there need be no feelings of superiority. We can laugh on being tickled, on seeing a magic trick, or on running into an old friend, all without self-evaluation. Indeed, if there is self-evaluation in laughing at the magic trick, the laugher would have to judge himself inferior, in at least one respect, to the magician who has fooled him. Much merely verbal humor, such as the use of excessive alliteration or the pun, can make us laugh without triggering any feelings of superiority. And the same is true of lots of absurd humor, such as the sight gag in which a physical law is apparently broken. The Superiority Theory, then, will not do as a general theory of laughter.

The second theory I want to look at is the Incongruity Theory, which had its beginnings in some scattered comments in Aristotle, but did not come into its own until Kant and Schopenhauer. The basic idea behind this theory is very simple. We live in an orderly world where we have come to expect certain patterns among things, properties, events, etc. When we experience something that doesn't fit these patterns, that violates our expectations, we laugh. As Pascal said, "Nothing produces laughter more than a surprising disproportion between that which one expects and that which one sees."[5] Or in Kant's terminology, "Laughter is an affection arising from the sudden transformation of a strained expectation into nothing."[6] Schopenhauer explained the incongruity behind laughter as a mismatch between our concepts and the real things that are supposed to be instantiations of these concepts.[7]

Like the Superiority Theory, the Incongruity Theory clearly covers many laughter situations. In fact, I think that with proper refinement it can account for all cases of humorous laughter. But it is not comprehensive enough to cover all the non-humorous cases. The laugh of the five-month-old baby at being tickled involves no incongruity, for the baby's cognitive capacities do not yet include noticing incongruity. Even adult laughter need not involve incongruity; consider our laughter on winning a game or on anticipating some enjoyable activity.

Here, too, we might mention one of the refinements which the Incongruity Theory would require to serve as an account even of humorous laughter, for it will be important when we come to construct our own general theory of laughter. It is that not just any incongruity which a person experiences will trigger laughter: the experience must be felt as pleasant by the person. An incongruity which evokes negative emotions such as anger, fear, or indignation, will not do the trick. If I opened my bathroom door to find a large pumpkin in the bathtub, for example, I would probably laugh. But if I found a cougar in the tub, I would not laugh, though this situation would be just as incongruous.

The last theory I want to consider is the Relief Theory. Though reference to the power of laughter to relieve us of nervous tension goes back to Aristotle's comments on catharsis in comedy, the notion that laughter is a release of nervous energy was not carefully worked out until the nineteenth century. In an essay called "On the Physiology of Laughter"[8] Herbert Spencer claims that our emotions are, or at least in our nervous systems take the form of, nervous energy. And nervous energy tends to beget muscular action. In fear, for example, we make incipient movements of flight; if the fear becomes great enough, we actually flee. As anger builds up we clench our fists and make other aggressive movements; if the anger reaches a certain intensity we may attack the person who has angered us. Now laughter differs from these kinds of release of energy, according to Spencer, in that the muscular movements in laughter are not the early stages of larger movements associated with some emotion. Laughter, even if intense, does not lead to practical action such as flight or attack. Laughing, rather, is *just* a release of energy. It occurs, Spencer says, when some emotion has built up but then is suddenly seen to be inappropriate. If someone feels fearful because she thinks she hears an intruder in the house, for example, then upon discovering that it was only the cat she might break into laughter.

Spencer's theory influenced many subsequent theorists of laughter, including Dewey and Freud.[9] Freud's theory is complex, and involves much more than the notion of the release of excess nervous energy. Indeed, to discuss it thoroughly would involve a discussion of Freud's general psychoanalytic theory. But it is not necessary for our purposes to explore all the details of Freud's theory. If we understand the basics, we can see how it qualifies as a Relief Theory.

Freud's theory of laughter is found in his *Jokes and Their Relation to the Unconscious*. Here he distinguishes three kinds of laughter situations, which he calls "jokes," "the comic," and "humor." The core of the theory is that in all laughter situations we save a certain quantity of psychic energy, energy that is usually employed for some psychic purpose but which turns out not to be needed. The discharge of this superfluous energy is laughter. In joking, he says, we save energy that is normally used to suppress forbidden feelings and thoughts; in reacting to the comic we save an expenditure of energy in thought; and in humor we save an expenditure of energy in emotion.

Freud's distinction between joking, the comic, and humor, turns out to be highly artificial, and his explanation of how the different forms of psychic energy become superfluous and are released, is implausible in many places. But we need not go into all the weaknesses of Freud's theory here, for the basic fault it shares with other Relief Theories—a lack of comprehensiveness—is enough to make it unsuitable as a general theory of laughter.

Clearly there is a connection between some laughter and the relief of nervous tension. We have all had the experience of being in danger, say of falling, and then laughing on regaining our security. But it is a big jump from observations like this to the claim that all laughter involves, or *is*, the release of nervous energy. In many cases of laughter at jokes, for example, it seems that no emotion or excess nervous energy needs to have built up before the joke is told, and that none is built up by the joke itself. Consider the following:

My car can stop on a dime—and leave a nickel change.

If Freud is right that our laughter at this joke is the release of energy normally used to suppress forbidden feelings and thoughts, then just what are the feelings and thoughts indulged in here that are normally suppressed?

Freud might try to handle this case by classifying it not as an instance of joking, but as an instance of the comic, where we are supposed to save an expenditure of energy in thought, or as an instance of humor, where we save an expenditure of energy in emotion. But these categories hardly seem more promising as ways of making this joke fall under the Relief Theory. And besides, Freud's treatment of the comic and humor is highly problematic, for it never justifies the transition from saying that a certain amount of energy, of thought or emotion, *is saved*, to saying that the energy saved *is a packet of actual energy* built up in the nervous system. When in a particular laughter situation we don't have to expend psychic energy in thinking or feeling emotion, "saved energy" need not refer to real energy that has been summoned, has been found superfluous, and now requires discharge: it may simply mean energy that was never generated. Freud's reasoning in all his discussions of the saving of expenditure of psychic energy is faulty in the same way as a sales pitch I heard once in a TV commercial for a company that sold swimming pools: "And with all the money you save on the pool and the filter, you'll be able to buy our deluxe diving board."

The Relief Theory, then, like the Superiority Theory and the Incongruity Theory, will not do as a general theory of laughter. But although these three theories are inadequate, each of them draws our attention to important aspects of laughter. A comparison of these theories, in fact, suggests two general features of laughter situations which can form the basis for a comprehensive theory.

The first feature is the change of psychological state involved in laughter situations. This change may be primarily cognitive, as the Incongruity Theory shows—from a serious state of perceiving and thinking about things that fit into our conceptual patterns, to a non-serious state of being amused by some incongruity. The change may be primarily affective, as in certain cases described by the Superiority and Relief Theories in which laughter accompanies a boost in positive feelings, a cessation of negative feelings, or the release of suppressed feelings. Or the change may be both cognitive and affective, as in cases of hostile humor. We'll say more about the various kinds of psychological change involved in laughter in a moment.

Not just any change in psychological state will trigger laughter, however. As the three theories considered earlier show, the change must be sudden. To laugh, we must be caught offguard by the change so that we cannot smoothly adjust to what we are experiencing. We can build this element of suddenness into our notion of a psychological change by henceforth talking not about psychological changes, but about psychological "shifts," which will be understood to be *sudden* changes.

The second feature which must be added to our characterization of laughter situations is that the psychological shift is felt as pleasant. Enjoying self-glory, being amused by some incongruity, releasing pent-up nervous energy—all these feel good, and can cause us to laugh. An unpleasant psychological shift, on the other hand, will not normally lead to laughter (though we shall have to say something later about the apparent counterinstance of laughter in embarrassment).

Now we can put these two features together into a single formula for characterizing laughter situations in general:

> Laughter results from a pleasant
> psychological shift.

I say "results" here because laughter is not the psychological shift itself, nor the pleasant feeling which the shift produces. Laughter is rather the physical activity which is caused by, which expresses, the feeling produced by the shift.

Now the formula above is very general, but that is just what we should expect. Narrower formulas that are limited to just one kind of psychological shift, as we have seen, are not comprehensive. Generality would be a problem here only if it made our theory vacuous as applied to specific laughter situations. But as I'll show, this is not the case. And to see how our theory applies to laughter situations in an illuminating way, I would like to use it to explain the development of different kinds of laughter in the child; for here, especially in connecting non-humorous laughter with humorous laughter, is where previous theories have failed.

When an infant first laughs at about three or four months, it is not as a response to humor, of course, because his[11] simple psychology does not yet include such things as the appreciation of incongruity. Indeed, he is not even able to perceive objects or distinguish his own body from what is not his body. The earliest kind of psychological shift which the infant experiences is not conceptual, nor even perceptual; it is merely a shift in sensory input. The baby's first laughter will probably be caused by tickling, in which he alternately feels stimulation on his skin and underlying tissues, and does not feel stimulation. Being tossed in the air and caught provides another kind of shift, this one in kinesthetic sensations, that brings on laughter in young infants.

As the baby learns to perceive objects a new kind of shift, a perceptual shift, becomes possible, as in the game of peekaboo. At the cognitive stage where infants laugh the most at peekaboo, they can perceive objects but are not yet aware that those objects continue to exist when they are not being perceived. Before the age of about eight months, as Piaget has shown, *esse est percipi* for infants. Peekaboo for them is not the alternate covering and uncovering of someone's face, but the alternate existence and non-existence of that face. Under the right conditions, this perceptual shift will be pleasurable to the baby and he will laugh. If the non-existence phase of the shift lasts very long, of course, the baby may feel distress at what from his point of view is his being abandoned; then he may break into tears instead of laughter. Indeed, even in peekaboo that amuses him, the shift is usually not merely perceptual but also affective — there is a mild, temporary negative feeling at the disappearance of the face, and a boost of positive feeling when it reappears. Babies enjoy peekaboo only with familiar faces of people they feel attached to.

The earliest kinds of laughter in the child, then, require no sense of humor but are based merely on sensory and perceptual shifts. Humor comes a few years later when the child is capable of enjoying another kind of shift, a conceptual shift. By the age of three or four, the child not only perceives objects but has a set of concepts for understanding them. He distinguishes people from animals, for example, and food from what is not food. He has a counting system, perhaps, and knows that some kinds of things, such as oranges, have typical colors. He has also learned other patterns among the things, properties, and events in his experience. Snow and cold go together, as do dogs and barking, and dropping glasses and their breaking. And you know the rest of the story from reading Hume. We do not need to get into the fine points of conceptual development here; for our purposes it is enough to understand that the child develops a conceptual system, or picture of the world, which is based on his experience and which is the basis for his expectations.

Once the child has such a scheme of the ways things are supposed to be, and has operated with it for awhile, he can begin to enjoy humor. If someone puts on a dog's head from a costume, he won't simply be surprised, as the baby might be, by the newness of this experience—he will be jolted by the incongruity of this dog/human. His conceptual system, in which a dog is one thing and a person another, will have been violated. The child, too, will run together incompatible ideas by himself, as in saying "Daddy (is) baby" and the like, to achieve this same conceptual shift. And as he gets older and his conceptual system grows more sophisticated, his capacity for enjoying and creating humor will grow. He will come to laugh at the incongruity in word play, in violations of social mores and the apparent violations of physical laws, etc. Wherever he develops a pattern in his thinking, in short, there is room for a violation of that pattern and so for humor.

Though humor always involves the enjoyment of a perceived or imagined incongruity, often this enjoyment is accompanied by and boosted by our simultaneous enjoyment of an affective shift. If I see a character in a film accidentally lean against the lever of a slot machine and thereby hit the jackpot, I might be amused by this incongruity. But if I were to do the same thing accidentally in a gambling casino, my laughter might be all the greater because my enjoyment of the incongruity would be boosted by my positive feelings toward my sudden good fortune. Similarly in hostile humor, our expression of feelings of superiority at our enemy's downfall, say, can boost our enjoyment of the incongruity involved. If I hate my neighbor because he flaunts his wealth, for example, then in watching him fall into his swimming pool in his new $500 suit, I might enjoy both the incongruity of this accident, and the suffering it causes him. A pleasant affective shift is never sufficient for humor, though it may be for non-humorous laughter; nor is a pleasant affective shift necessary for humor. And so both the Superiority Theory and the Relief Theory are off the mark in seeing the essence of humor in an affective shift rather than in a conceptual shift. Any particular instance of humorous laughter, nonetheless, *may* involve a pleasant affective shift boosting the enjoyment of the conceptual shift.

Our formula that laughter is an expression of pleasure at a psychological shift, then, applies in an illuminating way to the development of different kinds of laughter in the child. And if we return to the diverse laughter situations mentioned at the beginning of this chapter, we can see that it applies to them as well. We have already discussed laughter at humor and laughter at tickling (though in older children and adults tickling is more complicated than in babies), so let's look at the other situations listed. The laugh on seeing an object appear or disappear is based on a shift similar to the perceptual shift experienced by the infant in peekaboo. We see an empty box, and then without any apparent change in the box, suddenly we see a tiger in it. All the other laughter situations mentioned, except for the laugh of embarrassment (which we'll treat at the end), involves shifts that are basically affective in nature. In regaining our safety, say after almost falling, what makes us laugh is the sudden change from feeling fearful and tense to feeling secure and relaxed. In solving a puzzle or winning a game, there is a similar shift. If the solution or victory comes easily, we are not likely to laugh. But if we have had to struggle and have been feeling frustration and tension, then the shift from that emotional state to the positive one of solving the puzzle or winning the game may well make us laugh.

The shift which causes laughter, moreover, need not be from a negative emotional state to a positive one. It may be from a non-emotional state to a positive emotional state. In the situation where I run into an old friend on the street, I may well be experiencing no emotion at all before I see her. But then as I recognize her face and rush toward her, I feel sudden excitement. The shift from feeling no emotion to feeling strong emotion here will be pleasant, and my hearty laughter will be the expression of my pleasure. Even the shift from a neutral emotional state to simply thinking about something that arouses positive emotions can be enough to trigger laughter, as when we laugh in anticipating some enjoyable activity or in recalling some particularly fond memory.

The last case on our list, laughter in embarrassment, at first seems to be a counterexample to our theory, for though we may experience a psychological shift when we suddenly feel embarrassed, clearly it is not a pleasant shift. To see how the laugh of embarrassment does fit into our theory, we need to realize that although laughing is the natural expression of amusement, it is also a piece of behavior which is to a certain extent under our control. An analogy may be drawn here with a purely physical semi-voluntary behavior like coughing, which, though it evolved as a physiological mechanism to clear the throat, can also be performed as an action when there is nothing irritating the throat. Laughing is the natural expression of amusement, and in this respect is, like "non-performed" coughing, an involuntary behavior. But the muscles involved in laughing are voluntary muscles, and so laughing can be performed as an action independently of our being in any particular psychological state. If we are in a play, we will laugh at the appropriate moment not because we're amused but because the script calls for us to perform this action. We often force a laugh, too, as when our boss tells a corny joke, in order to make someone think that a joke amused us. And this can work, of course, only because there is a natural connection between involuntary laughter and amusement.

Laughing in an embarrassing situation is likewise a case of feigning amusement by feigning involuntary laughter, though in most people it is probably less calculated than laughing at the boss's jokes, because it is a behavior learned earlier in life and used more habitually. (In this respect it is similar to the itchless scratching many people do when they're nervous, and of which they're not aware.) When we are embarassed we feel self-conscious and uncomfortable, but don't want to *appear* self-conscious and uncomfortable to the other people in the situation, for that would only make things worse. And so we perform the action of laughing as if it were not an action but an involuntary expression of amusement. If we are laughing and therefore are amused, the implicit message is, we must be enjoying the situation and not be uncomfortable.

Our account of laughter as a natural expression of amusement, to conclude, is not vitiated by laughter in embarrassment. It is a fact that the muscles involved in laughter are also under our voluntary control, so that we can feign involuntary laughter; but this does not invalidate our theory any more than our ability to cough on cue makes it false that coughing is a physiological mechanism for clearing the throat.

Notes

1. Plato, *Republic*, III, 388: *Republic*, V. 452; *Laws*, VII, 816; *Laws*, XI, 935-936. Aristotle, *Rhetoric*, II, 1389b, 10-11; *Nicomachean Ethics*, IV, 1128.

2. Thomas Hobbes, *Human Nature*, in Molesworth edition of *Works* (London, 1840), p. 46. Cf. *Leviathan*, I, 6.

3. Albert Rapp, *The Origins of Wit and Humor* (New York, 1951), p. 21.

4. Voltaire, Prefact to *L'Enfant Prodigue* (Paris, 1829).

5. Quoted in Anthony M. Ludovici, *The Secret of Laughter* (New York, 1933), p. 27.

6. Immanuel Kant, *Kritik of Judgment*, tr. by J. H. Bernard (London, 1892), p. 223.

7. Arthur Schopenhauer, *The World as Will and Idea*, tr. by R. B. Haldane and J. Kemp (London, 1964), Vol. 1, p. 76.

8. In *Essays on Education, Etc.* (London, 1911).

9. John Dewey, "The Theory of Emotion," *Psychological Review*, 1 (1894), p. 559. Sigmund Freud, *Jokes and Their Relation to the Unconscious*, tr. by J. Strachey (New York, 1976).

10. In Freud's account of joking, the psychic energy discharged in laughter is not the energy of the emotion that is no longer repressed, but the energy usually used to repress that emotion. This technicality does not affect our criticism here that we may laugh without releasing any repressed emotions.

11. I'll presume a boy baby here.

17 Michael Clark

Clark evaluates the Superiority, Relief, and Incongruity Theories as theories of humor, not as theories of laughter. In their classic versions all three are open to counterexamples, he argues, although the Incongruity Theory can be modified to be adequate. In developing his own version of that theory, Clark proceeds by looking for the "formal object" of amusement—that is, the description under which anything must be thought if it is to amuse us. This formal object is "that which is seen as incongruous." Clark's full formula for capturing the essence of amusement is that it is "the enjoyment of (perceiving or thinking of or indulging in) what is seen as incongruous, partly at least because it is seen as incongruous."

Humor and Incongruity

I

The question "What is humor?" has exercised in varying degrees such philosophers as Aristotle, Hobbes, Hume, Kant, Schopenhauer, and Bergson and has traditionally been regarded as a philosophical question. And surely it must still be regarded as a philosophical question *at least* in so far as it is treated as a conceptual one. Traditionally the question has been regarded as a search for the essence of humor, whereas nowadays it has become almost a reflex response among some philosophers to dismiss the search for essences as misconceived. Humor, it will be said, is a family-resemblance concept; no one could hope to compile any short list of essential properties abstracted from all the many varieties of humor—human misfortune and clumsiness, obscenity, grotesqueness, veiled insult, nonsense, wordplay and puns, human misdemeanors, and so on, as manifested in forms as varied as parody, satire, drama, clowning, music, farce, and cartoons. Yet even if the search for the essence of humor seems at first sight unlikely to succeed, I do not see how we can be sure in advance of any conceptual investigation; and in any case we might do well to start with the old established theories purporting to give the essence of humor, for even if they are wrong they may be illuminatingly wrong and may

139

help us to compile a list of typical characteristics.

In this essay I want to outline a more defensible version of what is probably the most plausible of the traditional theories, the Incongruity Theory, and to use my version to elucidate the nature of some of the theories which are its apparent rivals. I do not know whether my Incongruity Theory is satisfactory, but I believe it is more satisfactory than previous versions and deserves to be considered in this stronger form. I shall begin, however, with a sketchy review of some of the main theories of humor and the standard objections to them, which usually take the form of providing counterexamples. The classification of the types of theory and most of the points made about them are drawn from D. H. Monro's admirably comprehensive book *Argument of Laughter* (Melbourne and Cambridge, 1951).

(1) *Superiority Theories,* notably Hobbes' view that laughter is "a kind of sudden glory." On such theories, finding something humorous necessarily involves a feeling of triumph and superiority, and this is why we laugh at human incompetence, clumsiness, clowning and misfortune. Sometimes the feeling is one of moral superiority, as when we are amused by incidents involving sex, drinking, or human greed.

Yet even in those cases where feelings of superiority seem appropriate they do not always seem to account for our amusement. When the behavior of children amuses us it isn't simply because we feel superior to them, nor are obscene allusions funny simply because we feel above sexual matters, for if we feel very much above them we are unlikely to find the allusions humorous. In other cases feelings of superiority do not seem to be involved at all, in word-plays and puns, for example, and in nonsense rhymes and words like "runcible," that are amusing in themselves. To say that in these cases we feel superior to the words or rhymes seems strained and implausible. Again, the humor of absurd Goon-style behavior is hardly to be found in any superiority we may feel as people who behave more rationally.

(2) *Relief from Restraint Theories.* It is equally difficult to account for the humor in children's behavior, word-plays, and nonsense on these theories. The sort of case which does fit quite well is the amusement evoked by oaths, but again it is objected that oaths are not funny *because* they provide relief from restraint.

(3) *Incongruity Theories* — the Humorous as the Incongruous. The same types of objection have been produced against these. In

the first place there are many cases of incongruity which are not humorous, including those in this liberal collection of Bain's, who wrote:

> There are many incongruities that may produce anything but a laugh. A decrepit man under a heavy burden, five loaves and two fishes among a multitude, and all unfitness and gross disproportion; an instrument out of tune, a fly in ointment, snow in May, Archimedes studying geometry in a seige, and all discordant things; a wolf in sheep's clothing, a breach of bargain, and falsehood in general; the multitude taking the law into their own hands, and everything of the nature of disorder; a corpse at a feast, parental cruelty, filial ingratitude, and whatever is unnatural; the entire catalogue of vanities given by Solomon, — are all incongruous, but they cause feelings of pain, anger, sadness, loathing, rather than mirth, (*The Emotions and the Will*, pp. 282-3.)

Nowadays perhaps some of these would seem funny to some people in some contexts — there are changing fashions in humor; but it could scarcely be maintained that all of Bain's examples are invariably amusing to everyone.

Again, those instances of incongruity which are humorous are not always found humorous just because of the incongruity. Why are we amused by the behavior of our children and not by the same behavior in other people's children? Presumably because our own children are more endearing to us. Many jokes are effective because of their topicality and are completely unfunny when their references cease to be topical.

The three classes of theory which I have mentioned are certainly not exhaustive and three of the most famous accounts of humor fit into them uneasily. Bergson's view that the source of humor is human inflexibility in social life is akin to the Superiority Theories, but it is less easy to attack since he is sensitive to the many varieties of humor and does not insist that every case rigidly fits this description; he claims only to have described the *leitmotif* of the humorous. Freud's theory is very complex and provides different accounts for different types of humor. The sort he calls "wit" is supposed to involve the gratification of repressed desires — a form of relief from restraint. Kant's view that amusement is frustrated expectation is closest to the Incongruity Theories. Without qualification it is quite obviously inadequate, for the humor of many comedy situations depends on the audience's knowing precisely what is going to happen. (Those who are familiar with a record by Gerald Hoffnung on which he impersonates a builder's mate will have a very good example of this.)

II

There can be no adequate account of the notion of humor without one of the notion of amusement. For the humorous is so characterized in virtue of the human attitude or response to it: we call something "humorous" if it is apt to, or should, or deserves to, amuse people, or some special sort of person. By "amusement" here I do not, of course, mean trivial diversion of any sort; I am using the word in the narrower sense in which amusement is amusement at the humorous or comic or witty. In this essay, then, I shall approach the question "What is humor?" via the question "What is amusement?"

As a preliminary it is necessary to introduce two pieces of logical apparatus, each of some antiquity. The first, which is due to Aristotle, is too well known to need any exposition. It is the genus-species schema: the members of a species belong to a proper subset of the members of a genus. Species are defined within a genus by means of the essential characteristics which distinguish them from other species, i.e., by their *differentiae.*

The second piece of apparatus is less well-known and less ancient. It involves the concepts of material and formal object, which have recently been exhumed from medieval metaphysics by Dr. A. J. Kenny. Suppose we have a sentence-frame "Someone ψ'd — " where "ψ" is a verb-variable. The gap can be filled by various descriptions of objects. If "ψ" is "clean" you can significantly replace the dash by "his car," for example, or "his shoes," "the windows," "the floors;" less informatively you can substitute "something dirty." If "ψ" is "dry" you can substitute "his car," his clothes," "his face" . . .; or less informatively you can put "something wet." If "ψ" is "divorce," you can put "Mary" or "the president of the club"; less informatively, "his spouse." The last suggestion in each case is less informative because you know that no one can (logically) ψ an object unless it satisfies that description: he can clean only objects which are dirty, dry only what is wet, divorce (in one sense) only someone who is his spouse. These relatively uninformative descriptions are said to specify formal objects (the others specify material objects). More technically, a description 'P' specifies the formal object of ψing (be-by) if and only if

(i)

(Someone ψ's/is ψ'd by a) entails, but is not entailed by, (a is P). This at any rate is the account that Kenny wants to give of the notion. He says:

(iK)

The formal object of ψing is the object under that description which *must* apply to it if it is to be possible to ψ it. If only what is P can be ψ'd, then "thing which is P" gives the formal object of ψing (*Action, Emotion and Will*, London, 1962, p. 189).

However, this is not entirely satisfactory. Where the formal object is specified by modalizing the relevant verb ("the edible," for example, gives the formal object of eating) no difficulty may arise. But such trivial specifications are not very interesting. The trouble is that if we are looking for an interesting specification we shall, in many cases at least, have different alternatives to choose from. For it is a consequence of the above definitions that, if "that which is P" gives the formal object of ψing and (a is P) entails (a is Q), "that which is Q" also gives the formal object of ψing; and at least where the entailment is not mutual, that is where (a is Q) doesn't entail (a is P), the description "Q" will not be equivalent in any relevant sense to "P." for example, (Someone divorces a) entails (a is his spouse), so that "his own spouse" would give the formal object of divorcing. But (a is his spouse) entails (a is a human being). So (Someone divorces a) entails (a is a human being), and the description "human being" seems to give the formal object of ψing. In other words, if we define "formal object" in the manner of Kenny, we have no right to talk of *the* (one and only) formal object of, for example, divorcing.

What we want, it might be thought, is the most specific description substitutable for "P" (for a given value of   ) in (i) to produce a true statement. The narrowest description would be one entailed by every other description whose substitution produced a true statement. But if we ignore the trivial specifications — like "the edible" for eating — and their close synonyms, I doubt whether it will always be possible to find *the narrowest* description. Only a sentient being can (logically) be divorced, but only if he is a human being, and only if the human being is the spouse of the divorcer, and only if he goes through what is taken to be a legally acceptable procedure, and so on. How far are we to stop short of the specification of the class of people who actually *are* divorced? Out of context there may be no answer to this question. Must we, then, abandon talk of *the* formal object of ψing?

A way of avoiding this conclusion is suggested in subsequent remarks by Kenny himself. He says:

> One way in which a species of action may be differentiated from other species of the same genus is by a difference in its formal object. Thus if we take (voluntary) killing as a genus, homicide differs from other species in this genus as being the killing of a *human being;* if we take homicide as a genus, murder differs from other species in this genus as being the killing of an innocent human being [*sic*]. If we take making as a genus, then cobbling differs from tailoring because the formal object of the one is footwear and the other is clothes (*op cit.,* pp. 190-1).

The species is specified by the conjunction of two spefications: (1) of the genus, (2) of the differentia(e). In these cases (2) is a specification of the formal object of the species. The formal object is uniquely determined by the genus under consideration — although there may be a number of different synonymous descriptions which give it. In the light of the considerations above it may well be that *the* formal object of ψing cannot be specified until a genus of which ψing is a species is also specified, and that ψing may have different formal objects according to the genus under which it is being considered. The notion of formal object can now be given as follows:

(ii)

> Specifying the formal object of ψing/being ψ'd by for a genus of which ψing/being ψ'd by is a species is specifying the differentia(e) of that species within the genus where the species is being differentiated solely in terms of the object of ψing. If "that which is P" delimits the species, ψing, within the genus in such a way, then this expression gives the formal object of ψing.

It is a consequence of (ii) that talk of the formal object of an act, etc., is appropriate only when we have a concept for a genus of which that act may be regarded as a species. Definitions which involve specifying formal objects are definitions of that traditionally respectable variety, definitions *per genus et differentiam*. If a species has no single set of differentiae (like *game* as a species of activity), then it will have no clear-cut formal object. In such cases it may well be that any talk of formal objects is misleading.

There is, in general, no such thing as *the* genus of a given activity, there is a hierarchy of genera; e.g., the species philosophy lecture falls under each of the following genera: lecture, instruction, communication (ideally), behavior. Since almost any activity can be considered under different genera, it can have different formal objects. If anyone claims that "thing which is P" gives the formal object of ψing, it always makes sense, I suggest, to ask, "under what genus?"

III

I think that it is illuminating to think of some traditional theories of humor as attempts to specify the formal object of amusement. Thought of in this way they will not be treated as complete accounts, since the genus under which amusement (that is, being amused by) is being considered has not been made clear. In setting forth my revised Incongruity Theory my procedure will be to introduce a plausible candidate for formal object of *being amused by* and then to consider the genus under which it must be understood. I will suggest that it is an essential feature of any object of S's amusement that it should be seen as incongruous by S. In other words, "that which is seen as incongruous" gives the formal object of *being amused by*. A related view can be found in Aristotle and one has been put forward more recently by Schopenhauer, part of whose account I shall quote, because he also goes a little way towards clarifying the notion of incongruity:

> The cause of laughter in every case is simply the sudden perception of the incongruity between a concept and the real objects which have been thought through it in some relation, and laughter itself is just the expression of this incongruity. It often occurs in this way: two or more real objects are thought through *one* concept, and the identity of the concept is transferred to the objects; it then becomes strikingly apparent from the entire difference of the objects in other respects, that the concept was only applicable to them from a one-sided point of view. It occurs just as often, however, that the incongruity between a single real ob-

ject and the concept under which, from one point of view, it has
rightly been subsumed, is suddenly felt. Now the more correct the
subsumption of such objects under a concept may be from one
point of view, and the greater and more glaring their incongruity
with it from another point of view, the greater is the ludicrous effect which is produced by this contrast. All laughter then is occasioned by a paradox, and therefore by unexpected subsumption,
whether this is expressed in words or in actions. This, briefly
stated, is the true explanation of the ludicrous. (*The World as
Will and Idea*, I, 13.)

I would substitute "object of amusement" for "cause of laughter,"
since, clearly, not every outburst of laughter is occasioned by the
humorous, e.g., laughing when tickled, hysterical laughter,
laughter under nitrous oxide; nor does every man always express his
amusement by laughing. Secondly, I would replace the narrower
term "ludicrous" or "laughable" ("Lächerlich") by "amusing"
because I believe that (apparent) incongruity[1] may be an essential
feature not merely of what we would call the "ludicrous" but of all
types of humor.

Now Schopenhauer's account suggests the following (a priori)
thesis:

(T) If an event/state of affairs etc. amuses someone, then he sees
it as involving the incongruous subsumption of one or more instances under a single concept.

Notice that I say he *sees it as involving* incongruous subsumption.
Whether the object really involves incongruity is immaterial; indeed
it is not even necessary for the amused person to *believe* that what is
amusing him is incongruous—all he needs to do is to see it in that
way. Someone who watched a gesticulating politician on television
with the volume turned down so that he couldn't hear him, might
try thinking of what he saw as the politician trying to sing a popular
song, and then find what he was watching amusing; but he needn't
believe that he is really watching an important politician singing a
popular song. Kenny says:

The description of the formal object of a mental attitude such as
an emotion, unlike a description of the formal object of a non-
intentional action, [i.e., an action which has no intentional object]

must contain reference to a belief. Only what is wet can be dried: but something which is merely believed to be an insult may provoke anger (*op cit.*, pp. 193–4).

He is surely wrong in thinking that this applies to all mental attitudes. Amusement need not contain that sort of reference to a belief, only to the way the object is perceived or thought of. I do not know whether what Kenny says would be true if for "reference to a belief" you substituted "reference to a belief or to the way the object is perceived or thought of," though it does seem plausible.

It is worth trying thesis (T) out on a few examples. Obviously I cannot expect to be able to substantiate my thesis in this way—a few examples prove nothing positive, for they may be tendentious; my intention is only to illustrate the thesis. Consider the following story:

(a)

One day, it is said, Sir Isaiah Berlin went to a magnificent concert at the Sheldonian Theatre and, as he was leaving, Professor Ryle happened to be passing Blackwell's. Ryle hailed him and shouted, "Hallo, Isaiah. Been listening to some tunes, then?"

The subsumption of mere tunes under the concept of symphony music is clearly incongruous. It is, of course, not always easy to say precisely under which concept the illicit subsumption is being made, because it need not be mentioned in a description of the object of amusement. There are the added complications that different people, and even the same man, may find the same thing amusing for different reasons. Consider a few more examples:

(b)

Conservative Party spokesman: "The Conservative Party is always ready to provide an alternative to Government."

(c)

"G. E. Moore doing philosophy is like a man dancing in treacle."

(d)

"The time has come, the walrus said,
To talk of many things,

Of shoes and ships and sealing wax,
Of cabbages and kings. . . ."

(e)

A woman asked a shopkeeper recently for a small packet of a certain
product. She was given a packet marked "Large." The shopkeeper
explained that the firm made three sizes, "Super," "Giant," and
"Large," the last being the smallest.

Example (b) is funny because the spokesman should have said
something different. Perhaps we might describe it as the subsumption of an utterance of a remark inimical to one's cause under the
concept of utterances typically made by spokesmen and favorable to
their causes. This may sound objectionably artificial, but talk about
concepts and their instances often sounds artificial, and, although it
may be healthy for us to suspect unnatural sounding accounts which
philosophers attempt to foist on us, it is surely at least as unhealthy
to assume that they must all therefore be wrong.

Example (c) seems to me to involve a double incongruity. A
man dancing in treacle is an odd case of a man dancing and, at
first sight anyway, an even odder instance to liken to the activity of
philosophizing. In (d), under what concept is the walrus subsuming
shoes, ships, sealing wax, cabbages and kings? Perhaps the whole set
is being subsumed under the concept of group of objects for discussion. Example (e) obviously involves the oddity of calling the
smallest item in a series "large."

IV

What sort of account is to be given of incongruous subsumption
of instances under a concept? Clearly the instances incongruously
subsumed are different in some way from the standard instances
falling under the concept. But in what way? Sometimes the subsumed instance just does not belong to the concept at all: the remark
made by the Tory spokesman is *not* a remark favorable to his party.
Sometimes indeed the instance isn't the sort of thing which could
belong to the concept in question, as in those cases involving
category mistakes: recently someone of my acquaintance stopped at
a garage to ask how to get onto a projected motorway which appeared on her A.A. map—a projected motorway is not a special sort

of motorway. On the other hand a man dancing in treacle *is* a case of a man dancing — the point is that it is not a typical case. Again, standard groups of topics for discussion differ from the walrus's in that the topics are coherently related. It is because conversations *should* be, or (more doubtfully) typically are, more coherent than that projected by the walrus that the latter is regarded as different from the former.

There is more than one way, then, in which incongruous instances differ from paradigm instances of the concept and no doubt these types shade off into one another. The objects of humor are so various partly because the modes of incongruity are various.

If incongruity amounts (for present purposes) to incongruous subsumption under a concept, and this is to be analyzed in terms of the difference between the subsumed instance(s) and the standard instances of the concept, why not dispense with all this admittedly artificial talk about concepts and just talk about the incongruous assimilation of instances to one another? This, however, would be inadequate, for any object may properly be assimilated to any other given a context which provides a concept under which both naturally fall, and we can always in principle find or form a concept under which both instances fall as standard instances. When there is a particular concept, however, under which one of the instances is thought, it helps to determine the limits of proper assimilation of other objects to that instance.[2]

In the majority of cases there seems to be some good reason for the subsumption of the wayward instance under the concept in question, apart from the intention to amuse. Perhaps from one point of view the subsumption is perfectly correct and congruous, or someone thinks that it is congruous (Cf. example (c).) However, I do not think that, *pace* Schopenhauer, this is absolutely necessary — (d) might serve as a counter-example. I think that it is a common but not invariable feature of the objects of amusement.

V

What about the stock objections to traditional versions of the incongruity theory, then? I think that it is quite easy to see that they cannot be invoked yet against the stronger version which I have begun to elaborate. All that has been claimed so far is that the ap-

parently incongruous is the *formal object* of amusement. It is no
good now saying that there are many instances of incongruity which
are not amusing, for in saying that the apparently incongruous is the
formal object of amusement all we are saying is that nothing can
(logically) amuse someone *unless* he sees it as incongruous, that seeing it as incongruous is a *necessary* condition of his finding it
humorous. We are not saying that it is a sufficient condition for his
finding it amusing, we are not saying that if he sees it as incongruous
he is bound to be amused by it. To say that "what is dirty" gives the
formal object of cleaning is to say that nothing can be cleaned unless
it is dirty, not that anything dirty *will* be cleaned.

Even so, it may still be objected that what makes (a) funny, for
example, is not just the queer assimilation of symphony music to
mere tunes, but our knowledge of Ryle's own character as revealed
in his behavior and writings. Example (b) is funny (to those with
non-conservative sympathies) because the remark seems to them to
come very near to the truth. And so on. But this objection need not
worry us yet since my revised account is not yet complete. All that
needs to be pointed out at the moment is that a specification of the
formal object of ψing need not contain a full explanation of why
things are ψ'd. Saying that only dirty things are cleaned is not to explain why certain things which are dirty are cleaned. Saying that
only what is seen as incongruous is found amusing is not to explain
why some things which are seen as incongruous are found amusing.

VI

To see something as incongruous, then, is not necessarily to be
amused by it. What is the difference between a man who finds
something he is doing, perceiving, or thinking about, odd and who
is not amused by it, and someone who *is* amused by it? What is a
man denying who, while admitting that he sees something as incongruous, says that it fails to amuse him? Or, more technically,
under what genus is the (apparently) incongruous[3] the formal object
of amusement? I shall suggest that amusement is *the enjoyment of
(perceiving or thinking of or indulging in) what is seen as incongruous, partly at least because it is seen as incongruous.* (A
qualification follows at the end of the paragraph.) This answer does
a little more than answer the question in the technical form I have
just put it. It gives more than the genus asked for: the last nine

words of the italicized phrase require that apparent incongruity should be a reason for the enjoyment which is involved in amusement. I think that this proviso is necessary, even though we are not left with a simple definition *per genus et differentiam* after all. A man might enjoy something which he incidentally regarded as incongruous, but if the incongruity were no reason for his enjoyment I see no reason to think he would be amused. A man who was enjoying some exotic food which he incidentally regarded as a very odd sort of food would not find the food, or eating the food, amusing if its apparent incongruity did not contribute towards his enjoyment. The object of amusement must be enjoyed partly at least for its apparent incongruity. Moreover, it is necessary to add that *the apparent incongruity is not enjoyed just for some ulterior reason* (say, because eating *odd* food is fashionable and you get pleasure from eating it because you know it is fashionable).

In order to be able to evaluate the suggested account of amusement it would be as well to have a satisfactory account of enjoyment, and I doubt whether one has ever been given. However, it does seem to me that the sort of account of enjoyment or pleasure which currently finds favor will fit quite nicely into the suggested account of amusement. Consider that offered by C. C. W. Taylor in his paper on "Pleasure" (*Analysis Supplement*, January 1963):

> Wanting something because one enjoys it is wanting it for itself
> . . . but to do what I want for its own sake is not necessarily to enjoy it. Someone may, for instance, want the good of humanity,
> but this is not to say that he wants the good of humanity because he enjoys it, since the assertion that anyone enjoys the good of humanity is senseless (p. 16).

What cases of wanting x for its own sake are cases of enjoyment, then? Taylor's answer is: those where x is an action or "passion" (in Hume's sense) of the subject. For example, to enjoy a football match is, strictly, to enjoy *watching* a football match. Any action which I perform or experience which I have, wanting to perform or have it for its own sake, is necessarily something which I am enjoying.[4]

Taylor considers that enjoyment is only a species of pleasure. Kenny has offered a thesis about pleasure in general, which is similar to Taylor's account of enjoyment: "If an action is done from pleasure, then it is done for its own sake with no ulterior motive or further end in view" (*op, cit.,* p. 144). Kenny seems to be making the same point about pleasure as Taylor is making about enjoyment, but he has formulated it inaccurately. For I can certainly get pleasure from something, for example, working, which is *also* done for some ulterior motive, for example, money. Compare also William Alston in an article on pleasure in Edwards' *Encyclopaedia* (New York, 1967):

> To get pleasure is to have an experience which, as of the moment, one would rather have than not have, on the basis of its felt quality, apart from any further considerations regarding consequences. (Vol. 6, p. 345.)

I shall make use of Taylor's formulation, which says that to enjoy some action, activity, or experience of one's own is to perform or have it, wanting to do so for its own sake. This must not be understood as implying that the action or experience is necessarily a fulfillment of an antecedent desire, for it is clear that some enjoyment is not *preceded* by any desire for what we are enjoying; but the object of the enjoyment must be something which we are wanting at the time of the enjoyment. Thus Ryle says of a man who enjoyed gardening: "he dug, wanting to dig and not wanting to do anything else (or nothing) instead" (*The Concept of Mind*, London, 1949, p. 108).

I do not believe that Taylor's account of enjoyment is entirely satisfactory, but I think that it may be on the right lines. I shall consider two possible deficiencies. Suppose I am watching a film at the cinema, wanting to watch it for its own sake, but that my enjoyment is completely spoilt by the sound of dance music coming from the palais next door. Here we seem to have a case which fits the proposed account of enjoyment and yet is not itself a case of enjoyment. But it may be granted that this is not a serious difficulty, and that it can be overcome by requiring a more determinate description of what is wanted. In the case envisaged I do not want to watch the film in those conditions: watching a film whose sound track is partially obliterated by dance music is not something I want for its own sake, I want to watch the film without the dance music and that is what I am not doing.

A more serious difficulty, however, cannot be met without modifying the account. It seems to me possible that a man may work as an academic philosopher, wanting to do this for itself, but that he may not literally enjoy his work; it will give him satisfaction, presumably, but that is not necessarily quite the same thing. Russell couldn't enjoy writing *Principia Mathematica* because of the immense intellectual effort involved in it. I agree that it is probable that what Russell wanted for its own sake here was the finished product rather than the actual process of composition (see footnote 4), but it is surely not impossible that he should have wanted the composing for its own sake. Or what about a puritan who values self-abnegation for its own sake and who fasts, wanting to fast for the sake of fasting; need he enjoy fasting? Perhaps, then, the absence of much effort or the absence of constraint is an essential feature of enjoyment. On the other hand it does seem possible to enjoy exerting oneself or tackling something which is really difficult. Maybe the enjoyment doesn't come until the exertion is well under way, or what is enjoyed is the realization that you are achieving something difficult. It would be optimistic to think that a clause added to Taylor's account to cope with the point about effort would result in an adequate definition of enjoyment, but in default of having a better one I shall make use of it.

We can now substitute this account of enjoyment in the suggested account of amusement. If the object of amusement for S is an action or experience of S, then he will want to indulge in that action or have that experience for its own sake because[5] he sees it as incongruous. If the object of amusement is an object of S's perception or thought, then he will perceive or think of that object for the sake of doing so because[5] he sees the object as incongruous. Furthermore, it must (in the appropriate sense) be easy, involve no great effort, to persist in perceiving the object, or in the acting or experiencing. If it does require such an effort, we may be said to appreciate humorous qualities in the object, but we may not properly be said to be amused at it. For example, to be amused at the man we see slipping on a banana skin is to enjoy watching him slip because we see this as incongruous — that is, to watch him slip, wanting to watch the (apparently) odd incident for the sake of watching it — and (in some sense) to be able to do this without effort. The account of enjoyment I have used seems to fit quite nicely.[6]

VII

I want now to revert to the second sort of criticism of Incongruity Theories, that incongruity is not always what really makes something funny. What Ryle says in my example (a) may well only seem funny because it is Ryle who said it, and so on. Now in claiming that amusement is roughly the enjoyment of what is seen as incongruous, we certainly do not explain why it is that *certain* things when seen as incongruous evoke enjoyment and others do not, we say almost nothing about the various features of the former which account for the enjoyment. It is true that I have insisted that a reason for the enjoyment in cases of amusement must be the apparent incongruity of the object, but I do not claim that it will always be the only reason or provide us with a full causal explanation of the enjoyment. It seems to me that Superiority and Relief from Restraint Theories provide partial answers to the demand for this sort of explanation and that it is not a demand that can be met by a purely philosophical theory. Some sort of empirical investigation is surely necessary to satisfy it. Seen in this light Superiority Theories and Relief from Restraint Theories are not competitors with my version of the Incongruity Theory but are complementary to it. Whether they are satisfactory complements is a matter for psychologists, biologists, and literary critics. On the face of it it seems unlikely that *all* amusement is in fact produced by relief from restraint, or that amusement always involves glorying in others' apparent inferiority, but at the same time it looks as if there are some cases of each.

VIII

I do not know whether there are any clear counterexamples to my account of the humorous, whether there are, for example, any cases of enjoyment of the apparently incongruous which are not cases of amusement. Suppose a man is looking at a picture and is enjoying this experience, and suppose he says he likes the picture because of the incongruity of its content. Moreover he likes the incongruity for its own sake, not for any insight, say, that the picture gives him into the nature of the world. Must we say he finds the picture amusing? I find it difficult to say.

There is a more systematic way of searching for counterexamples than the random construction of imaginary cases. Monro tests each of the theories he considers by trying them out as accounts of a number of different types of humor—breaches of the usual order of events, forbidden breaches, indecency, importing into one situation what belongs to another, word-play, and so on. I shall not attempt this somewhat tedious task in the present paper, but it is a task which is available to any sceptical reader.

Notes

1. I shall use the expression "apparently incongruous" for what is seen as incongruous, although it is not as appropriate as I would wish.

2. I think it is likely that there are alternative, but fundamentally equivalent, accounts of incongruity, say in terms of conflicting concepts under which an instance is being subsumed, or simply in terms of an instance's being subsumed under a concept under which it does not fall. My remarks on incongruous subsumption are not intended to give a complete, non-circular definition of "incongruous."

3. See note 1.

4. Taylor points out that it must really be the action or passion itself that is wanted, not an end-product of it, unless this is also an action or passion. Thus, if I write a philosophical paper wanting to do so for its own sake, I may want either (i) "my writing this paper," or (ii) "there being a paper on this topic written by me," and only in the first case will I necessarily enjoy writing it. Obviously I can write a paper I want to write for its own sake without particularly enjoying what I do, but in that case I will want (ii) as distinct from (i).

5. But it needn't be *only* because.

6. I think it may be possible to define some other concepts in the same family as amusement in a similar way — I am thinking of some particular species of amusement. What is it to find something ludicrous or farcical or comic or witty, for example? Sometimes a definition can be obtained by narrowing the genus, enjoyment: *e.g.*, finding something hilarious or mirthful is a species of more *intense* enjoyment, or perhaps of enjoyment the expression of which is typically uninhibited. Sometimes the formal object under the genus enjoyment can be restricted: to find something comic is not just to find it incongruous but to find it obviously and unsubtly so. In the case of finding something witty either procedure seems available: it is not just enjoyment but intellectual enjoyment, enjoyment requiring some exercise of the intellect. Again, if something is found to be witty it is found to be subtly incongruous. In this case the two methods of definition are equivalent.

18   Roger Scruton

Although Scruton titles his essay "Laughter," it is really only about laughter at humor. He agrees with Clark that it would be helpful to find a "formal object" of humorous laughter—the description under which anything must be thought if it is to amuse us. But he rejects Clark's claim that incongruity is this formal object. Consider, he says, counterexamples like our amusement at a caricature, in which it is the fit, and not any incongruity, between the representation and the person that we enjoy. Scruton ultimately offers not a formal object of amusement, but a pattern of thought characteristic of amusement. This pattern is the enjoyable de-valuing, demolition, of something human. In exploring the nature of amusement, Scruton makes several interesting observations. Two of the most important, in relation to the other essays in this book, are that amusement is a kind of aesthetic interest, and that amusement differs significantly from standard cases of emotions. The first of these claims will be challenged by Mike Martin in the essay after this, and the relation of amusement to emotion will be the topic of all three essays in part III.

Laughter

1

Man is the only animal that laughs, but it seems that laughter belongs also to the immortals. A starting point for all enquiries into laughter must therefore be the hypothesis that it is an attribute of reason (which is the quality that distinguishes men and gods from animals). That gets us no further than our definition of reason. If all we can say is that reason is the feature which distinguishes men and gods from the humorless animals, then it gets us nowhere. As a matter of fact, however, it has become clear in recent years that much can be said about the concept of the "rational being." Although analytical philosophy has yet to give a theory of rationality that has the grandeur and consequence of those of Aristotle, Aquinas, or Kant, it can nevertheless make gestures which carry some promise of system. In this paper I shall make such a gesture, and hope that the intimation of a distant theory will compensate for the sketchiness of my account.

156

It is evident that a theory of sensation that said nothing about the nature of sentient beings would not be a theory of sensation. It should be equally evident that no theory of laughter can dispense with an account of the being that laughs. It is not a misfortune of animals that they are so humorless. The cackle of the hyena would not be turned into laughter by a little more effort on his part. However hard he tries, the day will never come when the dismal sound is irradiated by the spirit of amusement. It is not that he should try harder at what he is doing, but that he should do something else. And this something else lies outside his nature. The discussion of animal mentality frequently brings to light these mental capacities that are "outside nature." It is this which compels us to recognize the vastness of the gap between the animals and ourselves. To possess reason is not to possess a further sense or "capacity": it is to be systematically different in *kind*. Reason permeates our nature, and transforms even our pains and pleasures into states that are peculiar to us.

2

"Laughter" is a misleading term. We use it to refer to the sounds emitted by someone who is being tickled, to certain expressions of scorn or dismay, to the "hollow laughter" that accompanies the perception of one's ruin. In this broad sense (in which it denotes a sound produced through the mouth of a sentient being) we even use the term of hyenas. Hence the preference among philosophers for less symptomatic labels: "amusement," which denotes a state of mind, and "humor," which denotes one of its objects. Neither of these terms is fully satisfactory: an amusing holiday, like an amusement arcade, may contain little humor, and no amusement. To feel our way towards the mental phenomenon that concerns us, we must recognize that common usage will be an inaccurate guide.

The first step towards imposing order on this usage is to stipulate that the phenomenon which we seek to describe has intentionality. It is not laughter, but laughter at or about something, that interests the philosopher. Given intentionality, "laughter," "amusement," and "humor" may designate a single state of mind. Laughter is its full expression, amusement its essence, and humor its intentional object. As we shall see, this is not quite right; but it serves to introduce the topic in a more or less orderly manner.

3

One familiar account of intentionality is in terms of thought. A state of mind is intentional if it contains, or is founded on (recourse to metaphor is difficult to avoid) a thought.[1] "Thought" here means what Frege meant by "*Gedanke*": the content of a declarative sentence; the bearer of a truth value. In certain cases this thought may be a belief. I am afraid of you because I believe that you intend me harm. But not all thoughts are beliefs; some are merely entertained, in whatever mode of imagination or suspended judgement.

One explanation of the humorlessness of animals might be that amusement contains, or is founded on, a thought of which animals are incapable. Thoughts that involve self-consciousness are peculiar to rational beings (which is why animals are never sentimental); so too are thoughts that involve morality (which is why animals never feel remorse). And so on. I make this suggestion not in order to endorse it, but in order to suggest an *easy* way in which rationality and amusement might be brought into connection. It is not the way that I shall recommend.

Is it true that all intentionality involves, and is explained by, thought? Unfortunately there seem to be intentional states that do not (in the sense intended) involve thoughts. The nearest a dog ever gets to laughing, is, I suppose, barking. But we make the distinction between barking *simpliciter* (a useless activity which most human beings deplore), and barking *at* an intruder or a friend. Is this second not an example of intentionality? It certainly seems that reference to the object of a bark can require an intensional context; in which case barking satisfies the most favored criterion of intentionality. If a dog barks at a cat, it does not follow either that there is an object at which he is barking (he might be barking up the wrong tree), or that, if there is one, it is, so to speak, as he "barks" it to be (it may be a mechanical cat with jaws of invincible steel, and he was certainly no such fool as to bark at *that*). Thus things barked at need not obey Leibniz's law; nor can one always quantify into a bark. Confirmation of the "intentional in-existence" of the barkee is to be found in George Eliot:

> The sincere antipathy of a dog towards cats in general, necessarily takes the form of indignant barking at the neighbor's black cat which makes daily trespass; the bark at imagined cats, though a frequent exercise of the canine mind, is yet comparatively feeble. (*Felix Holt*, ch. XV).

Whatever we say about the case, however, it is clearly not likely to provide us with a model for amusement. In the same sense in which dogs bark *at* cats, we can imagine hyenas laughing *at* each other. But it is quite another thing to say that hyenas thereby express their amusement (although we may hear them as expressing ours). This must lend weight to the theory that amusement is an expression of thought. So is there any specific thought, characteristic of amusement as such? If so, we will be able to characterize the "formal object" of laughter — the description under which anything must be thought to fall if it is to be laughed at.

4

The case for the formal object has been admirably set out by Michael Clark in an article which also offers a theory of amusement.[2] Clark rightly criticizes those, like Schopenhauer and Bergson, who have tried to provide sufficient conditions for something's being funny, and to explain amusement as the perception that those conditions are fulfilled. If there is a place in the analysis of amusement for such a perception it is, Clark argues, as a necessary and not as a sufficient condition. That is to say, it may be necessary to perceive, think of, or imagine an object in a certain way in order to laugh at it: but one might well so conceive it and not laugh. Clark argues that the traditional theories are more acceptable if regarded as attempts to give the thought that is characteristic of amusement — the "description under which" an object is laughed at — rather than the whole character of laughter.

Clark rightly points out that the thought which characterizes amusement does not have to be a belief: I can be amused by what is merely imaginary. Following Schopenhauer, he proposes the "incongruous" as the formal object of amusement, and argues that whenever I am amused, I must "see" the object "as" incongruous, in a manner that he tries to specify. That is not sufficient for amusement, but it is necessary. In order to be amused I must also enjoy this incongruity, the incongruity must be the cause of my enjoyment, and (I here paraphrase radically) I must enjoy the incongruity at least partly *for its own sake*. I shall return to these further observations later.

5

I wish first to examine the suggestion that the formal object of amusement is to be captured by the idea of "incongruity." Clark, following Monro[3], distinguishes three common accounts of amusement: superiority theories (exemplified by Hobbes's view of laughter as "sudden glory"), "relief from restraint" theories (such as Freud's explanation of jokes), and "incongruity" theories, of the kind given by Schopenhauer. He rejects the first two kinds—rightly I believe. For either they cover all examples of amusement by being made so vague as to be insignificant; or else they are given a precise meaning only to exclude many of the things at which we are prone to laugh. But why is the incongruity theory not open to a similar objection? Clark, inspired by Schopenhauer, explains incongruity as "incongruous subsumption under a concept," which amounts to some kind of striking discrepancy between the object subsumed and the standard instances with which it is thereby brought into relation. Is it likely that such an idea could be made precise without also excluding central cases of amusement? In order to test the theory I shall return to Schopenhauer, and attempt to gloss the idea of "incongruity" in terms which are not Clark's but which capture, I think, Clark's meaning.

Schopenhauer explains incongruity thus:

> Two or more real objects are thought through *one* concept, and the identity of the concept is transferred to the objects: it then becomes strikingly apparent from the entire difference of the objects in other respects, that the concept was only applicable to them from a one-sided point of view. It occurs just as often, however, that the incongruity between a single real object and the concept under which, from one point of view, it has been rightly subsumed, is suddenly felt. Now the more correct the subsumption of such objects from one point of view, and the greater and more glaring the incongruity with it from another point of view, the greater is the ludicrous effect which is produced by this contrast.[4]

This is not the place to embark on an interpretation of Schopenhauer. However, the passage makes several suggestions about incongruity: for example, that it is revealed or understood through a conflict of points of view; that it lies, or can lie, in an incongruity between object and concept. Neither suggestion is clear. I suspect that the real incongruity of which Schopenhauer speaks lies not between object and concept but between points of view: the reference to concept and object being no more than an attempt to squeeze his analysis into the brave metaphysical system of which it is designed to form a part. There is an instance, however, that could be held to illustrate Schopenhauer's meaning: that of the mimic. Mimicry is amusing partly because of its successful presentation of *two* things in one — the mimic, and the person being mimicked. The "funny man" presents his victim at the same time as distorting him, with the odd result that one sees the victim *in* the distortion.[5] You might say that this is like the simultaneous subsumption of an object under, and exclusion of that object from, a single concept. From one point of view the mimic's gestures fit the concept "indolent man." From another point of view (that which does not penetrate to the representation), the subsumption is absurd, for the very exaggeration of the gestures denies it.

But the language of "concept and object" belongs to the metaphysical theory, and looks plausible only because of its vagueness. Consider a caricature of the Prime Minister: it may represent a non-deviant example of a woman, but still be a caricature of *her*. So what is the concept with which this instance is compared? Should we say: the concept of Mrs. Thatcher? should we refer, that is, to the Leibnizian "individual notion" which she uniquely satisfies and from which the caricature, in however minute but significant a way, departs? It may seem so, since what is funny in a caricature is its simultaneous proximity to and deviation from an individual. But then the reference to "concepts" is no more than a ruse. And when this reference is dropped, it is no longer clear that we have a case of incongruity. The caricature amuses, not because it does not fit Mrs. Thatcher, but because it does fit her, all too well. it is true that it must also contain an exaggeration: but the exaggeration is amusing because it draws attention to some feature of *her*. If one wishes to describe the humor of a caricature in terms of incongruity it must be added that it is an incongruity which illustrates a deeper congruity between an object and itself.

If that is vague, it is because the word "incongruous" is vague. The point of the example was merely to draw attention to the general difficulty: either you make the concept precise, and then risk leaving out important cases of amusement. Or you leave it vague, and content yourself with a vacuous characterization of the formal object of laughter—vacuous because to know what is meant by the "incongruous" you would have to consult, not some independent conception, but the range of objects at which we laugh.

Further examples can be adduced to confirm that thought. Consider the action which is so much *in character* that we cannot but laugh. Wit may not be quite what Pope said it is—what oft was thought but ne'er so well expressed—but satire at least possesses, when successful, the quality of accuracy, and satire has its equivalent in everyday life, when a character acts true to himself. What amuses us, it could be said, is the total congruence between the idea of the man and his action. We might be enraged or hurt by it: but I do not see why we might not also be amused.

It would be wrong to expand those observations into a "congruity" theory of amusement. For that would be to risk just the same kind of censure that I have been expressing. Rather I wish to suggest that the problems with Clark's analysis stem, not from a faulty identification of the formal object of amusement, but from a misleading implication in the idea of a formal object.

6

I have taken for granted a certain understanding of the phrase "formal object"—a medieval term of Aristotelian provenance, recently applied to the discussion of intentionality by Kenny.[6] When describing states of mind we transfer the idea from the material to the intentional realm. The relation between emotion and object is—to use the misleading term—"internal." It is not a material relation. In the material sphere the idea of a formal object is not so hard to understand: only what is wet can be dried, only what is solid can be thrown, and so on. But you can *try* to dry what is not wet: "trying to dry" designates an intentional relation, and its object is characterized by what Brentano called "in-existence." So too with emotions. If the formal object of fear is "what is harmful," then this designation must be understood to qualify only the intentional object. It specifies a limitation not on the material object of fear, but on the thought through which the material object is presented. I can fear only what I *think* to be harmful. It has been argued that many emotions have formal objects, since they are identified in terms of the beliefs on which they are founded. For example, we distinguish jealousy from envy by referring to the belief, present in the first, but not in the second, that the subject is *cheated* by another's possession of some good. Some, Clark included, go on to construe the existence of the "formal object" of emotion as a product of our classifications of states of mind.[7]

It is necessary to distinguish formal from proper objects. The formal object of fear (say) is given by the description under which something must be thought if it is to be feared: it is what *can* be feared. The proper object is not what *can* be feared, but rather what it is right, proper or justified to fear. The "harmful" is (perhaps) the formal object of fear; its proper object is the fearful. To justify the description "fearful" is to justify fear. Confusion between formal and proper objects leads many—including Sartre[8]—to consider emotions to be a kind of judgement. Fear then becomes the recognition of the fearful, anxiety the recognition of the *angoissant*, amusement the recognition of the amusing. It begins to seem as if nothing of the *emotion* remains, other than this act of (admittedly passionate) appraisal. The characteristic of a formal object is that someone may think something to be an instance of it, and yet feel no prompting towards the emotion which it partially characterizes. The formal object is given by a description which falls short of embodying the peculiar emotional characteristics which it serves to focus. The proper object is not so given. It is my belief that the temptation to build into the description of the formal object ideas that belong to the proper object is responsible for many fallacies in ethics, aesthetics and the philosophy of mind. In particular it seems to have precipitated renewed sympathy for the philosophy of "moral realism," according to which the possession of values resides in an ability to recognize peculiar (and peculiarly elusive[9]) features of reality.

7

Does amusement have a formal object? How do we settle the question? We could, I suppose, list all the possible candidates and attempt to find counter-examples. One pleasing candidate is offered by Bergson: the formal object of amusement is life overcome by mechanism, or mechanism perceived in the heart of life (a special case of the incongruity theory).[10] This seems vulnerable at once to the counter-example of the character who amuses because he is true to himself. But perhaps there is some better method than that of listing proposals and then attempting to demolish them. If the formal object is a *merely* nominal feature, if it results *only* from our attempts to classify, then the question would hardly matter. We could arbitrarily designate amusement as that form of enjoyment which has the situation described by Bergson as its object, and use *Le Rire* as a kind of extension to our dictionary entry on "laughter." But the subject would hardly have aroused such interest if there were not some real basis to our classifications, and if the choice of a formal object were not restricted by some independent reality that we are attempting to describe.

It is important to understand, in this connection, a peculiar feature of amusement, which serves to distinguish it from the common examples of emotion: it is a matter of indifference whether the object of amusement be thought to be real. Most of our emotions are founded not just on thoughts, but on beliefs. We may also suffer them in imagination; but the imagined version is a derived case, to be understood in terms of the real, active emotion of which it is the shadow. Consider jealousy. There is no doubt that jealousy has a formal object: in order to be jealous of Alfred I must believe Alfred to be a rival. (That is only one part of the full description of the formal object, but it will do.) Without that belief I may hate Alfred, despise him, or envy him; but I cannot be jealous of him. The formal object is given by this belief. I can also entertain the thought of "Alfred as rival" in imagination; and I may then feel some imaginative simulacrum of jealousy. But it is quite clear that real jealousy and "imagined" jealousy are different states of mind. The first is necessarily terrible; the second may be titillating, even pleasant. The first involves a definite stance towards the world, and a tyrannical invasion of experience; the second is sealed off in a private reserve of fantasy.

In the case of amusement no such distinction between the real and the imagined can be sustained. If I laugh at someone's remark, and if I imagine the remark and laugh, then in each case my laughter has the same object, and expresses genuine amusement.

Whether the object of my amusement be believed or imagined, my amusement remains the same; it has the same consequences, and the same place in my experience as a whole. Belief seems to be irrelevant. Or at least, what relevance it has is not that of distinguishing imagined amusement from the genuine article.

I think that this "indifference to belief" is an important feature, and explains our reluctance to describe amusement as an emotion. In the case of normal emotions the belief which identifies the formal object has an important role in determining the structure and significance of the feeling. For normal emotions are also motives to action. Jealousy seeks not just to interpret the world but to change it. Amusement may cause us to do things, but it is not itself a motive. (I do things *for* amusement, but not *from* amusement.) We classify emotions not arbitrarily but according to their role in the explanation of behavior. As motives they are intermediaries between belief and action. Human nature being what it is, we have fixed expectations concerning the actions that will follow upon certain beliefs. Our classifications of emotions therefore stem from our perception (however indistinct) of real and recurrent causal relations between certain beliefs and the desires and projects which express, confirm and purge them. It is not merely a nominal matter that jealousy has the particular formal object that it has. It is a matter of the real essence of a state of mind active in the generation of human conduct, in which a belief is found locked in the heart of a perduring motive to action.

The indifference of amusement to belief suggests that we should not expect it to exhibit the kind of structure that we observe in fear, anger and jealousy. Sometimes, it is true, belief plays a role in precipitating amusement: amusement (if it is indeed such) that expresses *Schadenfreude* arises only in response to a belief that one's rival, enemy, or thorn in the flesh has suffered injury. The mere thought of him doing so is never satisfactory. But we hesitate to call *Schadenfreude* amusement, and this suggests that my thesis is correct. Such examples could not possibly establish, either that a belief is necessary to normal amusement, or that any *particular* belief is always active in producing it. It is partly this that makes it so difficult to attribute a formal object to amusement: for we lack the motivational structure that is present in normal emotions, and hence can never feel confident that anything is *explained* by our identification of this or that predicate as the description under

which an object must be laughed. We should therefore hesitate to
elucidate the intentionality of amusement in terms of some single
directing thought common to its instances. It *may* be that there is
such a thought; but it is hard to say whether its designation is a
merely nominal matter, or whether, on the contrary, there is some
real (and explanatory) essence that is being picked out by means of
it.

8

Nevertheless the intentionality of laughter is not like the intentionality of a bark. Amusement *is* a mode of thought. What mode of
thought? It is noteworthy that the traditional theories were not
theories of the formal object of laughter. They were, for the most
part, attempts to specify its proper object (the ridiculous): that at
which it is appropriate to laugh. Laughter and amusement were
described in terms, not of some basic thought that is necessary to
them, but in terms of the pattern of thought which renders the object ridiculous in the subject's eyes. This is fairly obvious in the
passage quoted from Schopenhauer: it is also evident in Bergson.
Perhaps there *is* no formal object of amusement. Perhaps there is no
general study of the intentional object that stops short of saying
when it is right to be amused.

There is a trivial sense in which every intentional mental state
has a formal object: only the believable can be believed; only the
thinkable can be thought. And these empty tautologies may be
given content by a theory of the "understanding," such as was envisaged by Kant. *The Critique of Pure Reason* offers a disjunctive
account of the thinkable (you can think X only if you think it under
the categories). But if this is all we mean by referring to a formal object — i.e. the *a priori* conditions of the thinkable — then the assertion that amusement has a formal object is highly uninformative.

We should, I think, recapture the motivation behind the traditional theories. We should look for a pattern or structure of thought
characteristic of amusement, without concerning ourselves too
much with the single necessary proposition in which all our laughter
is based. It may be that there is such a proposition, but, since
amusement is not an emotion, it is hard to say how we might
discover it. When we seek the pattern of thought characteristic of

laughter, two peculiar features impress themselves on us. The first is that, while everybody likes to laugh, nobody likes to be laughed at. The second is that a direct connection exists between amusement and the aesthetic point of view. The second feature is illustrated by the contrast between comedy and tragedy. There is no difficulty in explaining why we laugh in the theatre: any theory of humor is also a theory of comedy. Aesthetic representations are as much objects of amusement as anything else, and amusement enters into the enjoyment of comedy without doing any violence to the aesthetic point of view. Tragedy, by contrast, creates a notorious problem for the philosophy of aesthetic interest. Why do we enjoy the representation of suffering? There seems to be no normal ("extra-dramatic") state of mind of which tragic feeling is a species: we do not feel grief, dismay or horror in the theatre (else why should we go there?). The experience of tragedy is, or seems to be, *sui generis*; some mysterious alchemy is at work in accommodating the representation of terrible things to the aesthetic point of view from which they become enjoyable. Hence philosophers have felt obliged to give some special account of tragedy, in order to explain the transformation effected by the stage. Comedy, however, has never seemed problematic in quite that way. I wish to comment on these two features and suggest a theory of amusement that will explain them.

9

To be amused by someone is not the same as to be amused at him; while the first is gratifying to its object, the second is not. Why is that? Here we should reflect on the peculiar importance of the human among the objects of amusement. One can be amused at animals, and even at inanimate things (for example, mechanical dolls). But there is a temptation to think that these kinds of amusement are anthropomorphic. One sees the object in human terms, either as a human being, or as the expression of human thought and action. (Thus there are amusing buildings, but not, I think, amusing rocks and cliffs, even though many rocks and cliffs are quite bizarre.) If I were to propose a candidate for the formal object of amusement, then the human (in its widest significance) would be my choice. But I am certain that I should be quickly forced to withdraw the suggestion, and to content myself merely with emphasizing the importance of the human, its centrality, among the objects of laughter, and perhaps hazarding the guess that someone who could be amused at nothing human could be amused at nothing.

If people dislike being laughed at it is surely because laughter de-values its object in the subject's eyes. This de-valuing may be much needed and it may even be desired by the object. It is difficult to love a great man with the warmth that characterizes normal human relations. In order to do so, it may be necessary to find in him that which can be (however gently) laughed at. A truly great spirit will no doubt be willing to exchange the absolute security of the unlaughable for the comfort of human affection. Else, like Christ, he must think of himself as divine, in order to bear his inner isolation. Without the mitigation of friendship it is painful to be the object of laughter. It is possible not to be afflicted only by feeling such contempt (or pity) for those who laugh as to count it a virtue to be de-valued in their eyes (cf. Christ's attitude to those who mocked him).

"Laughing at" has many modes. Absolute mockery and reviling scarcely constitute amusement. Here every merit is stripped from the victim in the subject's eyes, and the laughter has that quality of malice which can be heard or overheard only with revulsion. Sarcasm likewise de-values and rejects in an unkind way, and again we feel that this "unkindness" distances it from the normal cases of laughter. But sarcasm must be distinguished from irony. Irony de-values without rejecting: it is, in that sense, "kind." For example, Joyce's ironic comparison of Bloom with the wily Odysseus de-values the former only to insert him more fully into our affections. His shortcomings are part of this pathos, since they reflect a condition that is also ours. Irony of this kind causes us to laugh at its object only by laughing at ourselves. It thus forces upon us a perception of our kinship. Flaubert called it "l'ironie qui n'enlève rien au pathétique"; it is the laughter between familiars, without which no domestic affection could rise.

In referring to a process of "de-valuing" that is integral to laughter I have spoken very imprecisely. But I am not sure how to remedy the defect. "De-valuing," however it is to be analyzed, seems to be neither a precondition of amusement nor the result of it. It is, rather, the amusement itself. It is difficult to encapsulate it in the form of a judgement or thought which might have existed without the disposition to laughter. This "pattern" of thought is constitutive of laughter. Amusement may thus be described as a kind of "attentive demolition." It is no accident that this pattern of thought should be enjoyable to us, since it reconciles us to our own condition. The connection between attentive demolition and enjoyment is real. The conjunction of the two in the definition of amusement is not the arbitrary specification of a nominal essence, but an attempt to isolate the causal process which structures a part of our mental life.

10

It is open to the defender of the formal object to find some way of translating my "pattern" of thought — attentive demolition — into a specific proposition entertained about its object. If that *could* be done, then I concede that amusement has been provided with its formal object. But I am sceptical. For I am impressed by the complexity of this "attentive demolition," which resides in no single thought, and which feeds insatiably on everything that serves to approximate the condition of its object to our own.

What matters, in any case, is the peculiar complexity of the thought that underlies amusement, and its distance from the thoughts which focus our emotions. There is no "discovery" at the heart of amusement. Amusement is, rather, a mode of reflection which presents its object in a certain light. It might now be thought that I have committed myself to the traditional "superiority" theory mentioned earlier. But my remarks about irony were intended to deny that charge. To lower the object is not necessarily to raise the subject; it might be to lower both together. It is by the universal lowering that one may come to feel "kinship" with the thing at which one laughs. The mistake, of "superiority" and "release" theories alike, is to find the meaning of humor in what it does for the subject, rather than in how it represents the object. Humor is not, normally, self-directed. Indeed one of its values lies in the fact that it directs our attention unceasingly outwards. If we are repelled by the humorless person it is often because we think of him as interested only in himself.

11

I turn now to the second feature of amusement: its ready subsumption under the aesthetic point of view. We laugh at real scenes,
and at their dramatic representation, but there seems to be no
transformation in the nature or quality of amusement as we proceed
from life to art. Whether we are interested in an amusing episode, in
the recital of it, or in its theatrical representation, we laugh always
at the same thing and for the same reason. If the last is an example
of aesthetic pleasure, then so is the first. Conversely, if amusement
at real situations is not aesthetic pleasure, then laughter in the
theater ought not to be so either: in which case, there *would* be a
problem of comedy after all. We should have to explain just how
and why amusement is transfigured in the contemplation of imaginary scenes, and how it becomes part of an aesthetic interest in
what is observed.

It seems to me that it is most plausible to say that amusement *is*
a kind of aesthetic interest — or at least, that it belongs to the genus
of which aesthetic interest is a species. This is suggested by the
thought (which I attributed to Clark, although the words are not
his) that amusement is a mode of enjoying an object "for its own
sake." My suggestion can be formulated in four propositions:

(1) Amusement is a mode of reflective attention to an object.

(2) It does not have the purpose of discovery (it does not concern
itself with the acquisition of new beliefs, or the verification of old
ones).

(3) It is not a motive to action (it does not regard its object as the
focus of any project or desire).

(4) Enjoyment is to be explained by the thought of the object, and
it is not felt (as Clark puts it) *"for some ulterior reason."*

It is, I believe, one of the major tasks of aesthetics to make that last
proposition clear. We know that there is a difference between the
laugh of triumph, which enjoys the sight of another's misfortune
because of what it seeks in it, and the laugh of amusement, which
takes pleasure simply in what it sees, and for "no other reason." But
it is hard to say anything systematic about the contrast.[11] But the
task is a general one for aesthetics. To the extent that amusement
satisfies the four conditions, to that extent is it already a mode of

aesthetic interest. For the conditions are precisely those which must be invoked in order to elucidate that peculiar kind of "disinterest" that has — since Baumgarten — been called "aesthetic."

12

The argument has touched on a subject that lies beyond its scope. So I shall end with a suggestion that returns us to the opening remarks of this paper. It is only rational beings who can be attentive without a motive; only rational beings who can be interested in that in which they have no interest. Whatever explains that fact explains why only rational beings have aesthetic pleasures, and why only rational beings are moral. I shall offer no theory. But it remains to point out that the humorlessness of animals is of a piece with their incorrigible lack of taste, and with their deplorable indifference to questions of morality.

Notes

1. See, for example, Richard Wollheim: "Thought and Passion," *P.A.S.* 1967-8.

2. Michael Clark: "Humor and Incongruity," *Philosophy*, 45 (1970), 20-32.

3. D. H. Monro: *Argument of Laughter* (Melbourne and Cambridge), 1951.

4. *The World as Will and Representation*, I, section 13.

5. See J. P. Sartre, *L'Imaginaire*, Paris, 1940, 2, III, in which the example of mimicry is discussed in detail.

6. *Action, Emotion and Will* (London, 1962), p. 189.

7. See Clark, *op. cit.*, p. 24.

8. See *Esquisse d'une théorie des émotions* (Paris, 1939).

9. cf. Mark Platts: *Ways of Meaning* (London, 1979), ch. 10.

10. H. Bergson, *Le Rire*.

11. I have tried in *Art and Imagination* (London, 1974), 143ff.

19   Mike W. Martin

This essay challenges two common views about humor—that amusement is the enjoyment of incongruity, and that amusement is a kind of aesthetic experience. Both views, Martin shows, need qualification. He challenges the first view by discussing Clark's "Humor and Incongruity." The enjoyment of incongruity for its own sake, he agrees, is a necessary condition for amusement, but it is not a sufficient condition, for we can enjoy incongruity—in the form of irony in Oedipus Rex, for example—without being amused. To develop a sufficient condition for at least the central cases of amusement, Martin argues, we need to add a condition based on the tendency of amusement to issue in laughter. Martin challenges the second view, that amusement is a kind of aesthetic experience, by showing that only some amusement is aesthetic. When the grounds for the enjoyment of the humor are sexual or aggressive, he says, amusement is not aesthetic enjoyment. It is only when the grounds for the amusement lie in the enjoyment of incongruity for its own sake that amusement constitutes aesthetic enjoyment.

Humor and Aesthetic Enjoyment of Incongruities

Classical philosophers frequently gave serious attention to humor in the course of unfolding a general speculative theory of metaphysics, epistemology, or human nature. Within these contexts analyses of humor often ended up fitting the speculative theory better than they fit the phenomenon. Bergson's view of humor, for example, as "something mechanical encrusted upon the living" emerged naturally from his metaphysics of vitalism, but his claim for this being the general leitmotiv of the humorous has little plausibility.[1] Much the same can be said concerning the relationship between Hobbes's psychological egoism and his claim that "the passion of laughter is nothing else but sudden glory arising from a sudden conception of some eminency in ourselves."[2]

In my view the most promising of the traditional theories is Schopenhauer's incongruity theory set forth in *The World as Will and Representation*.[3] This theory was given a careful reformulation by Michael Clark in "Humor and Incongruity", a reformulation which freed it from Schopenhauer's particular speculative interests.[4]

172

Yet Clark's version is far from adequate as it stands, and my first main concern will be to develop an improved version.

Humor has also aroused philosophical interest as a special topic within aesthetics. Here the context made it easy to assume that enjoyment of humor is always a variety of aesthetic appreciation. Thus by the time *The Encyclopedia of Philosophy* appeared, D. H. Monro could begin his entry under "Humor" by taking it for granted that to find something humorous "is to have a special kind of aesthetic emotion."[5] More recently John Morreall argued that to appreciate humor is to have an aesthetic experience, although not necessarily an emotional one.[6] My second concern will be to reject this generalization and to replace it with a criterion for when enjoying humor is an aesthetic experience.

I

Throughout I shall follow Clark in using the word "amusement" in a narrow sense to mean "amusement at the humorous," and not just any kind of light entertainment or diversion. By contrast, the word "humor" will be used in a very wide sense to cover anything funny (i.e., "funny ha-ha" rather than "funny peculiar"). This means setting aside the narrow usage in which humor is contrasted with wit (which is more intellectual and relies on verbal ingenuity), sarcasm (which is more derisive), satire (which aims to discredit vices and follies), slapstick (typically based on boisterous action), and farce (generated by one-dimensional characters and improbable situations).

Clark's guiding intuition, which I share, is that humor can be elucidated by clarifying amusement. If no one was ever amused by humor then humor would not exist. For "the humorous is so characterized in virtue of the human attitude or response to it: we call something 'humorous' if it is apt to, or should or deserves to, amuse people, or some special sort of person."[7]

What, then, is amusement at humor? Clark believes (and here I will later disagree) that it is possible to state necessary and sufficient conditions for amusement. To begin with, amusement is a specific type of emotion which must have a particular type of object. The object is pinpointed by Schopenhauer's Incongruity Theory. To be amused is to perceive, think, or imagine something incongruous, and this involves applying a concept to something with which it is not fully congruent. Or as Clark paraphrases Schopenhauer, incongruous subsumption under a concept amounts to viewing one or more objects as "different in some way from the standard instances falling under the concept."[8] Hence the object of amusement always involves something viewed as unusual or odd. The incongruity, it should be emphasized, need not actually exist in the objective world. It is the phenomenological, intentional, object of thought that is spoken of as incongruous.

Clark proceeds by arguing that apprehending an incongruity is only a necessary, but not by itself a sufficient, condition. His full set of defining features may be summarized as follows: (1) A person perceives (thinks, imagines) an object as being incongruous. (2) The person enjoys perceiving (thinking, imagining) the object. (3) The person enjoys the perceived (thought, imagined) incongruity at least partly for itself, rather than solely for some ulterior reason.

This account has three major strengths. First, it enables us to keep distinct the conceptual and empirical issues concerning amusement and humor. There are innumerable causes and influences which lead people to experience amusement, and to experience it with varying degrees of intensity. On the subjective side there is the person's particular mood, psychological set, perception of the situation, desires (such as to ridicule), and needs (such as to release tension). On the objective side there is the timing, emphasis, wording, and degree of originality and freshness of a joke. Cultural and social conditioning and even genetic inheritance would presumably have to go into a complete causal explanation of amusement.

Some classical theories of humor are best viewed as partial causal explanations. This is true, for example, of Relief from Restraint Theories which treat enjoyment of humor as an act of emotional and physical release,[9] and Superiority Theories, like Hobbes's, which treat it as an act of elevating oneself in one's own eyes at the expense of someone else.

Second, Clark's view avoids a simplistic treatment of the relationship between laughter and amusement. Schopenhauer's discussion, for instance, was hamstrung from the outset by equating the question "What is humor?" with "What evokes laughter?". Thus he construed the task of clarifying enjoyment of the humorous as the same as providing an explanation of the origin and meaning of laughter. His thesis was that "In every case, *laughter* results from nothing but the suddenly perceived incongruity between a concept and the real objects that had been thought through it in some relation; and laughter is just the expression of this incongruity."[10]

There are several obvious objections to this claim. Not all laughter is prompted by humor and perceived incongruity. There is the laughter of joy at one's good fortune; hysterical laughter at a tragedy one cannot bear; and the sadist's chuckle of happiness in response to the suffering of his victim. Sometimes laughter is not *at* anything at all, for it can be a purely physiological response to nitrous oxide or electrical stimulation. Laughter expressing amusement at humor, however, always takes an intentional object. Conversely, much enjoyment of humor is never expressed in laughter, either because an inclination to laugh is suppressed or because the humor is enjoyed without so much as a felt inclination to laugh. Moreover, incongruities such as those involved in human deformities and disasters often produce pain and sadness, rather than laughter.

Third, the Incongruity Theory has the breadth needed to capture the enormous variety of things we are amused by. It applies to amusement at unusual dress, grooming, and speech. It covers sexual and scatological jokes which make reference to subject-matter thought inappropriate in polite society. It accounts for the humor of the bungling oaf, the victim of the banana peel, the thumb-hammerer, and others who fail to execute effective action. It extends to amusement at Falstaff's departures from his society's ideals. And it captures amusement at puns, where one meaning of an expression deflects from another more suitable or normal sense of a passage. In short, without being thinly vacuous, it allows for the many variations suggested in the OED's entry for "incongruity": "(i) disagreement in character or qualities; want of accordance or harmony; discrepancy; inconsistency. (ii) Want of accordance with what is reasonable or fitting; unsuitableness, inappropriateness, absurdity. (iii) Want of harmony of parts or elements; want of self-consistency; incoherence."

II

In spite of these strengths, however, Clark's account suffers from a serious deficiency. It is vulnerable to a wide variety of counter-examples which show it to be insufficient for distinguishing amusement from other forms of enjoying incongruities for their own sake.

The most compelling cases are non-humorous aesthetic enjoyments. Clark himself seemed to suspect the existence of these cases when he expressed the following doubts at the end of his essay:

> Suppose a man is looking at a picture and is enjoying this experience, and suppose he says he likes the picture because of the incongruity of its content. Moreover he likes the incongruity for its own sake, not for any insight, say, that the picture gives him into the nature of the world. Must we say he finds the picture amusing? I find it difficult to say.[11]

This passage contains a good description of aesthetic enjoyment of an element of discord, contrast, or irony in a picture. Surely, however, the enjoyment of such elements need not constitute amusement at humor.

Grant Wood's *American Gothic*, for example, is a painting of a man and woman on a farm standing in a formal and rigid pose. The woman's hair is combed neatly and firmly pulled back, and yet — ironically and incongruously — there is one prominent wisp of hair curling loosely downward. The irony is enjoyable for its own sake, whether or not it seems funny. (For me, sometimes it does and sometimes it does not.) Again, one need only recall the stunning incongruities permeating Picasso's work, such as in the disjointed, mangled, and tragic — though not humorous — figures in *Guernica*.

Incongruities present in other art forms can be enjoyed in the absence of amusement. Thus the ironies present in the plot of *Oedipus Rex* can be aesthetically enjoyed, although they are anything but funny. With respect to music, there is the delight at non-humorous incongruities experienced by connoisseurs of dissonant and atonal music. We would also understand a description of Oriental music as having an enjoyably "incongruous beauty." A character in a John Hersey novel says just that about the song of a tracker pulling boats up the Yangtze river: "He sang songs of an incongruous beauty" and "wove melodies of an incongruous haunting gaiety in and out, in and out."[12]

Aesthetic appreciation, however, is not the only "pleasure domain" providing counter-examples. Incongruities in erotic objects can be enjoyed for their own sake in a purely sexual way. Freud described a foot fetishist who became sexually excited upon seeing a certain kind of scraggy and incongruously shaped foot.[13] If the person sometimes enjoyed this incongruity-directed pleasure for its own sake, whether or not it also led to further sexual activity, then Clark's conditions would be met. It can be argued, of course, that there are ulterior unconscious reasons for the fetishist's enjoyment. But Clark's condition 3 would still be met, since it merely requires that the incongruity be enjoyed at least partly for its own sake.

Imagine too a culture of people who lacked a sense of humor, but who stood motionless for long durations staring with pleasure at objects that we would be amused by, or listening for hours to the repetition of jokes that we would find funny. If they did this within a religious context, we might describe their enjoyment as some bizarre kind of religious delight or awe about incongruities; other contexts might lead us to think they found aesthetic satisfaction in the objects; and we would be hard pressed to classify their enjoyment if it derived from a continuous pleasure in their big toes that occurred at the sight of incongruities.

III

Our problem, then, is how to distinguish amusement from these other ways of enjoying incongruities for their own sake. What is it to enjoy incongruities specifically as humorous and for their humor?

I will not attempt to uncover some new necessary condition which when added to Clark's list will yield a set of necessary and sufficient conditions covering all cases. For my intent is to abjure the search for a simple set of necessary and sufficient conditions for amusement and humor. Instead, I propose to clarify amusement by providing the sufficient conditions for only the central cases. Other cases will then qualify as amusement to the extent they bear a family resemblance to these central cases.

Let us reconsider Schopenhauer's emphasis upon laughter — the element which dropped out altogether in Clark's account. While laughter is neither a necessary nor sufficient condition for amusement, as we saw earlier, surely it is not an accident that the word "laughable" is a very close synonym for "funny" and "humorous." Laughter is the most characteristic way of enjoying humor. Because of this it provides a focus for understanding our concepts of humor and enjoyment of humor.

It is sufficient for amusement, I suggest, that Clark's conditions are met *and* at least one of the following occurs. (a) The person laughs spontaneously at the incongruity. (b) The person has a spontaneous inclination to laugh in response to the perceived incongruity, but suppresses it. (By "spontaneous" is meant unmediated by a judgement that the incongruity should be laughed at or is suited to be laughed at.) (c) The person laughs or has an inclination to laugh following an explicit judgement that the incongruity is worthy of laughter. (d) The person experiences episodic cheerfulness (without an inclination to laugh) in response to the incongruity and does so because he or she judges the incongruity to be laughable, i.e., worthy of or suited to be laughed at.

With these central cases in mind we might formulate a disjunctive condition and add it to Clark's three conditions: (4) The person responds to the perceived incongruity with laughter, or with an inclination to laugh (whether or not it is preceded by an explicit judgement that the incongruity is worthy to be laughed at), or with an episodic cheerfulness in response to the incongruity as being suited for laughter, or with closely related forms of enjoyment. The open-endedness of (4) should tempt no one to treat it as a strictly necessary condition. It merely sketches several paradigms and indicates that other instances may qualify if they are significantly similar to these central cases.

As thus modified, Schopenhauer's twin emphasis on perceived incongruity and the laughable does succeed in clarifying the concept of amusement, and thereby the concept of humor.

As a kind of intuitive check of this theory, return for a moment to Clark's man looking at a picture whose incongruous content he says he enjoys for its own sake. Imagine he is looking at Picasso's *Weeping Woman*, a picture of a bizarrely disjointed face painted in wildly incongruous colors. Imagine further that he is puzzled about precisely why he enjoys perceiving the incongruities and unsure whether he finds them amusing. Then something clicks, and suddenly he realizes he is amused. What happened?

It seems to me most likely that at this moment he either laughed, felt like laughing, or experienced an episodic cheerfulness because he tacitly or explicitly came to view the incongruities as laughable. These would be the central cases. But it is also possible that he experienced a milder sort of enjoyment than actual episodic cheerfulness. Such might be the case when he soberly declares to us that the picture is not really laughable — though it is perhaps worth a smile. His experience might count as amusement even though it is not one of the more central cases we would use to clarify the concept of amusement.

By contrast, the man's eye could focus on the tears and the expression of pain in the mouth. His amusement may turn to sadness. Or more likely it may transform into non-humorous enjoyment of the painting for its interesting way of expressing or capturing grief. The grief, of course, as expressed in the painting may be aesthetically enjoyed without actually causing the man to feel sadness or grief. Likewise, next imagine that the man comes to enjoy the humorous incongruities in the picture as aesthetic properties without actually being amused by them. That is, he enjoys the humor in the painting — enjoys the incongruity as laughable — without actually being amused by it. My guess is that in this case he will not experience either an inclination to laugh or episodic cheerfulness in direct response to seeing the incongruity as laughable.

Three further comments need to be added. First, if I am correct it is important for laughter to enter into an account of amusement as we know it. But it does, nevertheless, seem to me conceivable that there could be amusement in a world without laughter to serve as a reference point for understanding it. All that would be needed is for some other typical behavior, sufficiently analogous to laughter, to be present as a new focal point for understanding it.

Second, laughter should not be regarded as an incidental outer behavior which leaves an experience of inner cheerfulness untouched. To laugh spontaneously is generally to undergo a distinctive form of physical pleasure. Or rather, it is to undergo one of a variety of such forms of pleasure. These include snorts, sniggers, and guffaws; cackles, giggles, and mellow belly laughs; howls, roars, shrieks, paroxysms, and convulsions. This is a further reason for not bypassing laughter in an account of amusement by making sole reference to inner cheerfulness.

Third, we have been discussing episodic amusement. There is also a use of "amusement" which refers to a long-term state. It makes sense to say a person was amused for weeks by a laughably bizarre turn of events.[14] Here the state of enjoyment is not a steady-state of the sort of enjoyment defined above. Instead it involves a belief that the events warrant laughter, and also a disposition to some episodic amusement.

IV

We have seen that many aesthetic enjoyments of incongruities do not involve amusement at something humorous. It is time to ask whether all amusement at the humorous constitutes aesthetic enjoyment or appreciation. I believe the preceding account enables us to respond to this question with more care than is usual, although the discussion will have to be somewhat tentative. A complete answer would presuppose an adequate theory of aesthetic experience, and providing such a theory is no easy task. My procedure will be to begin by criticizing John Morreall's defense of the view that amusement always constitutes aesthetic experience given certain traditional conceptions of aesthetic experience. Following this I will show that on one fairly broad definition of aesthetic satisfaction not all amusement qualifies, although much does.

There are some noteworthy general similarities, several of which Morreall discusses with insight, between the exercise of a sense of humor and what are commonly accepted as aesthetic experiences.

(a) Both amusement and aesthetically enjoyed experiences can occur in response to either works of art or things which are not works of art. Thus, human behavior, natural objects, comic plays, and novels are equally capable of serving as objects of aesthetic or humorous enjoyments.

(b) Amusement, like aesthetic enjoyment, can be directed towards intentional objects experienced in various sense-perception modalities and also towards objects of thought. Both come in response to things seen, heard, and (less frequently) to things touched, tasted or smelled. And the experience of either need not be a perceptual one at all, as when the object is an idea or story.

(c) Both generally involve the play of the imagination in getting us to view common objects or situations in novel ways, and in leading us to consider enriching possible worlds.

(d) While there is disagreement over whether aesthetic experiences should be regarded as necessarily enjoyable,[15] a weaker view is that those aesthetic experiences which we prize for their intrinsic worth are enjoyable experiences. Non-enjoyable ones are valued only for some instrumental value or further good effect on our lives. Here there would seem to be a comparison with amusement. We should add that both amusement and aesthetic appreciation may involve an admixture of considerable pain. Among the most intense experiences of art are the anguishing jolts from complacency or moral blindness. Just as honest responses to the work of Dostoevsky or O'Neill typically involve something other than pleasant diversions, so too the humor of Shaw and Kafka can sting.

(e) Not only are amusement and aesthetic appreciation both sources of desirable experiences, but we tend to see it as a deficiency for persons to lack a developed sensitivity either to humor or aesthetic appreciation. The grounds for these value judgements are typically not moral ones, and indeed moral values sometimes come into conflict with them. Occasionally we employ moral terms in appraising both the telling of jokes and the creation or displaying of works of art, such as when they are blatantly racist or sexist. Again, there are times when it would be morally wrong to indulge in aesthetic experiences or amusement. Thus we are appalled by a person who could stand by enjoying the striking color display created by a bleeding accident victim when he ought to be calling an ambulance, and even more appalled by a person who chose to crack some jokes in place of providing help.[16] There are also instances of both jokes and art dealing with ethnic or sexual themes or human deformities which may leave our reactions confused and ambivalent because of the clash of our moral interests with desires for other sorts of enjoyments or for understanding.

(f) The responses of amusement and aesthetic appreciation are equally matters of taste, and in both the subjective and objective senses of "taste." One the one hand, aesthetic experiences involve objective discrimination and perceptiveness of properties like unity, gracefulness, tension — and incongruity. This discrimination is an achievement, unlike the mere ability to perceive colors, lines, and sounds. The perceptiveness can be cultivated by practice and formal training in studying humor and art.[17] For there are objective reasons which can be referred to in explaining the images of incongruity created in subtle wit, just as a critic can help us identify features of a work of art that we have missed. On the other hand, such reasongiving is ultimately undergirded and limited by personal preferences. What we appreciate and for what reasons differs as much with respect to humor as with respect to art.

What should be said about these similarities? Are they enough to warrant viewing amusement as a special case of aesthetic appreciation? I think not. Most of the same comparisons could be drawn between amusement and mystical experiences, and yet that would hardly justify assimilating the one to the other. We need to turn to the features of aesthetic experiences which have been suggested as special or unique to the aesthetic, and then see if amusement shares them.

Morreall accepts the traditional characterization of aesthetic experiences as involving a "distancing" of an object in the sense of attending to its detailed features in abstraction from utilitarian interests. "We must be sufficiently 'distant' from the aesthetic object so that it is not part of our practical life where we think about what we can do with objects, how much they cost, and so forth."[18] Amusement, he suggests, also fits this description: "to the extent that we can laugh about something, we have achieved a measure of objectivity and emotional neutrality toward it."

Now whether or not this is true of all aesthetic experiences, it is not always true of amusement. A great deal of amusement arises as integral to the expression of desires and interests of a very practical sort: to deride, degrade, shock, cheer up, comfort, or impress someone. To laugh at the foolishness of the neighbor we detest is often to enjoy viewing him in a demeaning way. Such amusement and laughter which involves sarcastic derision of others does not reveal an achievement of objectivity or emotional neutrality. Again, the enjoyment of an unmitigatedly smutty joke is more akin to low-grade pornographic pleasures which have generally been denied the status of aesthetic pleasures because they evoke primarily a sexual interest.

The same considerations are fatal to Morreall's claim that appreciation of humor and aesthetic experience involve a "disinterested attending to some object of awareness for the sake of the experience itself."[19] Disinterestedness presumably means unbiased and lacking motives which are ulterior to enjoying the incongruous aspects of the object itself. But surely a good deal of humor involves ulterior motives connected with the sorts of practical interests mentioned in the previous paragraph.

Let us set aside Morreall's use of traditional characterizations of aesthetic experiences by reference to special ways of attending or motives and intentions in attending to objects, characterizations which in any case have been given sharp criticism by Dickie and others.[20] Consider instead Urmson's more plausible thesis that the specific sorts of satisfactions derived from experiences might appropriately be called aesthetic given certain types of grounds for those satisfactions.[21]

I do not know how to define with precision what those grounds must be, and so I will rest content with roughly Urmson's characterization. Thus, in simpler cases a satisfaction is aesthetic if the primary reasons for the satisfaction are, *per se*, the features constituting the object's appearance or, in the case of literature, the object's abstract pattern of ideas, images, and characters. The idea is that the grounds for aesthetic enjoyment have to do with the way an object appears to our senses or contemplation, rather than with purely economic, moral, religious, sexual, or self-interested considerations.

It seems to be plausible to say that amusement constitutes aesthetic enjoyment when the grounds for the amusement lie primarily or entirely in enjoyment of perceived or conceived incongruities for their own sake. With this as a criterion, amusement will not always constitute aesthetic satisfaction, although much of it will. When the grounds or motives for the enjoyment of humor are, e.g., mainly sexual or aggressive, the amusement is non-aesthetic. Accordingly, it is possible for the same object of amusement to be enjoyed by one person aesthetically and another person non-aesthetically, or by the same person in either of these ways on different occasions. This view blocks Morreall's overgeneralizations while uncovering the truth in his view: amusement is aesthetic when the primary reason for enjoying incongruities is the incongruities *per se*, rather than further ulterior reasons.

V

Consider, in conclusion, the objection to the Incongruity Theory that as rational beings we never enjoy incongruities to any extent for their own sake. For "incongruity and degradation, as such, always remain unpleasant" and "by their very nature they must at all times" displease us. Instead, when we enjoy the incongruities in, say, a comedy, it is owing to "the inward rationality and movement of the fiction" and to "the stimulation and shaking up of our wits."

The objection and quoted words are those of Santayana.[22] Apparently what led him to make these remarks is a special picture of what it is to be a rational being. In the same context he remarks that "man, being a rational animal, can like absurdity no better than he can like hunger or cold."

The best response to this view is to reject the picture of rationality as overly rationalistic. Indeed, so long as we value much of the capacity to enjoy incongruities for themselves, including the inappropriate, the absurd, and even occasionally the degrading, we can turn Santayana's picture on its head. Our delight in humorous incongruities reveals something about the kind of rational beings we are.

If, however, we were to follow Santayana in narrowly conceiving of human reason as that part of us which seeks and appreciates order and *congruity*, then it would be worth recalling one of Schopenhauer's barbs. Amusement, he tells us, reveals that it is "delightful for us to see this strict, untiring, and most troublesome governess, our faculty of reason, for once convicted of inadequacy" in its attempt to discern a perfectly reasonable universe.[23] And who could deny that this delight is eminently healthy when confronted daily with a world so abundantly rich with the absurd and the incongruous?[24]

Notes

1. Henri Bergson, *Le Rire* (Paris, 1900). Printed in *Comedy*, ed. Wylie Sypher, trans. Cloudesley Brereton and Fred Rothwell (New York, 1956).

2. Thomas Hobbes, *Of Human Nature*, Ch. 9.

3. Arthur Schopenhauer, *The World as Will and Representation*, trans. E. F. J. Payne (New York: Dover Publications, 1969), Vol. I, pp. 58-61 and Vol. II, pp. 91-101.

4. Michael Clark, "Humor and Incongruity," *Philosophy*, 45 (1970), pp. 20-32.

5. D. H. Monro, "Humor," *The Encyclopedia of Philosophy*, ed. Paul Edwards (New York: Macmillan Publishing Co., 1967), Vol. IV, p. 90.

6. John Morreall, "Humor and Aesthetic Education," *Journal of Aesthetic Education*, 15 (Jan. 1981), pp. 55-70.

7. Clark, p. 22.

8. Clark, p. 27.

9. For example, Sigmund Freud, *Jokes and Their Relation To The Unconscious*, trans. James Strachey (New York: W. W. Norton and Company, 1963).

10. Schopenhauer, Vol, I., p. 59.

11. Clark, p. 32.

12. John Hersey, *A Single Pebble* (New York: Bantam Books), pp. 30, 34.

13. Sigmund Freud, *The Complete Introductory Lectures on Psychoanalysis*, trans. James Strachey (New York: W. W. Norton, 1966), pp. 34ff.

14. Thus I differ from David Pears who viewed amusement as always a momentary reaction, "Causes and Objects of Some Feelings and Psychological Reactions," reprinted in *Philosophy of Mind*, ed. Stuart Hampshire (New York: Harper and Row, 1966), pp. 143-169.

15. For opposing views see M. Beardsley, "Aesthetic Experience Regained" and P. Kivy, "Aesthetic Perception," both printed in *Art and Philosophy*, 2nd edition, ed. W. E. Kennick (New York: St. Martin's Press, 1979).

16. Monroe Beardsley, "The Aesthetic Point of View," reprinted in *Philosophy Looks at the Arts*, ed. Joseph Margolis (Philadelphia: Temple University Press, 1978). p. 22.

17. See Robert A. Sharpe, "Seven Reasons Why Amusement is an Emotion," *Journal of Value Inquiry*, 9 (1975), pp. 201-3; and F. N. Sibley, "Aesthetic Concepts," *The Philosophical Review*, 68 (1959), pp. 421-50.

18. Morreall, pp. 60-61.

19. Morreall, p. 62.

20. See especially George Dickie, "The Myth of the Aesthetic Attitude," printed in *Art and Philosophy*.

21. J. O. Urmson, "What Makes a Situation Aesthetic?," *Proceedings of the Aristotelian Society*, Supp. Vol. 31 (1957).

22. George Santayana, *The Sense of Beauty* (New York: Dover Publications, 1955), pp. 248-9.

23. Schopenhauer, Vol. II, p. 98.

24. Earlier versions of this paper were read at the Pacific Division Meetings of the American Philosophical Association, March 1981, and the National Linguistic Humor Conference, Arizona State University, April 1982. I am grateful for helpful comments from Kurt Bergel, Shannon Martin, John Morreall, Joseph Runzo, and Thomas Stewart.

III. Amusement and Other Mental States

20 John Morreall

Regardless of the problems faced by any particular version of the Incongruity Theory, it seems clear that in some sense or other amusement is a reaction to incongruity. In this essay Morreall suggests that we can better understand amusement if we contrast it with two other reactions to incongruity—negative emotion and "reality assimilation" (puzzlement at the strange). When we react to the incongruity with emotions like anger or fear, or else when we try to make sense of the incongruity, it disturbs us; we feel uneasy about it. This uneasiness stems in part from a feeling of loss of control, and it motivates us to regain control by doing something. In negative emotion, we try to change the incongruous situation or our relation to it; in reality assimilation, we try to change our understanding of it. Amusement contrasts sharply with both negative emotion and reality assimilation on all three counts. When amused, we are not disturbed by the incongruity; we do not feel a loss of control; and we are not motivated to change the incongruous situation, our relation to it, or our understanding of it. Once we see the special nature of amusement as a reaction to incongruity we can better appreciate its value in human life.

Funny Ha-Ha, Funny Strange, and Other Reactions to Incongruity

In most European languages there is a word for "humorous" that also means "strange" or "odd." The English word is *funny*—"funny ha-ha," as we say, and "funny strange." What the humorous and the strange have in common is that both involve incongruity: Some thing or state of affairs which we perceive, remember, or imagine, strikes us as out of place. But we do not find all incongruity funny; many incongruities evoke negative emotions like fear or anger instead. I would like to explore some of the ways we react to incongruity, with an eye to showing what is special about humor. I will use three main headings: Negative Emotion, Reality Assimilation (for our puzzlement at the strange), and Humorous Amusement.[1]

Before discussing these three reactions to incongruity, though, let's spend a moment on the idea of incongruity itself. I will use the term "incongruity" in a very general way to mean a relation of conflict between something we perceive, remember, or imagine, on the one hand, and our conceptual patterns with their attendant expectations, on the other. What we perceive, remember, or imagine is often easily assimilated into our mental flow. It is consistent with our understanding of the way things are supposed to be; it "fits our picture of the world." We bite into a banana, for example, and find it soft and bland. But sometimes our mental input is not easily assimilated — or maybe not assimilable at all — into our understanding of the way things are supposed to be. What if the next banana you bit into were hard and granular and gave you an electrical shock?

Incongruous experiences such as biting into an electric banana would clash with our established, long-term conceptual patterns and expectations. But there can also be incongruity when much less established, merely short-term patterns are violated. In one psychological experiment, for instance, a person is asked to pick up a series of metal bars. All of the bars are of the same size and appearance, and the first several bars the person picks up are of the same weight. A pattern and so an expectation are set up very quickly, but then seven or eight bars along, the person picks up a bar that is much heavier or lighter than the ones earlier in the series. Jokes, too, may violate either long-term expectations about the world which we brought with us to our hearing of the joke, or short-term expectations built up as we listened to the joke itself.

The expectations which are upset in cases of incongruity also vary in their generality. Sometimes our expectations are very specific — your friend Diane has agreed to stop by at noon, and so when the door bell rings at noon, you open the door expecting to see Diane. If it turns out to be a man dressed in a moose costume, or even just the postman, that would be incongruous. If you had not made the arrangement with Diane, weren't expecting any visitors, and the door bell rang, then you would still have expectations in answering it, but of a more general kind — perhaps only the very general expectation that it will be a person in ordinary dress. In that case the appearance of the postman would not be incongruous, but the man dressed as a moose would still be. Indeed, a moose costume is almost always incongruous just because there is almost no situation in which we expect to see one. The nature of the incongruity in seeing a moose costume will vary, of course, with the expectations of the person who sees it. If you are expecting Diane and get a moose, that's different from just expecting *a person* and getting a moose.

Now there are many more distinctions which can be made be-tween types of incongruity,[2] but for our purposes we need not go in-to them. Rather than pursuing such distinctions further, then, let's use our general notion of incongruity — a conflict between some mental input and the framework into which that input is received — to explore the different reactions we have to incongruity.

I. Negative Emotion

The first reaction to incongruity we will consider is negative emotions, such unpleasant or painful emotions as fear, anger, disgust, and sadness. I'll be using the term "emotion" in its occur-rent sense to refer to episodic states and not long-term attitudes, and the analysis of emotion I'll be assuming is the farily standard one outlined by Jerome Shaffer, according to which an emotion is "a complex of physiological processes and sensations, caused by certain beliefs and desires."[3]

If we understand incongruity in a suitably wide way as devia-tion from "the way things are supposed to be," then we can see in-congruity as an aspect of the intentional object of all negative emo-tions which have an intentional object. In these negative emotions we are upset by a violation of what we see as the proper order of things, the order on which our expectations are based. Phrases like "the proper order of things" and "the way things are supposed to be" can be understood here in either a moral or a non-moral sense. Sometimes the state of affairs violating our expectations is caused by a moral agent, as when we react with anger at the mugger who has just assaulted and robbed us. At other times the upsetting state of affairs is a non-moral, natural event, as when we are saddened by a friend's dying of natural causes. It seems that we have a wider range of emotions in reaction to the actions of persons than we have in reaction to natural events, but as emotions the latter may be just as strong and upsetting as the former.

The incongruity to which I react in negative emotion, of course, need not be in someone else's actions or in some state of af-fairs outside of me. It may just as well be in a moral or non-moral condition of my own, as when I regret having treated a friend in a way that I now see was highhanded, or I feel embarrassed at discovering a hole in the seat of my pants.

In different negative emotions the kind of incongruity upsetting us varies. In fear the person or object is perceived as dangerous to us, in anger it is perceived as frustrating or harming us, in disgust it is perceived as intensely distasteful, etc. But in all negative emotions there is some kind of practical concern about the incongruity.[4] Some situation that matters to us is judged not to be as we want it to be, and we are motivated to react in various ways that have the potential of improving the situation itself or at least our relation to it. The world has somehow slipped out of our control, and we are motivated to bring it back into control. In fear, for example, we are motivated to protect ourselves, in moderate fear by fleeing the situation, in stronger fear by covering our face and screaming for help, by "freezing" so as to escape notice, or by "playing dead." The physiological changes occurring in fear, such as the heightened muscle tension in moderate fear and the rigidity in extreme fear, equip us for these defensive actions. In anger, the motivation is not to flee or to protect ourselves, but to eliminate the person or thing frustrating or threatening us; and again there are bodily changes to equip us for aggressive action. The motivation in jealousy is to maintain our hold on what we have. Human jealousy can be seen as evolving out of the sexual possessiveness and territoriality of lower animals. Indeed, a sexually jealous man acts much like a jealous walrus, say, in keeping close watch on his mate and fending off intruders.

With some other negative emotions it is not as easy to discern the practical dimension; if we consider their evolutionary history, nonetheless, I think that a good case can be made for this dimension. Sadness, to take the emotion which may look least practical, is a defensive reaction like fear, only here some major injury or loss has already been suffered. The motivation in sadness is to prevent further injury or loss, and the action taken is to slow down and withdraw from normal activities. Human sadness, we might speculate, had its origins in the parallel reactions of lower animals to injury or sickness by immobilizing the affected part of the body and reducing bodily movement generally, the practical function of which is to conserve the animal's energy and facilitate healing. Separation from a mate, mother, or offspring may at first produce distress and motivate the animal to search for the loved one, just as it does in humans. But if the search is ineffective, or the loved one turns out to be dead, the animal may slow its activity and experience something akin to human sadness. The negative feeling tone of

sadness serves as a negative reinforcer, motivating the animal to prevent a recurrence of separation or loss in the future, by sticking close
to and protecting its loved ones. In a social species like our own,
then, sadness would have survival value for the individual and the
species.

In tracing these human emotions back to their counterparts in
subhuman animals, I am not claiming that human emotions today
always do turn out to benefit the person in the emotional state.
Some negative emotions like jealousy, indeed, seem more often than
not to get in the way of successful human interactions. What I am
claiming is that these emotions have a practical orientation, in that
they evolved as a way of getting an animal to do an appropriate action in a practical situation, and that today they are still ways of
handling situations in which the world has slipped out of our control, to bring it back into control.

II. Reality Assimilation

Our second reaction to incongruity is puzzlement at the
strange, or as Paul McGhee has called it, "reality assimilation."[5]
Here the incongruity is treated not as emotionally upsetting, nor as
amusing, but as a problem in cognitive processing, a problem in
making sense of what has been experienced. Something has been
presented to our consciousness that does not fit our conceptual
schemata, and we try to make it fit. Consider, for example, Roentgen's discovery of X-rays, which came about while he was ex-
perimenting with cathode rays and he noticed that a barium
platino-cyanide screen in the room glowed when the cathode rays
were discharging. Here was a phenomenon Roentgen did not expect, and which he had no way of explaining. Of course, a scientist
may have a predominantly practical attitude toward an experiment,
and treat it as a plumber would treat the installation of a toilet bowl.
And then anything out of the ordinary which happens may be
viewed as frustrating the project, and so be reacted to with negative
emotions. But for our purposes, let's assume that at least on the day
he discovered X-rays Roentgen was the ideal scientist brimming over
with sheer curiosity, so that he reacted to the incongruous glowing of
the screen not with frustration or anger, but with that desire to
understand which Aristotle told us we all have.

In contrasting the emotional response to incongruity with the response of reality assimilation here, I don't want to overlook their similarities. Indeed, I want to stress them for two reasons. First, these similarities show us something about how our cognitive processing, no matter how theoretical, is connected with our practical side. And secondly, most of the features that are shared by negative emotion and reality assimilation as responses to incongruity, will not be shared by our third response — humorous amusement. So by linking these first two responses, I'll have a foil for my treatment of humor.

The most obvious similarity between negative emotion and reality assimilation is that both involve an uneasiness or tension based on unfulfilled desires. Just as we speak of negative emotions as uncomfortable or distressing, we speak of "itching" or even "burning" with curiosity about the solution to a puzzle. The difference between negative emotion and reality assimilation here is that in the former we want the incongruous situation to be different, while in the latter we want our cognitive state to be different. In negative emotion it's the incongruous situation that bothers us, while in reality assimilation it is our not being able to fit the incongruous situation into our current schemata. If I opened today's mail to find a letter from an enemy threatening my life, for example, I would feel fear; what I would want to change is the situation of my life being in danger. But if I opened my mail to find $1000 in cash from an anonymous source, I would probably react with reality assimilation, I would try to figure out who could have sent me this money. Here what I would want to change is not my receiving the money, but my ignorance about who sent it.

To a large degree the desires we have in negative emotion and in reality assimilation that cause our uneasiness, stem from a certain loss of control which we feel.[6] When we are attacked or we lose a loved one, our loss of control is obvious. But to be perplexed by some incongruity is also to suffer a loss of control. In such a state we stop what we are doing, for we don't know how to proceed. In Roentgen's case, for instance, the unexpected glowing of the screen disrupted his experiment. Anomalous events like this can be disturbing because they suspend our confidence in our ability to predict, and so to anticipate, what will happen next.

We don't have hard evidence about the evolution of reality assimilation in humans, but it seems reasonable to trace it to the more general orienting reflex in lower animals. When faced with an unfamiliar situation, an animal typically stops what it is doing, freezing momentarily in surprise. Surprise serves as a way of clearing the cognitive channels for new input. The eyes are opened wide; the ears and other senses are directed toward the strange stimulus. Now the strangeness of the stimulus may be extreme, in which case the animal will experience fear. But if fear isn't aroused, the animal will probably experience curiosity instead. It will look and listen and smell, move around and perhaps manipulate strange objects, until features of the situation that the animal can recognize emerge, or at least until it develops a new schema into which this situation fits—until, in short, what was initially unfamiliar becomes familiar.

In this orienting reflex in animals, the "What is it?" question is always bound up with the "What is to be done?" question, and herein lies the practical value of orienting behavior. For an animal not to be able to make sense of some situation is for it not to know what action is appropriate, and so might be to risk harm, or at least to miss an opportunity for, say, a new kind of food.

In humans today the orienting reflex serves our basic survival needs in many situations, just as in the lower animals. But we have developed it, along with the rest of our cognitive repertoire, far beyond our daily practical needs. We want to make sense not only of the immediate situations in which we find ourselves, but of the wider situations we're in—all the way up to the cosmic level, and including the past and future as well as the present. Indeed, there seem to be no bounds to what human beings want to understand. Unlike our distant ancestors, we have the luxury of asking the "What is it?" question all by itself, without the "What is to be done?" question.

As in the orienting reflex of lower animals, our drive to figure things out when confronted with an incongruous situation leads to various kinds of activity. And here we have another parallel between reality assimilation and negative emotion. In negative emotion we act to change the incongruous situation, or our relation to it—by fleeing, attacking, withdrawing, etc. In reality assimilation we try to change our own cognitive state of puzzlement, our inability to relate the incongruous situation adequately to our previous experience. The latter may be attempted in several ways. We may just sit in our armchair and think about what we have experienced. Or we may engage in more observation, along with manipulation of the situation, as I'm sure Roentgen did after getting the anomalous glow on

his screen. We may also, of course, ask other people for an explanation. While some of these ways of trying to figure things out may involve little observable activity, reality assimilation responses to incongruity are frequently much busier than negative emotion
responses.

Our first two responses to incongruity, then, are distinguished
by the practical concern in negative emotion, which is lacking in
reality assimilation; but in the other respects we considered, they are
similar. The three main parallels I've drawn are these. First, in both
negative emotion and reality assimilation there is an uneasiness
based on our desires. Second, the uneasiness and our desires in both
are due in part to our feeling a loss of control. And third, both lead
to actions, in negative emotion action to change the incongruous
situation or our relation to it, and in reality assimilation action to
improve our understanding of the situation.

III. Humorous Amusement

With these three parallels between negative emotion and reality
assimilation in mind, we can now turn to humorous amusement,
which, as I suggested earlier, is "odd man out" among our three
reactions to incongruity. We can see this by considering the three
features shared by negative emotion and reality assimilation.

In contrast to the disagreeableness of the incongruity typical of
negative emotion and reality assimilation, in amusement the situation that does not meet our expectations is not disturbing to us, nor
is the fact, if it is a fact, that we are unable to figure out the
incongruity. We do not have desires for the incongruous situation to
be different, or for our understanding of it to be different. Indeed,
we *enjoy* the incongruity. Think again of Roentgen in his
laboratory. Earlier I supposed that when the screen glowed, he
reacted to this anomaly with puzzlement, taking it as a cognitive
challenge. But, as I said, he might have reacted with anger at this
hitch in his previously smooth-working experiment. In either case,
however, the incongruity would not have been satisfactory to him.
Yet suppose for a moment that the glowing struck Roentgen neither
as an obstacle frustrating his experiment, nor as funny strange — an
incongruity to be figured out, but instead as funny ha-ha. In that
case, not only would he not have been emotionally or cognitively

upset by the screen's glowing, but he would have taken a certain delight in its incongruity.

The second parallel I drew between negative emotion and reality assimilation was that the uneasiness we feel in these reactions is due in part to our loss of control. In amusement, on the other hand, we are not uncomfortable, in part because we do not feel that the world has slipped out of our control. When we are amused, just as when we react to an incongruity with negative emotion or reality assimilation, we were not expecting the anomalous state of affairs, and we may not know what is coming next; but in amusement none of this threatens our feeling in control. And because we do not feel a loss of control, it is not troubling to us that our expectations have been violated. Indeed, that is the source of our pleasure in amusement.

The third feature shared by negative emotion and reality assimilation, as we saw, is that both motivate us to change something—the incongruous situation or our relation to it, in negative emotion, and our understanding of the incongruous situation, in reality assimilation. And here again there is a contrast with amusement, in which we enjoy, and so are satisfied with, the incongruity. Because we enjoy the incongruity in amusement, our only motivation might be to prolong and perhaps communicate the enjoyable experience; we do not have the practical concern to improve the incongruous situation, nor the theoretical concern to improve our understanding of it. There is nothing to be done in amusement as there typically is in negative emotion and reality assimilation.

Let me go into more detail about the lack of practical concern and the lack of theoretical concern in amusement. We can begin with the latter. Here the main thing I want to establish is the most obvious—that it is possible to be faced with some incongruity and simply enjoy it, without feeling compelled to figure it out. I make this obvious point only because a number of respected philosophers and psychologists have portrayed human beings as creatures which automatically seek conceptual order and shun disorder. A tradition stretching back to Plato insists that it is perverse to enjoy the frustration of our reason, which is what enjoying incongruity amounts to. Santayana, for example, speaks of an "undertone of disgust" found in amusement at humor, and claims that "man, being a rational animal, can like absurdity no better than he can like hunger or cold."[7] Among behavioral and social scientists, we can find the same theme. "Anomaly is inherently disturbing," writes Barry Barnes, "and automatically generates pressure for its reduction,"[8] In an influential work, *A Theory of Cognitive Dissonance*, Leon Festinger uses the category of "cognitive dissonance" much as I have been using "incongruity," for "nonfitting relations among cognitions"; his thesis is that cognitive dissonance, like hunger, automatically motivates us to reduce it and to "avoid situations and information which would likely increase the dissonance."[9] If claims like these were true, there would be no such thing as the nonperverse enjoyment of incongruity. Most psychologists have not claimed that incongruity is never enjoyed, but many have gone almost that far and claimed that only young children enjoy incongruity per se. According to Thomas Schultz, for instance, children over the age of seven and adults require not just incongruity in order to be amused, but the resolution of that incongruity. Mature humor, that is, requires the fitting of the *apparently* anomalous element into some conceptual schema. Indeed, Schultz is unwilling to call unresolvable incongruity "humorous" — instead he calls it "nonsense."[10]

Against all the views I have been describing, I would insist that not only do many adults enjoy incongruity for its own sake, but there is nothing perverse or immature in doing so. In looking for cases of the enjoyment of unresolved incongruity, we should not limit ourselves only to jokes, as many psychologists have done. In most jokes, it is true, the incongruity is resolved on some level. There is a punchline which upsets our expectations about how the joke would turn out, that is, but we *get* the joke because we switch to another schema in which the punchline fits. Not all jokes, however, have punchlines. Consider the joking question "What's the difference between a duck with one of its legs both the same?" Here the fun lies precisely in our inability to switch to an alternate schema which turns the joke into a coherent question. Many single-frame cartoons are also based on unresolved incongruity. In the cartoon below by Charles Addams, for instance, our amusement is at the absurdity of the ski tracks passing around the tree.[11] To adopt the attitude of reality assimilation and try to figure out how those tracks could have been made is to lose the humor of the cartoon. Indeed, I chose this cartoon as an example here because when it was published in a German magazine in the late 1940's, many readers wrote in with their "solutions" to it. Instead of being amused by the drawing, they took it as a cognitive challenge.

Drawing by Chas. Addams; © 1940, 1968
The New Yorker Magazine, Inc.

Humor based on unresolved incongruity can be found not only in jokes and cartoons, but also in real life. Consider, for example, situations in which we have overlooked the obvious, as when we spend several minutes searching for our glasses, only to discover that they are on our head.[12] To be amused by such situations, we do not need to be able to resolve their incongruity—indeed we usually find them funnier if they seem simply absurd. Most actions we call "wacky" or "zany," too, such as donning an outlandish mask, are gratuitously silly, offering no resolution of their incongruity.

Even in nonabsurd humor, moreover, where we can switch to some alternate schema into which the incongruity can be fit, the new schema will itself be incongruous in some way or other. Consider Henny Youngman's classic one-liner "Take my wife—please." The first three words set us up to think that Youngman is referring to his wife as an instance of something or other. But then we are hit with the "please," which is incongruous because it suddenly turns the sentence into a request. In switching from the citing-an-instance schema to the request schema, we resolve the speech act incongruity, but the request itself—to get rid of Youngman's wife for him—is incongruous. And it is this incongruity of hostility coming out of nowhere that makes the joke amusing. If the joke had simply relied on the switch from one speech act to another, where all the incongruity could be resolved by switching to the schema of the second speech act, it would fail as a joke. "Take my wife—this letter" or "Take my wife—to the doctor's tomorrow," just because their incongruity is completely resolvable, are not funny. *Getting* a joke, in short, even where it involves switching of schemata, is never the complete elimination of incongruity.

Having seen something about the lack of theoretical concern in amusement, then, let us turn to the lack of practical concern. To be amused by some incongruity, I suggest, is to have a measure of practical disengagement from it. The person who can enjoy the incongruity in a situation is, as we often say, "distanced" from that situation. Suppose, for example, that the incongruity is a deficiency in some machine, say a car that won't start. In order to find the futile sound of the cranking starter motor funny, we must not feel an urgency about this deficiency being corrected. Or if the incongruity is a moral fault in ourselves or another, we must not be morally concerned with it in order to find it amusing. That's why, of course, we object to people who "laugh off" criticisms about, say, their habitual drunk driving—if they are sincerely amused by such a habit, that shows that they don't care about the serious consequences of their actions and see no urgency about changing their actions.

The incompatibility between finding an incongruity funny and having practical concern toward it shows up even in the physiology of laughter as contrasted with the physiology of negative emotions. In moderate fear, for instance, there are incipient movements of flight, and the bodily changes prepare the person for fleeing. In anger there are incipient aggressive movements and the bodily changes prepare the person for violent action. But in amusement there are no incipient movements of larger actions to come, and the physiological changes are not a preparation for any action. Indeed, heavy laughter is incapacitating—breathing is interfered with and less oxygen is taken in, muscle tone is lost, our legs may buckle and we may be reduced to a spasmodically writhing heap on the floor. Our bodies here show that we are disengaged from the world of doing and caring.

We often exploit this incompatibility of amusement with practical concern to block negative emotions. We joke with people to reduce their fear or anger, and to cheer them up when they are sad. By inducing amusement we can keep people from getting emotional, or can often break the hold which existing emotions may have on them. There is even a psychiatric technique called "paradoxical therapy," used to help people overwhelmed by emotional problems, in which the psychiatrist presents the problem in such an exaggerated form that the patient finds it funny.[13]

IV. The Value of Humor

With this understanding of the contrast between amusement and our other two reactions to incongruity, we are now in a position to see the value of humor in human life. We can proceed by considering how humor might have evolved in our species. The practical value of negative emotions and reality assimilation has already been traced, and it is easy to see how they would have enhanced the chances of survival of early humans. But how is it that a reaction to incongruity like amusement, which is incompatible with negative emotions and reality assimilation, could also have had survival value? How could a reaction that involved the *enjoyment* of incongruity, and that disengaged early humans from practical and even theoretical concerns, have become part of human nature?

I think that part of the answer to these questions lies in the connection between our enjoyment of incongruity and our drive to seek variety in our cognitive input. This drive is not unique to humans, but is found to some extent in all animals with sophisticated nervous systems. Rhesus monkeys will perform a task like bar pressing just to bring about more complexity in their environment, for example, to see photographs instead of a field of plain light, or movies instead of photographs.[14] The nervous systems of mammals, indeed, require varied stimuli even to develop properly. (The brain of a young rat or child deprived of sensory stimulation even weighs less than the brain of its normal counterpart.) If children and adults are deprived for long of varied sensory stimulation, and cannot generate their own stimuli in thought, memory, or imagination, they get very uncomfortable. Variation in stimulation is important because we quickly get acclimated to an unvarying stimulus, so that its effect as a stimulus diminishes. An unvarying sound or smell, for instance, can fade into the background of our attention so that we no longer realize that it is still there.

The survival value of our seeking variety in our cognitive input is that it makes us curious, exploring creatures, and thus motivates us to know our environment better. Improved knowledge of our environment, of course, enhances our ability to cope with it and so to survive. An animal, at least a higher mammal, that was without curiosity, would be at a disadvantage in the evolutionary struggle.

Our craving for varied stimulation would not serve us well, however, if it were unconditional. An animal that sought just any new stimulation whatever, that would, say, walk into a bear's cave or jump out of a tall tree for the sheer novelty of the experience, would not last long. And so the drive for stimulation must be counterbalanced by the avoidance of situations known to be dangerous, and by caution in situations that are so unfamiliar that the animal does not know what actions are appropriate in them. This counterbalancing is achieved largely by the reaction we know as fear, which involves the shunning both of stimuli recognized as dangerous, and of excessively novel stimuli. (Fear of the excessively novel has been neglected in the traditional philosophical literature on fear, but in sub-human animals it is perhaps the more common kind.)

The optimum kind of novelty for animals and early humans, then, would be novelty that is not threatening, both in that it involves nothing known to be dangerous, and in that it is not so extreme as to be disorienting. What is desired is freshness in experience where one's overall control is maintained. And here is where humor comes in, for it involves a kind of novelty — incongruity — under the desired circumstances. When we are amused our expectations are violated, but we do not feel in danger or otherwise practically concerned, and we do not feel disoriented. Incongruity which arouses practical concern, as we have seen, produces fear or other negative emotions; incongruity which puzzles us may produce fear, or where the concern is theoretical rather than practical, reality assimilation.

Incongruity is not only a kind of novelty, but a sophisticated kind. For something to strike us an incongruous, it must not only be different from what we are used to, but it must violate our conceptual patterns. To appreciate incongruity we have to be capable of more than mere animal surprise — we have to be able to compare things and events, at least implicitly, with things and events of the relevant kind. A creature capable of humor, then, needs to have a system of mental representations, especially a system of class concepts. It also needs to be able to operate with its concepts in a nonpractical, non-theoretical, in short a *playful*, way, so that the violation of its conceptual patterns won't evoke negative emotion or disorientation. Subhuman animals, with the possible exception of the few apes that have been taught language, are not capable of humor because they lack either class concepts, or the ability to operate with these concepts in a non-serious way. Even where they have something like a conceptual system in an organized set of expectations, they cannot enjoy the violation of their expectations, because their thinking is only about the practical aspects of their current situation. Humans are capable of humor, by contrast, because our thinking is abstract, both in being general and in transcending both practical and immediate considerations.

Because of the abstract thinking in humor, it would have appeared late in evolution, long after emotions (which were already present in subhuman mammals), and probably along with language. It seems reasonable to speculate that language and humor would have developed in a mutually reinforcing way, just as they do in children today.[15] Language is especially important for creating humor: by far the most common, most versatile, and most convenient ways we have of creating incongruity for enjoyment are through language, and it is impossible to imagine non-linguistic creatures developing humor nearly as sophisticated as humans are capable of. We can, of course, introduce incongruity into our experience by producing incongruous things or causing incongruous events to occur, as in many practical jokes. Most of our joking, however, is done not by manipulating things but through language. With language we can create incongruous fictional situations, exaggerate features of real situations, call things by the wrong name or put them in an inappropriate category, say the opposite of what our listeners know we believe, and so on. We can also create incongruity by playing with the morphological, phonological, and semantic features of words themselves, as in puns.[16] Early humans probably stumbled onto these and other humorous techniques, but the delight they experienced would have motivated them to remember and develop them, and so to develop their linguistic abilities. In this way they would have developed their cognitive abilities generally (it is no accident that "wit" originally meant all our mental powers), and thus become more rational. Rationality, of course, has been the master survival strategy of our species.

Humor today goes hand in hand with our rationality, too, and not just rationality in the sense of cognitive sophistication, but also in the sense of a rational attitude toward the world. Part of this attitude is viewing things critically, and people with a well-developed sense of humor naturally look at things critically, because they are looking for incongruity. To be able to create humor, too, they need to cultivate imagination so as to be able to view things from unusual perspectives and create incongruous fictions. This imagination combined with a critical view of the world gives those with a rich sense of humor a flexible, versatile perspective and helps them overcome narrowness in their thinking. One of the most obvious traits of unimaginative, doctrinaire people is their lack of humor.

Space does not permit me to trace all the other values of humor here,[17] but we can see the essence of most of them if we think of humor as our higher cognitive functions operating in a play mode. At the most general level, the value of humor is that it liberates us from practical and even theoretical concerns, and allows us to view the world from a higher, less entangled perspective, as a kind of aesthetic field. This change from our more ordinary frames of mind is a luxury, to be sure, but in creatures like us, with our seemingly infinite capacity to worry about the past, present, and future, perhaps a necessary luxury. Were we able to experience incongruity only in serious ways, our lives would be fraught with urgency. But because we can also enjoy incongruity, our lives have a certain play to them, "play" in the obvious sense, and also in the older sense of slack or looseness. Voltaire said that heaven had given us two things to allow us to get through life: hope and sleep. Kant, who otherwise seems pretty dour, wisely added a third—laughter.

V. Amusement and Other Forms of Enjoying Incongruity

Having presented a quite general characterization of amusement in contrasting it with our other two reactions to incongruity, let me close by going into a bit more detail about the kind of enjoyment amusement is.

As Mike Martin has pointed out,[19] enjoying incongruity is not a sufficient condition for amusement, for we enjoy incongruity in other ways than by being amused. We may enjoy the events in a Richard Brautigan novel, for example, for their sheer bizarreness, without finding them funny. And we have other aesthetic categories besides the bizarre that cover non-amused forms of enjoying incongruity, most notably, the fantastic, the grotesque, and the macabre. Here I won't develop a full account of the difference between amusement and these categories, but let me suggest a sketch for such an account, putting to use our typology of reactions to incongruity.

Our enjoyment of the grotesque and the macabre, to begin, is in part a reaction of negative emotions, most importantly repulsion or disgust, and sometimes fear. There is a traditional question here—a generalized form of the paradox of tragedy—about how we could enjoy or find satisfaction in such emotions, but I can't go into that puzzle here. Suffice it to say that under certain circumstances, most notably in our appreciation of fiction, experiences of repulsion and fear can be enjoyed.[20] The grotesque may be treated as the wider category here, and the macabre as a subcategory involving our repulsion and fear of things associated with death, especially corpses.

Our appreciation of the bizarre and the fantastic, to take our other two categories for non-amused enjoyment of incongruity, is marked by a reaction of reality assimilation. What we enjoy here is being surprised and puzzled by strange things and situations. The difference between the fantastic and the bizarre is one of emphasis. As the name suggests, in calling something "fantastic" we are relating it to imagination — the imagination of the artist who created it, and our own imagination in recreating and trying to make sense of it. In appreciating something as bizarre, the emphasis is on the phenomenon itself and its strangeness. Nobody need have created the bizarre, and even where someone did, there need be no even implicit relation of the bizarre to someone's imagination. What we enjoy is simply the recalcitrance of the phenomenon to fit into our ordinary conceptual patterns.

What distinguishes the amusing from the grotesque, the macabre, the bizarre, and the fantastic is an absence of negative emotion or reality assimilation. Something which is just amusing — without overlapping these other categories — is something we enjoy merely for its incongruity, without the practical concern of negative emotions or the theoretical concern of reality assimilation. It is something we approach with a playful rather than a serious attitude, not caring about the incongruity but simply letting it delight us.

These distinctions are often difficult to apply to actual cases of enjoying incongruity, because the amusing often overlaps the grotesque, as in black humor, and overlaps the bizarre, as in Brautigan's novels. And different people, of course, can react in quite different ways to the same incongruity, some being amused by it, some feeling repulsion or fear, and some puzzling over it.

That we can enjoy incongruity at all, as I noted earlier, is quite an accomplishment in *homo ludens*. That we can enjoy it even when it evokes repulsion or puzzlement, shows how profoundly aesthetic a species we are.

Notes

1. Whenever I use the term "amusement" it will be in the sense of amusement at humor and not the broader sense of passing one's time in an agreeable manner, as by, say, playing cards.

2. See my *Taking Laughter Seriously* (Albany: State University of New York Press, 1983), ch. 6.

3. Jerome Shaffer, "An Assessment of Emotion," *American Philosophical Quarterly*, 20 (1983), 161-62.

4. See my "Humor and Emotion" *American Philosophical Quarterly*, 20 (1983), 297–304, for a fuller account of the practical dimension of emotions in general.

5. Paul McGhee, *Humor: Its Origin and Development* (San Francisco: W. H. Freeman, 1979), p. 57. My use of "reality assimilation" is narrower than McGhee's.

6. Barrie Falk has recently developed a whole analysis of fear on the idea of loss of control: ". . . to fear a situation is to take it as exhibiting the fact that the world is out of one's control." "What Are We Afraid of?" *Inquiry*, 25 (1982), 186.

7. George Santayana, *The Sense of Beauty* (New York: Scribner's, 1896), p. 248. For other philosophers' attacks on humor, see my "Humor and Philosophy," *Metaphilosophy*, 15 (1984), 305–317.

8. Barry Barnes, "The Comparison of Belief-Systems: Anomaly Versus Falsehood," in Robin Horton and Ruth Finnegan (eds.), *Modes of Thought* (London: Faber and Faber, 1973), p. 190.

9. Leon Festinger, *A Theory of Cognitive Dissonance* (Stanford: Stanford University Press, 1957), p. 3.

10. Thomas Schultz, "A Cognitive-Developmental Analysis of Humor," in Tony Chapman and Hugh Foot (eds.), *Humor and Laughter: Theory, Research and Applications (New York: Wiley, 1976), pp. 12*–13.

11. The editors of *The New Yorker*, where this cartoon originally appered, kindly gave me permission to use it.

12. This example is from Merrie Bergmann's paper "How Many Feminists Does it Take to Make a Joke?" Other examples from real life of humor based on unresolved incongruity can be found in my *Taking Laughter Seriously*, pp. 11–12.

13. See Viktor Frankl, *The Doctor and the Soul*, tr. Richard and Clara Winston (New York: Alfred Knopf, 1960), pp. 204–15; Allen Fay, *Making Things Better by Making Them Worse* (New York: Hawthorn, 1978).

14. Richard Restak, *The Brain the Last Frontier* (New York: Warner, 1980), p. 29.

15. See also McGhee, *Humor*, pp. 120–23.

16. See *Taking Laughter Seriously*, pp. 69–82, for more linguistic forms of humor.

17. See ibid., ch. 7-10.

18. Immanuel Kant, *Critique of Judgment*, tr. J. H. Bernard (New York: Hafner, 1951), p. 179.

19. Mike W. Martin, "Humor and Aesthetic Enjoyment of Incongruities," *British Journal of Aesthetics*, 23 (1983), 74-85.

20. See my "Enjoying Negative Emotions in Fiction," *Philosophy and Literature*, 9 (1985), 95-103.

21　Robert Sharpe

From Plato on, the traditional way of classifying amusement has been to treat it as an emotion. Sharpe here justifies this classification by pointing out seven parallels between amusement and standard emotions like fear and love. Both amusement and standard emotions have intentional objects; that is, they are *about* something. Both admit of degrees. With both we may suppress the behavioral manifestations. Both allow for self-deception. Both are intrinsically pleasant or painful. With both there is a distinction between the object of the mental state and its cause. And with both we can cultivate taste.

Seven Reasons Why Amusement Is An Emotion

Contemporary philosophers have had little to say about the concept of humor. This is a pity since there are some interesting philosophical questions that can be asked about it. I shall ask two. Firstly, is amusement, the correlative response to humor, an emotion and secondly, in what ways is amusement similar to our response to aesthetic objects? Amusement I take to be the appropriate response to humor. Laughter is a sign of amusement but, of course, amusement is neither a necessary nor a sufficient condition of laughter. I may be amused secretly and there is such a thing as a forced or hollow laugh.

There are some obvious parallels between amusement and standard cases of emotions. First of all both have an object. I love something or somebody or hate something or somebody. In the same way I am amused at something or somebody. To be amused at nothing at all is as odd or possibly pathological as to be afraid of nothing at all. Of course, one might be amused at or frightened of something which one mistakenly thought to be the case. In these circumstances one's fear or amusement has an object, though it is an object which corresponds to nothing in reality. A child may be frightened of the Bogeyman, or love Santa Claus in this way. These, though non-existent, are the objects of his fear or love. We should therefore regard the objects of amusement as intentional objects, as we do the objects of paradigm cases of emotion.

Secondly, amusement admits of degrees; the response to something funny may range from mild amusement to paroxysms of mirth and we may judge the intensity of somebody's response from his behavioral reactions. Just as somebody who is seen to be agitated, whose hands and knees shake and whose complexion is pale as he waits for an interview, is very fearful, so the person who rolls on the floor roaring with laughter is clearly very amused.

Thirdly, in the case of amusement as in the case of standard emotions such as fear, we may suppress these behavioral manifestations. When the fear or amusement is great, it may of course be impossible to conceal, as most of us know to our cost. At lesser intensities my amusement or my fear may be only known to myself or to those who know me well enough to recognize the very minute behavioral signs which give me away. I may tap my foot in annoyance, for example, or tighten my lips. Similarly I may suppress a smile at a particularly ridiculous remark in a seminar, but be unable to conceal a creasing about the eyes. On many occasions we may use our knowledge of how a person's behavior reveals his mental state to override his avowals and this is the case with amusement as well as with fear, anger, etc.

Fourthly, many emotions are the subjects of self-deception. I might not wish to admit to myself that I am jealous or envious, because it does not accord with my self-image. Self-deception over amusement is perhaps less frequent but it can occur. If I feel that to be amused at an obscene or blasphemous joke is morally wrong then I might wish to disguise to myself the fact that I was amused.

Fifthly, many emotions are intrinsically pleasant or painful. I would say that jealousy is intrinsically painful and joy intrinsically pleasant. Although a modicum of fear may be pleasant in an artificial situation, such as reading a ghost story or watching a Hitchcock film, terror is intrinsically unpleasant. Amusement I regard as intrinsically pleasant. There may, of course, be circumstances where it is not pleasant. If I find the ceremonial at a Degree congregation ludicrous, then I might find my amusement at it not at all enjoyable since I am on view and expected to keep a straight face. But, in the absence of such countervailing circumstances, amusement is pleasant and this is what I mean by calling it intrinsically pleasant.

Sixthly, it is usual to distinguish cause and object in emotion. My death may be the object of my fear but hardly the cause, since it has not yet occurred. The cause might be the lugubrious stories told to me when young. There are, I suspect, refinements required in this distinction but its essentials are plausible. Can the same distinction be made for any cases of amusement? At one point in Gerard Hoffnung's telling of the story of the bricklayer's mate at the Oxford Union, the audience, anticipating what is to come, roars with laughter. The object of their amusement is what he is about to say. But that could not be the cause of their amusement since it has not yet happened. The cause is their guessing what his next remark will be.

My final reason for treating amusement as an emotion at first struck me as a fairly conclusive objection to the suggested classification. So perhaps the best way to deal with it is to present it first as an objection and then work around to seeing how it actually picks on a logical characteristic which some emotions share with amusement. The objection is that amusement is similar to our response to aesthetic objects in being a matter of taste, and taste may be cultivated. I may enjoy Strindberg but find Ibsen boring. I may find Shaw amusing but not Dickens. Within limits I may change my taste. I may discover features in a work through repeated reading and by consulting critics and connoisseurs. In this way, it is possible to develop a taste in humor. Art and humor share also the fact the development of taste progresses towards the more subtle forms. A friend once remarked that he used to enjoy ground coffee but had of late developed a taste for Nescafe. This seemed to me a very odd thing to say. It would be rather like saying that whereas I used to love Mozart, my taste has now developed to the extent that I much prefer Tchaikovsky, or that my taste has developed away from Jane Austen and towards Kingley Amis. This is a degradation rather than a development of taste.

It is meaningless to say that I can cultivate a taste in objects of fear, terror, or jealousy in the way I can develop a taste in objects of amusement. Joy, fear, envy, jealousy, and terror strike willy-nilly and there is not a lot one can do about them. One can, of course, steel oneself not to fear one thing or another, and I may find out that something is not as frightening as I thought but we would hardly say of somebody who has trained himself not to fear torture that he is cultivating a taste. The development of taste is a matter of finding out what we like and what will repay our concentrated attention perhaps over a lifetime.

However, one *can* make out a case for certain emotions being susceptible to cultivation. Significantly these are the emotions which are appropriate responses to art. It is perfectly in order to speak of loving a work of art; I, or anybody else, can make a list of works of art of which I am particularly fond and for which, in expansive moments, I may perfectly properly announce my love. Now I can cultivate a love for the novels of Conrad. I do this typically when I read one of the better stories, enjoy it and find that I reflect on it after reading it. I then read other novels by the same author, discuss them with my friends, reread them, read a few good critics, and find my love for Conrad's novels developing. I nurture this affection by rereading and extending my knowledge of Conrad and so on.

My choice of what works I love and also of what people I love is, at least in part, also a matter of taste and taste may develop. In the same way what amuses me is also a matter of taste and it is a taste which can alter and develop. This suggests to me that amusement is a response which is not only often the apt response to works of art but shares other characteristics with other responses to works of art. We may note in this connection that we often admire jokes for the same sorts of reasons as we admire works of art. We like our jokes to be economical and unified, jokes in which every sentence counts. Judging from a rather rapid survey, it is as difficult to describe necessary conditions for producing jokes as it is to give necessary conditions for producing works of art. There seems to be no common character in virtue of which they are funny. And of course, this feature is very obvious in those works of humor which count without question as works of art, such as the plays of Aristophanes.

22   John Morreall

This essay challenges the traditional classification of amusement as an emotion by re-examining the similarities between amusement and standard emotions mentioned by Sharpe, and pointing out major dissimilarities. Two similarities—that amusement and standard emotions have an object, and that both may be pleasant—are shown to hide dissimilarities. While we have a positive or negative attitude toward objects of love, hate, and other emotions, we need have no such attitude toward objects of amusement. And while an emotion like love is pleasant in that the loved person or thing pleases us, amusement is not pleasant because the amusing thing pleases us. Indeed, amusing things are often somewhat repulsive. Further dissimilarities between amusement and emotions are brought out by examining the conceptual sophistication of amusement and its non-practical orientation. These dissimilarities, in fact, indicate that amusement and emotions probably had quite different evolutionary histories.

Humor and Emotion

Of all the phenomena which come under the investigation of empirical and philosophical psychology, humor is easily one of the least understood. Part of the difficulty in getting clear on the nature of humor is that laughter, the bodily manifestation of our amusement at something funny, is also our reaction to many nonhumorous kinds of stimulation, such as tickling, winning the lottery, and embarrassment. Here I am not going to offer a complete theory of laughter, nor even a complete theory of humor.[1] I simply want to clarify one issue which often trips up those working on these larger theories, and that is the connection between humor and emotion. In particular I want to challenge a view common in the literature on humor that our amusement at humor is a kind of emotion.

I

First, we need to make a terminological point. I will be using "amusement" only for our response to humor, and not in the broader sense in which a person is amused if his or her attention is simply agreeably occupied, as in, say, working on a jigsaw puzzle.

The view that amusement is an emotion, as I said, is a common one. It is found in Plato, Aristotle, Hobbes, and Beattie; in our own century in the work of Sully, Eastman, and Monro; and in many contemporary psychological studies.[2] (It is especially prevalent where laughter at humor is not distinguished from other kinds of laughter, as in the Superiority Theory and the Relief Theory.)And it must be admitted that there are a number of similarities between amusement and standard cases of emotions; the most basic, perhaps, is that both amusement and standard emotions involve physiological disturbances. Robert Sharpe offers seven other parallels as reasons for classifying amusement as an emotion.[3] First, amusement and standard emotions have an intentional object. Second, both admit of degrees. Third, we may suppress the behavioral manifestations of each. Fourth, both are objects of self-deception. Fifth, amusement and many emotions are intrinsically pleasant. Sixth, we can distinguish cause and object with both. And seventh, we can cultivate taste in amusement and in at least some emotions.

Two of Sharpe's parallels, the first and the fifth, I find illuminating, though as we shall see, a dissimilarity lies beneath the similarity in each. And there is a general problem with all seven of these parallels—they are not based on features which distinguish amusement and certain standard emotions from other states of a person. The fact that amusement and standard emotions have an intentional object, for example, does not make amusement an emotion; for other states, such as beliefs, have an intentional object, and they are clearly not emotions.

It could be objected here that there may not be features which pick out emotions and only emotions; the strongest connection that may exist between the various states we call emotions is that they have family resemblances. If this is true, of course, then Sharpe would be on the right track, for the most anyone could do to justify the claim that amusement is an emotion is to point out family resemblances between amusement and some standard cases of emotion. But even if we accept a family resemblance analysis of emotions, it is clear that not everything which is similar in any way whatever to a standard emotion is going to count as an emotion; not all similarities are family resemblances. In considering possible members of the emotion family, we must do more than look for similarities between X and standard cases of emotion. We must also evaluate the relevance of the feature shared by X and standard emotions to being included in the family of emotions. We must look too for dissimilarities between X and standard emotions, and weigh their relative importance or triviality. My thesis is that when we do all this with amusement, we find good reasons for ruling it out of the emotion family.

To see the dissimilarities between amusement and emotions, we might take two of Sharpe's parallels and probe beneath the surface similarity. His first was that both amusement and standard emotions have an intentional object. "I love something or somebody or hate something or somebody. In the same way I am amused at something or somebody."[4] And his fifth parallel was that many emotions are intrinsically pleasant or unpleasant, and amusement is intrinsically pleasant.

Let us begin with the nature of the object of an emotion and of the object of amusement, to see the important differences. To love something or to hate it[5] is to have a positive or a negative reaction to that very thing. If I feel love for the woman next door, then I am attracted to her; if I hate her chihuahua, then I am repelled by the dog itself. Fear, anger, and other emotions involve different evaluations of their various objects, but a positive or a negative attitude of some kind is always taken up toward the object of the emotion. To be angry at someone is in part to be repelled by some action or feature of that person; to be envious of someone's new house is in part to be attracted to that house; and so on with other emotions. But objects of amusement are different. If I am amused by something I need not have a positive or a negative attitude toward that thing. Suppose, for instance, that while driving through a tract of pastel, look-alike houses I suddenly come upon a gaily painted house with windows in the shapes of zoo animals. I may be amused by the house without thereby either liking or disliking the house itself. I like the experience of amusement, but that is a different matter.

Not only need I not have a positive or negative attitude toward an object of amusement, moreover, but I need not have beliefs about what properties it actually has. And herein lies another contrast between amusement and standard cases of emotion. As has often been pointed out, an emotion like love or fear for some object

X involves beliefs about X. To be afraid of some dog, for example, is in part to believe that the dog is likely to hurt you. Now amusement, as we'll see in a moment, is based on incongruity, but we need not *believe* that the object amusing us is in fact incongruous — it is enough to simply *look at* the object as incongruous. To use an example of Michael Clark's, if I am watching a political speech on TV and I turn the sound off, I may view the silent picture as if the gesturing politician were trying to sing a song; and viewed in such a way, the politician may amuse me.[6] But to be amused I don't have to believe that the politician is singing, or believe anything else about him either. It is not enough, of course, for me to look at the dog I fear *as if* it is dangerous; I have to believe that it is.

It is because of this belief element in emotions and its absence in amusement that an emotion can be inappropriate to a situation in a way that amusement cannot. If I experience fear because I think that there's a bear outside our tent, then I will see that my emotion was inappropriate when you show me that it is only a raccoon. If I were to continue in my fear even after my false belief had been corrected, then you would rightly think that there was something wrong with me. But if I am amused because I think that there's a dead bumblebee on your salad, then there's nothing comparably inappropriate in my continued amusement when you point out that it is only an olive. For me to be amused I don't have to believe that that thing is a bumblebee; I merely have to be able to see it as one.

All these differences between amusement and emotions can get overlooked if we talk about the objects of amusement and the objects of emotions in the same breath. We can also be led astray by the fifth parallel which Sharpe cites, that amusement, like positive emotions, is pleasant. Here, too, a difference lies beneath the surface similarity. An emotion like love is pleasant and one like annoyance unpleasant in that the object we love is pleasing to us and the object which annoys us is displeasing to us. Amusement, by contrast, is pleasant not in that the thing which amuses us is pleasing to us — often amusing objects are unattractive and even potentially repulsive — but in that our observing it or thinking about it is a pleasant experience. The gaily painted house with the odd windows, for instance, may strike us as grotesque; what is pleasant is seeing it among the other houses with which it obviously doesn't belong. What amuses us is the incongruity of this house in this setting.

II

The notion of incongruity has been discussed often in the literature on humor, and I have little to add to that discussion. I would go along with the standard view that something amuses us because it does not match up with what we expect things of that kind to be, or because it is out of place in the setting in which we find it. Something amuses us if it somehow violates our picture of the way things are supposed to be, and if we enjoy this violation.

Now although the essence of humor lies in this enjoyment of incongruity, it is important to note that in many laughter situations our enjoyment of incongruity is boosted by our simultaneous enjoyment of something else. If I am watching a movie in which a character falls into a swimming pool fully clothed, for example, then I may laugh simply in enjoyment of the incongruity of this event. But if I dislike my neighbor for the way he flaunts his wealth, and I see him fall into his pool in his new $500 suit, I may laugh harder, enjoying both the incongruity and his suffering. The enjoyment of someone's suffering, or the expression of pent-up feelings, however, never *constitute* humor, as the superiority and the relief theories of laughter might lead us to believe. By themselves, these other kinds of enjoyment are not kinds of humor even though they may issue in laughter. It is the enjoyment of incongruity that is both necessary and sufficient for humor; no other kind of enjoyment is either necessary or sufficient for humor.[7]

Returning to our contrast of amusement with emotions, I would now like to consider the relative sophistication of the enjoyment of incongruity. Objects of amusement do not strike us funny *simpliciter*, as objects of love may attract us *simpliciter* and objects of disgust repel us *simpliciter*. To be amused we have to be able to compare things with each other, at least implicitly, and we have to have class concepts. For a dilapidated car to strike us as incongruous, for instance, we have to have an idea of what cars are supposed to look like. Humor also often involves incongruity based on spatial, temporal, and causal relationships. And so a creature with even a basic sense of humor needs much more than a creature capable merely of emotions — it needs a fairly sophisticated conceptual system. Infants and many animals experience fear, love, anger, and other emotions, but do not experience amusement at humor, for they do not have the abstract level of thought required for appreciating incongruity.

Our capacity for humor is based not just on our having a conceptual system, but on our ability to operate with it in a nonpractical way. Even where infants and higher animals have something like a primitive conceptual system in an organized set of expectations, they are not able to enjoy the violation of those expectations in the way we can enjoy the violation of our expectations. Chimpanzees, for example, will react when presented with a model of a chimpanzee's head unconnected to a body, but the reaction is always anxiety or terror, never amusement. Human thought, by contrast, is abstract not only in its generality but in its ability to relate us to something other than our current situation. We abstract not just from the concrete but from the present. Unlike infants and animals, whose cognitive operations are directed toward whatever situation they are in at the moment, we are able to deliberately think about the past and the future, and about possibilities as well as actualities. And we can do so not only to learn practical lessons from the past or to plan for the future, but simply for the fun of it. We can reminisce and daydream and speculate; we can even create incongruous events in thought and present them to each other as jokes. All this is done, of course, primarily in language, which explains why children acquire a sense of humor around the time they master the basics of language use, and why the development of their sense of humor parallels their linguistic development.

III

The cognitive system which makes amusement possible orients us to the world in a way quite different from the way emotions orient us to the world. An emotion involves our practical concern, usually with our current situation or that of someone to whom we are attached, but also with situations in the past and future where we can "bring them back" or look forward to them with sufficient vividness that for the moment they are as real as our current situation. Amusement, by contrast, involves a non-practical attitude toward some present or non-present (often even non-real) situation, that need have no relation at all to us.

Emotions evolved in animals, our own species included, as ways of dealing with practical situations. They had survival value because they involved motivations for specific actions which benefitted the individual or the species, and they involved physiological changes which prepared the animal for those actions. We can see this most clearly, perhaps, in the three unlearned emotions of fear, anger, and love.

In fear an animal is motivated to flee a dangerous situation, or if that is not possible, to "freeze" so as to escape notice, or to play dead. The physiological changes which occur in fear, such as the heightened alertness and muscle tension, prepare the animal for these actions. Even the evacuation of the bladder and intestines, still found today in intense human fear, evolved in lower animals as a way of reducing body weight to facilitate flight.

In anger we are motivated not to flee but to fight, when someone has threatened or injured us or someone to whom we are attached. Noradrenalin is secreted to increase blood pressure and respiration and to prepare the animal in other ways to fight. Now the aggressive stance and movements of anger are often enough by themselves to get the offending party to back off or change to submissive behavior; but where the anger continues to grow, it naturally leads to violent action.

The two basic kinds of love — that between mother and offspring, and sexual love — have an obvious survival value. Without the mother's attachment to her offspring found in birds and mammals, and the actions which it motivates, the young would simply die, for they would not be fed or protected. Sexual passion, of course, leads to mating, which keeps the species going.

When we consider other emotions more influenced by human culture, their practical dimension may be harder to discern. Indeed, if we look at an emotion like jealousy only from our contemporary human perspective, we might be led to question whether it has any practical value. But this would be to ignore the evolutionary history of such an emotion. Though human jealousy is more complicated than jealousy in animals (largely because we have added various conventional forms of expression), it seems reasonable to speculate, judging from its function among animals today, that jealousy began as a mechanism for preserving an animal's hold on its mate(s) and territory. It involves the motivation to fight off intruders, and prepares the animal physiologically to do that (just as it does in humans today). If the animal is strong and able to produce healthy offspring, it will probably defend its territory successfully and retain its mate(s). If it is too old or weak, it will probably be replaced by the stronger intruder, who will make a better contribution to the continuation of the species. Jealousy would serve humans in the retention not just of territory and mates, of course, but of all the many kinds of possessions and status we have developed.

If we adopt this evolutionary perspective, we can also see the practical value of seemingly unpractical emotions like joy and sadness. Joy is a positive state attendant upon a creature's getting or experiencing something it desires — in animals usually a mate — or its anticipation of such acquisition or experience. In the former case it reinforces whatever we have done to obtain this good, and in the latter case it motivates us to obtain the good. Sadness, on the other hand, attends our losing something valuable or our experiencing something harmful. As with other emotions, we have no direct evidence about the evolution of sadness, but we might speculate that it had its origins in the self-protective reaction of sub-human animals to injury or sickness. This reaction, which involves an immobilization of the affected part of the body and a general reduction in movement, reduces the chances of aggravating the injury, conserves the animal's energy, and facilitates healing. In its developed form in humans and higher animals, the negative feeling tone of sadness also serves as negative reinforcement, motivating the creature to prevent a recurrence of a similar situation in the future, if that is possible.

Still other emotions are not found in animals at all because they involve a cognitive sophistication which only humans have. Animals get angry but not resentful or indignant, for instance, because they lack the self-awareness required for the latter emotions. Similarly, though they experience depression akin to human sadness, they do not experience regret because they lack the requisite self-awareness and ability to think about what might have been. While such "higher emotions" are found only in humans, however, they need not seem anomalous if we view them as developing out of cognitively simpler emotions. Resentment and indignation, for example, can be seen as sophisticated forms of anger occasioned by certain kinds of judgments and evaluations of which only humans are capable. Regret can be seen as sadness occasioned by a desire that things had happened differently than they did (most often because one's own actions would have been different). These "higher emotions" still have a practical dimension, too, both in that they are a response to something harmful done to or by a person, and in that they serve as negative reinforcement for the one perpetrating the harm not to repeat the action (either the person on the receiving end of resentment or indignation, that is, or the person feeling regret).

In sharp contrast to this practical orientation of emotions is the purposelessness of amusement, which is evident in many aspects of amusement, starting with its physiology. While in fear or anger we get prepared physiologically to flee or to fight, and we make incipient movements of flight or aggression, in laughing at something amusing we don't get prepared to do anything at all. The movements of the diaphragm, face, and the rest of the body in laughter are not the early stages of any larger action.

The contrast between the practical orientation of emotions and the non-practical orientation of amusement comes out, too, in the way emotions can overwhelm us and even make us their "slaves," while nothing comparable is the case with amusement. Sexual passion, anger or jealousy, can involve the motivation to kill someone, for example. When our rational faculties would judge that the killing is not a reasonable action to perform, but our emotion wins out and we do the killing, we say that we (identifying ourselves here with our rational faculties) were overcome by emotion. If our actions are habitually governed by our emotions in opposition to what our rational faculties would dictate, we say that we are slaves to our emotions. Amusement, on the other hand, because it does not involve the motivaiton to take action, cannot make us its slaves.

My claim here that emotions motivate activity while amusement does not needs a bit of qualification. In a broad sense of "motivate," the experience of amusement may motivate us to prolong or to repeat that experience. On seeing the funny house mentioned earlier, for instance, we might be motivated to take a snapshot of it so that we can enjoy its funniness later on with friends or by ourselves. In this broad sense of the word, of course, any experience that we like — even aesthetic experience and the contemplation of theoretical truth, those paradigms of non-practical activity can motivate us. Our aesthetic appreciation of a piece of sculpture might motivate us to return to the museum to see it again; our learning a little astronomy might motivate us to sign up for an astronomy course, or even buy a telescope.

The sense I have in mind in saying that amusement, unlike emotions, does not motivate us is not this broad sense, however, in which any experience that we like stimulates us to prolong and to repeat that experience. It is the narrower sense in which an experience stimulates us to do something *other than* have that experience, as fear motivates us to preserve ourselves and jealousy motivates us to protect our possessions or status. In this sense, amusement, like other kinds of non-practical experience, does not motivate us.

IV

The practical nature of emotions and the non-practical nature of amusement make them not just different kinds of experience, but experiences which suppress one another. Earlier I admitted that some case of laughter may involve both the enjoyment of incongruity and the enjoyment of some emotion. But here we should note that where this happens, the emotion must be relatively weak, or it will involve a practical concern which will block amusement. If I do not merely dislike my neighbor, but feel occurrent hatred for him, as I watch him fall into his pool, for instance, I'll be taken by practical interest in the situation: I'll crane my neck to see if he might actually be drowning, and I'll be thinking of ways I might prevent his rescue. And in this frame of mind I won't experience amusement. Similarly, it's not at the moment we are angrily fighting with someone that we find something he or she does laughable. We'll be amused, if at all, when there is a pause in the fighting, or later in retrospect, when the anger has subsided.

Not just negative emotions but also positive emotions like sexual passion can get in the way of amusement. When a person is overcome by sexual passion in lovemaking, for example, he or she will not find incongruities amusing. Indeed, for one sexual partner to laugh at anything—even something unconnected with their lovemaking—is usually taken by the other partner to indicate that the person was not feeling passionate.

We often exploit this incompatibility of humor with strong emotions by using humor to block emotions. We joke with people to inhibit or reduce their fear, to calm them down from an angry state, and to cheer them up when they are sad. Indeed, in this incompatibility I think we can see how amusement may have evolved in our species. For many theorists of evolution the development of humor is puzzling—how, they ask, could something that disengaged early humans from practical concerns, and even at times physically incapacitated them, have had survival value? Humor, I suggest, did not have survival value in the same way emotions did, by motivating people to do or refrain from certain actions in certain situations. Its value was more indirect, and was tied to our race's general survival strategy of being *rational* animals.

Our capacity for amusement developed along with our other higher cognitive functions, long after the evolution of emotions, which were already present in earlier mammals. The story of the development of human reason was the story of its becoming more and more abstract; and abstraction, as noted earlier, is thinking beyond not just individual objects but one's current situation. For reason to develop, early humans had to go beyond merely recognizing the practical aspects of the individual situations in which they found themselves. They had to be able to understand situations not just for the ways those situations impinged on them at the moment, but also for their general features, both practical, and more importantly, non-practical. Now in this development of reason, emotions would have been not a boon but an encumbrance, for in an emotional state a person looks at a situation practically and as related to himself or herself. Amusement, by contrast, like artistic activities and science, would be helpful in the development of reason because it involves a breaking out of a practical and self-concerned frame of mind, and an attention to things not only as related to us but as related to other things of their kind and to other things generally.

All this is not to say that amusement *brought about* abstract thinking, of course, any more than we would say that art or science brought about abstract thinking. It is probably closer to the truth to say that once a certain minimal level of abstractness in thinking was reached, humans were capable of enjoying incongruity; and the pleasure of amusement reinforced their noticing incongruity, stimulating them to look for and even create it, at progressively more abstract levels. (This stimulation does not make amusement practical like emotions, as I noted above, because it is a stimulation simply to prolong and repeat the experience of amusement.) Now a creature developing the capacity for amusement at progressively more abstract types of incongruity (from pratfalls to *double entendres*, e.g.) would be a creature developing a more and more sophisticated conceptual system. The development of amusement, then, would be part of the development of rationality.

The capacity of humor to block emotions would also have facilitated the development of rationality, for emotions, which served pre-human animals so well, would often get in the way of rational thinking, as indeed they still do. To be able to face incongruity in one's experience — especially one's own failure — with amusement instead of anger or sadness, allows a person a more objective and rational perspective on what is happening. With this more rational perspective, too, comes a more flexible and resilient attitude toward experience in general. Amusement even has medical benefits — because the person with a good sense of humor is less inclined toward negative emotions, he or she is less susceptible to stress and all the ailments brought on by stress.

Both humor and emotion, then, are human ways of getting along in the world. But they represent different survival strategies, and of the two humor is the more distinctively human. Emotions can be valuable in providing automatic, practical responses in concrete situations. But precisely because they engage us in a practical way in individual situations, they do not promote the cognitive orientation to the world we call rationality. In amusement, by contrast, our cognitive processes operate not in a practical but in a playful mode, where there is room for theoretical understanding, imagination, and creativity. Creatures that had no practical concerns of the kind we find in emotions would have died out quickly, of course; humans could not have evolved as full-time humorists, any more than as full-time scientists or artists. But creatures so engaged in the world that they were controlled by emotions would not have developed rationality to any significant degree and so would not have become human beings.[8]

Notes

1. See my "A New Theory of Laughter" in *Philosophical Studies*, Vol. 42 (1982), pp. 243-54, and Ch. 5 of my *Taking Laughter Seriously* (Albany, N.Y., 1983).

2. Plato, *Republic*, III, 388; *Laws*, VII, 816: Aristotle, *Rhetoric*, II, 12, 16; *Nicomachean Ethics*, IV, 8. Thomas Hobbes, *Human Nature*, Ch. 9 in Molesworth's edition of the *Works*, Vol. IV (London, 1840), p. 46; cf. *Leviathan*, I, 6, Molesworth, Vol. III; James Beattie, "On Laughter and Ludicrous Composition," in *Essays*, 3rd ed. (London, 1779), p. 420; James Sully, *an Essay on Laughter* (New York, 1902), esp. p. 308; Max Eastman,

The Sense of Humor (New York, 1921), esp. p. 22; and D. H. Monro, *Argument of Laughter* (Notre Dame, 1963), p. 255. For psychological studies see, for example, Magda Arnold, *Emotion and Personality*, Vol. II (New York, 1960), p. 323; George Mandler, *Mind and Emotion* (New York, 1975), p. 142; and Charles Cofer, *Motivation and Emotion* (Glenview, 1972), p. 68.

3. Robert Sharpe, "Seven Reasons Why Amusement Is an Emotion," *Journal of Value Inquiry*, Vol. 9 (1975), pp. 201-03.

4. *Ibid.*, p. 201.

5. Many emotion words—e.g., "love," "hate," and "jealousy"—can be used to refer both to episodic emotional states and to long-term attitudes. Because I'm contrasting emotions with amusement, which is an episodic phenomenon, I'll be using such emotion words in the episodic sense.

6. Michael Clark, "Humor and Incongruity," *Philosophy*, Vol. 45 (1970), p. 25.

7. I argue this point at more length in *Taking Laughter Seriously*, Ch. 5. Since writing this paper, however, I have come to see—thanks to Mike Martin—that enjoying incongruity is not sufficient for amusement, though it is necessary. See Martin's essay, ch. 19, sections II and III; and my essay, ch. 20, section V.

8. I am grateful to John Deigh for his comments on an earlier version of this paper.

IV. The Ethics of Laughter and Humor

23   Ronald de Sousa

In this chapter from his forthcoming book on emotions, de Sousa explores some social aspects of humor, especially of joking, in order to develop an ethics of humor. In stressing the social nature of humor, de Sousa is like Bergson, who saw laughter as a social gesture. But while Bergson (like Morreall in the last chapter) claimed that there was a certain incompatibility between humor and emotions, de Sousa revives the older Platonic-Hobbesian idea of a phthonic (malicious) element in humor. Telling and enjoying sexist and racist jokes, for example, is based on having certain emotional attitudes. And where the attitude presupposed by a joke is morally objectionable, then telling the joke or laughing at it is also morally objectionable.

When Is It Wrong to Laugh?

> *I laughed in all Cathedrals, knowing they were mine.* — Ellen
> Estabrook Taylor

The gift of laughter is often described as central to human nature. Rabelais, who had a stake in thinking well of laughter, said it defined the human essence: "Le rire est le propre de l'homme." Of the many differentiae suggested for our species, this has proved among the hardiest. "Featherless Biped" wouldn't do, as Diogenes proved by plucking a chicken, and our claim to be exclusive users of language and tools has been squeezed thin of late between apes and computers. The human cachinnophile will grant other species a sense of fun, a taste for play and even a capacity for mischief. But without repudiating the continuity of animal life, they will insist that if other animals turn out to laugh, this marks just one more way in which their intelligence and sociality is closer to ours than we thought. Before I proceed, a caveat about what I take my topic to include. Laughter is no mere class of sounds, not even if one of the defining conditions of the class is that they be produced by humans. Hysterical laughter is not laughter (though my account may implicitly sugge≤t what the relation is between them), nor are the happy noises an⸤ ⸤ries of infants, or "laughing with pleasure." Laughter

226

as I am concerned with it is a response of which the Formal Objects are the funny, the comical, the ridiculous.[1] I shall lump these together as *the Funny*. I shall be mostly interested in the Funny and our emotional response to it, rather than in laughing behavior. But the expression of an emotion may be of constitutive importance in defining the emotion itself, both as social reality and as subjective experience. So I shall not avoid speaking sometimes of actual laughter.

I shall not attempt to explain this fact, nor to provide a comprehensive account of laughter. Instead I shall ask how we can apply to it my contention that emotions can be rationally evaluated. Or rather, since we obviously do sometimes think it is irrational or even morally wrong to laugh, I shall ask whether we can rationalize the principles behind such assessments to construct an *Ethics of Laughter*.

This inquiry is intended as a prolegomenon to a more general discussion of the role of emotion in the moral life. In particular, it explores the idea that some principles of rationality constrain what emotions can coexist in relation to the same object. Most importantly, it will reveal an interesting characteristic that differentiates, I shall argue, emotional *attitudes* from mere beliefs. Finally, it will add a facet to our understanding of the ambivalence so prevalent in our emotional life. If indeed the Funny and our capacity to perceive it are central to human nature, that ambivalence is not surprising. For human nature has always been regarded, epecially in our tradition, as both angelic and demonic. Our vocabulary for the main emotions often comes in pairs of almost identical emotions, differing only in their sign. Love and Lust: Admiration and Envy; Indignation and Resentment. You know that one is good and one is bad, but you're neither quite sure which is which, nor even how to tell them apart. And that's how it is with laughter: "You're laughing at me!" — "No, I'm not laughing *at* you, I'm laughing *with* you." That there is a distinction seems clear; but how do we tell in practice when that retort is true?

Many a quotable word has been spoken by those who have focused exclusively on one side or the other of the ambivalence, praising or condemning laughter as such. The motto of Italian and French comedy, as one might expect, places laughter on the side of the angels: "Castigat Ridendo Mores," or loosely translated, the point of laughter is moral improvement. On the other hand, one Father of the Church claimed that while laughter was not itself a sin, it leads to sin. The poet Shelley seems to have agreed. He once wrote to a friend: "I am convinced that there can be no entire regeneration of mankind until laughter is put down."[2] Most of us are not so single-mindedly on one side or the other. We think of laughter as an occa-sionally risky pleasure, like sex, which is a good thing in itself, or at least when done in the right way and kept in its place. Like mon-archs, we sometimes license fools to tell us truths which our friends will be too well brought up to speak. And apart from such licensed fools, the common sense Ethics of laughter goes something like this: Laugh when it's funny, grow up and stop snickering at dirty jokes, don't laugh at cripples (unless you are one yourself), and *show respect*. To show respect means not to laugh, snicker, titter, chortle, giggle, or even chuckle when it's Too Sad, when it would be Unkind to, when it would Offend a Sacred Memory, and when it might be taken to Insult a Mother, a Country, or a Religion. But a few precepts don't add up to an Ethic. Can anything, indeed, properly be called the "Ethics of Laughter"?

Three Arguments Against Taking the Subject Seriously

I see three arguments that might be adduced against the very idea: that laughter is *involuntary*, that its consequences are *trivial*, and that its demands are at best *merely aesthetic*.

Laughter is Involuntary. The first argument stems from the familiar doctrine of the emotions as passions, therefore passive. It urges that nothing that is not voluntary could be the subject of moral constraint. For, it is often repeated, ought implies can. But the sense in which morally significant actions must be in our power is not, as Aristotle pointed out, one that requires each one of our ac-tions to be directly chosen among psychologically genuine alter-natives. It is enough sometimes that we are responsible for being the kind of person who no longer has a choice in this situation. That's why a driver—who could less avoid the accident drunk than sober—is thereby not less but more culpable. To be sure, it is not unusual to hear that someone "ought to know better" than to find a certain sexist or racist joke funny. Besides, actual laughter (as op-posed to the inclination to laugh) may generally be inhibited. And as Aristotle again sagaciously remarked with regard to a certain Adeimantus, who once burst out laughing but is not otherwise known, we don't blame someone for laughing if he's tried really hard not to.[3]

Triviality. Still, it might be said that even if laughter betrays character, and even if we ought on occasion to contain it, this is merely a minor social duty, like the duty not to fart or burp. Failures of restraint can inconvenience others, perhaps embarrass or even offend them; but surely this is a matter of etiquette, not of Ethics. Rules of etiquette are typically relative to a particular group: "It's all right to use such language when you're at camp with your buddies; but it just won't do at your sister's wedding." The suggestion that there are categorical Laws of Etiquette is a familiar device of the comical — either ingenuous, as in the injunction to "Never Give a Lady a Restive Horse," or ingenious, like Oscar Wilde's rule that "the only way to make up for being occasionally a little overdressed is to be always immensely overeducated."[4]

This won't do, for two reasons, as a characterization of the difference between Ethics and social convention. For one thing, it is one of the anthropologist's tasks to find underlying universal structures beneath the surface of particular social conventions. And on the other hand, a case might be made that some genuinely moral rules are relative to conventional social structures. But surely it is a necessary condition of moral significance that an act and its consequence not be *trivial.* Can laughter pass this test?

The association of laughter with the frivolous means that we may be tempted to assume that it cannot be serious. Yet for many people laughter is a great revealer of character. It is natural to assume that in these cases information is coming to us through the object of the laughter: we can react positively, as to revealed affinity, or negatively with shock and revulsion to the fact that someone finds a certain sort of joke or situation funny. In this way laughter is a powerful sorter. But it isn't always easy thus to pick out the object. To say what someone is laughing at, in the sense of exactly what target or scenario provokes laughter, is not always to specify *what's funny about it* — the motivating aspect. Moreover a sincere answer to that question is not always a true one. A partial guide to the nature of the true object is the character of the laughter itself, its actual sound, considered in isolation from its occasion. (Sometimes the sort of occasion it is can be easily inferred from the sound.) Imagine a man whose habitual sound of laughter is a *cackle,* or a *snicker.* Would you like your daughter to marry him? Even more interesting is a

second-order thought experiment that can be carried out here. The
example just given, to be imaginatively convincing, had to be
gender specific. Our gender stereotypes dictate that it is not very
feminine to *guffaw*, nor very manly to *giggle*. There are assumptions
buried in these reactions to the sound of laughter which cut much
deeper than etiquette:

> Self-loathing ladies titter; Hags and Harpies roar. Fembots titter
> at themselves when Daddy turns the switch. They totter when he
> pulls the string . . . Daddy's little Titterers try to intimidate
> women struggling for greatness. This is what they are made for
> and paid for. There is only one taboo for titterers: they must
> never laugh seriously at Father—only at his jokes.[5]

The Funny is Merely Aesthetic. Those categories of expressiveness are coarse, as they have to be to be even roughly
describable. But our ear is sensitive to much finer and less easily
describable nuances of expressiveness. We can be attracted or
repelled by the sound of a laugh even more surely than by that of a
speaking voice, without quite knowing why. "Tell me what you
laugh at and I will tell you who you are," but "Let me hear you
laugh and I will know if I like you." When I find a personality
disagreeable, it is a normal effect of moderate vanity to hope it is
because there's something wrong with them, and not with me. Thus
it is always satisfying to find the accident of personal distaste sup-
plemented by a sound motive for moral disapproval. Is this possible
here? Or are the preferences evoked by the expressiveness of
laughter just aesthetic ones? This question is quite a different one
from that concerning the triviality of laughter; for aesthetic questions can cut very deep, and still not be held to be moral. That we
are dealing with merely aesthetic preferences is suggested by the
variety of our reactions and by the difficulty of articulating them in
terms of general principles. If this is so, the affinities or differences
they reveal may not have moral significance.

Origins and Consequences

To determine whether our attitudes to laughter can be governed by genuinely moral principles, let us first look at different types

of moral consideration. Central to most moral systems is an interest in consequences, actual, probable, or merely possible. This contrasts with aesthetic interest, which characteristically focuses on some object in itself. Laughter, it may be conceded, does not have very significant consequences. The French philosopher Henri Bergson calls it a kind of "punishment," but stresses that it is only a social gesture: "society cannot here intervene with any material repression, since it is not hurt materially" by what laughter is intended to punish.[6] Leaving aside the curious optimism that prompts Bergson to assume that society will punish only symbolically what harms it only symbolically, what we should note here is that the material consequences of laughter are attributable only to the *meaning* of laughter: in this way laughter is essentially a sign, whose effect is based on convention. Yet — and this is the other side of the variety manifested by the sounds and object of laughter — laughter itself is natural to humans. It is universal, not just as a sound, but as a mode of communication. At least one important variety of this mode, as we shall see, presupposes sociality in that it requires a recipient or butt: someone to whom the laughter is liable, perhaps indeed intended, to give offense.

Not any action that gives offense is thereby morally offensive. Its evaluation requires that we consider the reason that it is found offensive. Mixed marriages frequently give offense to racists, but that does not warrant moral regard. Explicitly sexual literature can be offensive to the "common decency"of "community standards." Such offenses are liable to draw upon themselves social and legal sanctions, but whether they warrant moral condemnation on the ground of offense alone is less clear. The power to create moral obligations should perhaps be ascribed to prevailing social conventions only insofar as they express or embody human values that depend on sociality itself. The existence of some particular social arrangement or public opinon would not be sufficient. Moreover what gives offense usually does so in virtue of its motivational origins. An observer acquainted with La Tourette's syndrome, for example, will not be offended by the verbal products (known as coprolalia, which is Greek for "shit-talk") which spring directly from a neurological disorder and not from any even unconscious intent to utter offensive words. Similarly hebephrenic laughter is not, for our purposes, laughter at all. The sound of laughter is significant as laughter only if it's produced in the right way. Does it make sense then to speak of an "Ethics" of some class of acts that is discerned not primarily by their consequences, but by their origins?

A distinction is needed between two kinds of relevant origins. There is a classic sense, of course, in which all ethical assessments of particular acts are not of actual consequences but of "origin" in the sense of *motive*. For the Kantian, this judgment of the goodness of the Will is the only truly ethical evaluation. But this is not the sense in which I speak of evaluating laughter in terms of its origin. For although we can sometimes burst out laughing—or omit to restrain our laughter—on purpose, specifically with the intention of wounding someone, this is not the usual case, nor is it very problematical. More interesting is the criticism of laughter which arises from treating it as a *symptom*. There are cases in which we say: "If you can laugh at something like that, you must be insensitive, boorish cruel . . ." Such strictures are related to the Kantian criticism of motives, but they are not the same. For the Kantian looks at the origin of the act only in the sense of looking at the goal which it aims at. The "naturalness" of laughter makes it inappropriate for that kind of criticism. If we can answer the question "What did you intend to *achieve* by laughing?" then it was no genuine laughter at all.

The better parallel is with the assessment of cognitive rationality, or the "Ethics of Belief." Belief, like laughter, is not typically voluntary: On the contrary if it aims at some result—apart from the attainment of its Formal Object—its claim to be genuine belief is undermined. The evaluation of belief is in terms of the correctness of the *procedures* in which it originated. So to believe something in the face of the evidence because the consequences of believing it would be good, is always a violation of the Ethics of Belief.

Such a violation might be required by overriding considerations; sometimes perhaps we should persuade ourselves of some comforting falsehood in order to preserve the moral strength to continue a worth while struggle. In some of those cases a "bootstrapping" principle may be operative, so that the belief seems almost to create its own justification.[7] and maybe it is even sometimes our duty to propagate a Noble Lie for the benefit of humankind. But these are cases where the intrinsic, universalizable Ethics of belief is overridden, not cases where it appeals to consequentialist criteria for the sake of its own Formal Object.

Much the same can be said of "Professional Ethics": medical, business, or legal. All of these, more obviously than the Ethics of Belief, may ultimately rest on consequentialist moral considerations, but they are rules about the best *procedures* in the transactions characteristic of each of these domains. And insofar as they admit of exceptions, they do not violate the principle of universalizability. For exceptions to principles of professional Ethics are due to features of circumstances, not to the vagaries of individual preference.

Might not the objection then be raised that all these "Ethics" are so called merely by courtesy, by convenience, or by analogy? A simple argument shows that this objection would be wrong. It is always an unequivocally ethical question whether in some particular case we should allow ethical considerations *simpliciter* to outweigh or override the principles of the special Ethics. If these "special Ethics" had no genuine ethical import, this would not be so. For suppose they merely had the status, say, of etiquette: then on most ethical principles they would automatically be of no weight at all if confronted with genuinely ethical objections. Although they might provide *indirect* reasons through people's reactions or hurt feelings, and so forth.

I conclude that there are genuine examples of Ethics where the considerations are ones of appropriateness in relation to origins, not of consequences either aimed at or achieved. That, in any case, is the sense in which I shall be speaking of the Ethics of Laughter. If the preceding considerations do not suffice to vindicate it, they may be taken merely to define it.

The Comic and the Tragic

When *Waiting for Godot* first made it to the suburbs of London, England, I went to a matinee performance at the Golders Green Hippodrome. During the intermission I struck up a conversation with an elderly woman in the next seat. She had laughed not at all, and she spoke mostly of how gloomy the play was. As she could no doubt see that I was only thirteen years old, she was anxious that I not be misled into thinking it a comedy. The theatre darkened again, and there came one of the play's moments of sheer clowning. The philosophical disquisitions of the two tramps are punctuated by

the rapid tossing of a bowler hat, with machine-like precision and ir-
relevance. There is nothing funny in the telling of it: it was not a
joke but pure slapstick, an excellently executed visual gag, which
brought the house down. Under cover of the loud laughter, the lady
bent down towards me and gravely hissed: *"But it isn't MEANT to
be funny!"*

But on the contrary: these actors had worked very hard to be
that funny.[8] The lady was right, I daresay, about the overall vision
of the play; but what interested me, and still does, was the presupposition of her reproof: *If something is tragic then it can't be funny.*

Note that this doctrine, if true, would be of great interest for
the present theory. For it would provide us with one of those elusive
principles laying down the constraints on the coexistence of emotions, which as I pointed out a logic of the emotions ought to be able
to provide. It is a doctrine that has in most ages passed either for
common-sense or at least for an indubitable principle of aesthetics.
There have been some exceptions: in the *Symposium* Plato reports
that Socrates, at the end of that long night of talking and drinking,
"forced his companions to acknowledge that the genius of comedy
was the same as that of tragedy." But he implies that they agreed
mainly because "they were drowsy and didn't quite follow the argument." By and large, the Greeks separated Tragedy from Comedy.
So did their classical French followers, who like most of the English
eighteenth century thought Shakespeare exceeding vulgar for not
knowing the difference. But even Shakespeare usually separated
comic scenes from tragic ones. And although some authors view
laughter as a substitute for tears, even they view them as incompatible, even though mutually substitutable: "Man alone," said Nietz-
sche "suffer so excruciatingly in the world that he was compelled to
invent laughter." And Byron: "If I laugh at any mortal thing, — T'is
that I may not weep."

But what could be the nature of such incompatibility? Let us
begin by distinguishing two sources, or types, of incompatibility.
Two emotions might be incompatible *in the subject* or *in relation to
the object*. The first type applies characteristically to *moods*. If one
cannot feel elated and depressed at the same time, this cannot be
because of any incompatibility between the objects of these
moods — for moods have no object. Depression and elation seem to
be real contraries, not merely "opposites" in some vaguer sense.
Thus if, in the traditional figure of the Tragic Clown, we are in-

clined to see someone that is both gloomy and merry, we can evade contradiction only by appealing to some sort of split level theory. Split levels, like Plato's Parts of the Soul, allow each level to be pure even while explaining the possibility of inner conflict. Plato's method is explicitly designed to split faculties two by two, and it has trouble generating more than two Parts of the Soul. There is also a problem about how, if it succeeds in that task, it avoids succeeding too well, and producing an indefinite proliferation of parts.[9] The application of the method, I argued, is fallacious, but the basic principle is just a version of Leibniz's law. It says that if some pair of properties are incompatible, then no *one* thing can have them both at the same time. And if one grants that there can be more than one "level," why not several?

If we adopt Plato's strategy, we implicitly construe the incompatibility on the model of the impossibility of being simultaneously and homogeneously red all over and green. But this can't be the correct account of the incompatibility between laughter and alternative reactions. For although we do occasionally get into a "laughing mood," under the influence of cannabis, for example, or following relief from great tension, laughter is not objectless, as moods are. To get a better idea of what is involved in inconsistency with regard to objects, let's return to the case of inconsistent objects of belief. It is not inconsistent to describe a subject as believing both that p and that not-p. But it does constitute an *ascription* of inconsistency. What's wrong with inconsistency? What's wrong with it is that it guarantees *at least one false belief.* This goes against the categorical imperative of the Ethics of Belief: *Believe (all and only?) what is true.* The criterion for that violation lies in the logical relations between the propositions believed — between the contents of the beliefs. In an emotional analogue to propositional content, the imperative of consistency would derive from the following principle of the Logic of Emotions:[10]

> *If two emotional contents are incompatible, then that will guarantee that at least one of them is inappropriate.*

Unfortunately examples are hard to pin down. For the objects of emotions have no criteria of identity even as dubiously clear as those of propositions. How then can we tell whether one's emotional contents are so structured as to guarantee that at least one is inappropriate? We must resort, it seems, to some unexplained notion of phenomenological incompatibility. Whether the comic and the tragic are phenomenologically incompatible seems a hopeless question: both are too complicated. Let us at least narrow the case down to the *funny* and the *bitter*. As practiced by a certain kind of comedian (Lenny Bruce, Richard Pryor) it seems as though the funniness is *in* the very bitterness itself. Some might find this unintelligible; but any disagreement here is likely to get bogged down in denials of each other's phenomenological reports. Let us then grant, at least, that some people sincerely report experiencing both responses at once. Should this report be disbelieved, or construed as self-deceptive?

We need some distinctions. Let us say that the Richard Pryor *schtick* is the *target*. The two *Formal Objects* are the Comic and the Tragic. The tricky question concerns *what's funny about* the target: I shall call it the *motivating aspect*. The problem, then, is whether there are two distinct motivating aspects, and if so, what their relations are to the Comic and the Tragic as Formal Objects. The claim of incompatibility must be refined to distinguish the impossibility of joint *satisfaction* (incompatibility) from the impossibility of joint *success* (inconsistency). Recall that success was defined as the possession by a motivating aspect of the property that defines the Formal Object (e.g., the property *for* which I want something's being actually a *good*-making one.) Satisfaction is the actual possession by the target of the motivating property attributed to it by the intentional state (e.g., for a want: the proposition wanted actually being *true*.) Now there are two possibilities:

(a) Suppose first that there are two motivating aspects, both present in the performance: the tone of Pryor's voice, perhaps, which is apprehended as Comic, and the content of his words, apprehended as Tragic. Then, since the Formal Objects (and the corresponding emotional responses) are being attributed to those different aspects, no argument could show them to be inconsistent. That would be like claiming that it is inconsistent to say of two different propositions that one is true and the other is false.

(b) But now take the second possibility: there is really only one motivating aspect. It is not only the same performance, but the very same *aspect* of it that arouses both emotions. Here true inconsistency is a possibility: perhaps the two Formal Objects are inconsistent *as criteria of success*.

The example of belief will help to make this clear. No single proposition could be both true and false, not because of some property that every proposition has which prevents it, but because that is part of the meaning of the opposition between truth and falsity. So might it be with Comic and Tragic: that they are by their very natures related as logical contraries.[11]

The trouble with this last supposition is that although it is coherent I cannot think of a way to establish its truth. This seems to be a place where nothing but phenomenology will give us any answer. And if indeed some people report having both types of response in regard to a single aspect, I find no argument to support the view that the two Formal Objects must be inconsistent.

But there remains to be explored a form of the charge of incompatibility, which proceeds with a quite different strategy.

Feeling and Thinking: the Walberg View

On this new version, the claim is not that Comic and Tragic are inconsistent emotions, but that the comic is incompatible with *emotion as such*. I shall refer to this as the *Walberg view*.[12] This is a radical view, not only because it is so sweeping, but for its claim that laughter itself does not stem from emotion at all, but contrasts with it.

Against the Walberg view I see two arguments. One is too simple. The other perhaps will seem too complicated. Such is the Philosophical Life.

The simple argument is that to compete with emotion, laughter needs to be *in the same game*. The Walberg view presupposes some sort of philosophical psychology, in which something like Faculties can enter into competition. Now obviously there might be models that do this which philosophers traditionally haven't thought of; but, the argument runs, all the models that have been thought of are basically variants of either the *Cartesian* or the *Platonic*. On the Cartesian, Intelligence (or Understanding) is viewed as a separate faculty from emotion (or Will). On the Platonic, they are more like the parts of the soul of the *Republic*: each one is in some sense dominated by a particular faculty and primarily identified with it, but every faculty is represented in each homunculus.

Consider first the Cartesian picture. It allows no competition between the faculties, for they perform quite different tasks. Their *organs* can of course compete for resources; but the *functions* themselves can no more conflict than the volume control of a radio can conflict with the tuning control.

But the Platonic picture fares no better. To be sure, it agrees well enough with the popular notion that some individuals are primarily analytical and others primarily empathic. But it gives us no particular reason to see this as an *incompatibility*. And that was just what we needed explaining.

The diagnosis I suggest is this. The distinction so far sketched confounds two different contrasts. One is between *evaluative engagement* and neutrality or *detachment*. The other is between *identification* and *alienation*. We tend to associate detachment with alienation, and identification with empathy and therefore with evaluative engagement. But these are no more than associations: one can be evaluatively engaged with what is alien and one can be cold even while identifying with another person. I can regard *myself* coldly, for that matter, without ceasing to be or feel *myself*. This distinction is particularly important with regard to laughter; for laughter can be dispassionate, as when it is evoked by mere wit, or emotionally involving, whether we are laughing "with" someone, (involvement with identification) or "at" someone (involvement with alienation). The evaluative involvement characteristic of laughter has traditionally   and, as I shall argue, at least some times correctly — been taken to involve some apprehension of evil. My hunch is that in an important class of cases there is an interaction between this element of evil and the dialectic of identification and alienation. This class of cases defines a kind of laughter that is particularly susceptible to moral condemnation, and which for reasons that I shall explain in the next section I call *phthonic laughter*. If this is right, then the Walberg view rests on a confusion between intellectualizing detachment, and emotionally involved alienation.

Phthonos, Wit, and Anhypothetical Humor

To begin with, let us exorcise the evil element in laughter, by giving it a name to distinguish it from wit and from mere amusement. I borrow from Plato the word *Phthonos*. The Greek word means something like "malicious envy"; it connotes both the involvement of something evil, and the ambiguity between identification and alienation that characterizes jealousy. Plato applies it to the kind of laughter typically experienced at some ridiculous spectacle. Malicious ridicule, in Plato's book, is properly directed against our enemies; but it is a pleasure mixed with pain when directed at our friends. Of the many philosophers that have emphasized this element of evil,[13] Hobbes saw especially clearly that the phthonic element is distinguishable from wit: "That laughter consisteth in wit, or as they call it, in jest, experience confuteth, for man laughs at mischances and indecencies wherein lieth no wit nor jest at all."[14] But how is the distinction between phthonos and wit to be drawn? In reaching for a hypothesis, I need a joke of undiluted nastiness; one that is as devoid of wit as possible. A rape joke will do.

> Margaret Trudeau goes to visit the hockey team. When she emerges she complains that she has been gang-raped. Wishful thinking.

I once had occasion to discuss this joke with a student editor who rather proudly claimed to be its author; an exaggeration, since all rape jokes are variants of the same basic joke. I pointed out to the "author" that the joke seems to imply certain beliefs. One is the belief that all women secretly want to be raped. But the "author" protested: I had entirely missed the point. What the joke was *really* about, he ingenuously explained, was the common knowledge that Margaret Trudeau was *promiscuous.*

In tendering this transparent reply, the young man was furthering my quest. That Margaret Trudeau is promiscuous is indeed a hypothetical assumption of the joke. And embedded in the very use of the word "promiscuous" in this context are something like the following propositions: that rape is just a variant form of sexual intercourse; that women's sexual desires are indiscriminate; and that there is something intrinsically objectionable or evil about a woman who wants or gets a lot of sex. These are sexist assumptions. But *merely to know this doesn't make the joke funny.* What's more, to laugh at the joke *marks you as sexist.* It is not a convincing defense to say: "I was merely going along with the assumptions required to get the point of the joke."

Why not? In every joke that is based on a story—as opposed to arising from some life situation—some assumptions, some background setting, need to be understood and accepted. "An Englishman," we begin, "A Scotsman, and an Irishman . . . ." So how are the sexist beliefs just mentioned unlike the ordinary presuppositions that every joke requires?

What seems to be needed is that the listener *actually share* these attitudes. This suggests an explanatory hypothesis:

> In contrast to the element of wit, the *phthonic* element in a joke requires *endorsement*. It does not allow of hypothetical laughter. The phthonic makes us laugh only insofar as the assumptions on which it is based are attitudes actually shared. Suspension of disbelief in the situation can and must be achieved for the purposes of the joke; suspension of attitudes cannot be.

We cannot come to find something funny by merely imagining that we share its phthonic assumptions. Nevertheless we intuitively know that sharing these assumptions is what would enable us to find it funny. This is a crucial point. For without the possibility of this sort of second order knowledge about the relation of attitudes to laughter there could be no *criticism* of other people's laughter. Indeed there probably could be no phthonic jokes at all. For in the standard case a phthonic joke requires a butt or victim, and the butt of the joke is someone who typically does not laugh but knows only too well what's funny to those who do.[15]

But perhaps someone remains unconvinced, because they do find the joke funny and disclaim the allegedly necessary attitudes. For such a man, no knock-down argument can be forthcoming, but a simple thought experiment might help. Just imagine either of two variants. In the first, some non sexual form of assault is substituted for rape. Apart from some tenuous connection with masochism by which one might try to restore the original point, it will undoubtedly cease to be funny to anyone. In the second variant, substitute some man who (a) is not assumed to be homosexual and (b) is not the object of any particularly hostile attitude. Again, the joke loses its point. And this cannot be remedied by my saying: "for the purposes of the joke, just ignore the sexist double standard, and pretend that you think that there is something evil or contemptible about a man who fucks a lot."

My last sentence embodied a second thought-experiment, which both supports my suggestion and imposes an amendment. If you snickered at my language, it's because you consider it *naughty*. That is an *attitude*. If you didn't, I'm unlikely to get a chuckle out of you by asking you, just for the present purposes, hypothetically to think my language naughty. Though there is apparently a possible exception here: but it is only apparent, and therefore "proves the rule." The supposition just made may raise a chuckle after all, but only because you agree with me, and therefore find it funny to suppose otherwise. So the chuckle would really only be raised by the meta-thought-experiment, and instead of a counterexample it would be merely an instance of the following principle:

> *It can be funny to suppose that something that is not at all funny might be funny, but only if you actually think it isn't actually funny.* [16]

(A number of Monty Python's jokes are based on this principle.) This confirms my hypothesis, as well as carrying the additional empirical implication that thinking something intrinsically funny (or unfunny) is itself an *attitude*, and not a mere belief. The modification to my thesis required by this last example is the following. My suggestion about the anhypothetical feature was originally confined to phthonic jokes, defined as those that in some way involved evil. But we now see that the moral is broader. Phthonic jokes are a species of jokes that rest not merely on beliefs, actual or hypothetical, but on *attitudes.* but not all attitudes involve evil, nor are such jokes all phthonic. How is an attitude different from a belief? The hypothesis I have defended yields the following definition: *attitudes are beliefs that one cannot hypothetically adopt.* [17]

This, I believe, reveals an interesting characteristic of the category of emotional attitudes: their anhypothetical nature.

The Social Factor

The anhypothetical nature of attitudes is related to another feature of emotions — their *social* nature. One aspect of this factor, only implicit so far, is the social relativity of jokes. This forms the subject of one of Bergson's "fundamental observations on the Comical":

A man was asked why he wasn't crying during a sermon which

had everyone else in tears. "I'm not from the parish," he
answered. What this man thought about tears is even more true of
laughter. However frank it may seem, laughter always conceals a
subconscious thought of community, one might almost say of complicity, with laughing companions real or imaginary." (Ibid., p. 5)

Since the community of laughers is allowed to be imaginary, it
would be hard to refute Bergson's claim here. But when we actually
laugh alone, what subsists of this imaginary community? At least the
fact that certain attitudes are endorsed, and that if anyone else were
also to endorse them they would presumably be laughing too. But
also, more generally, there remains a set of social-biographical facts
that constitute the paradigm scenarios definitive of the particular
sort of Funny involved.

The notion of community is of independent importance,
however; for in some circumstances the question of whether one
belongs to a certain community, or shares in certain assumptions
made in that community, admits of no ready answer. After long
enough among the natives, the anthropologist might feel a sufficient
sense of community to laugh at their jokes, even though in sober
conscience she does not share their attitudes: she does not really
believe, say, that chickens are dirty and pigeons are pure. A feeling
of community can substitute for as well as engender a genuine adoption of attitudes, just as the adoption of certain attitudes can be
both a criterion of membership and a sufficient ground for being
adopted as a member. Here then we have a concrete example of the
possibility of changes in emotional dispositions. The convertibility of
emotional attitudes and community involvement ensures that in at
least some cases new paradigm scenarios can continue to enlarge
and refine our repertoire of emotions. But I need to say more about
the significance of this notion of *community involvement.*

Identification and Alienation: Inside and Outside

We have seen that the notion of community is related both to
the endorsement of common phthonic premises, and to the contrast
of identification and alienation. It's time now to look more closely at
the distinction between "inside" and "outside."

There are two characteristic manifestations of this distinction.
First, there is our claim to have a right to laugh, by virtue of shared

experience or community, at some things but not others. Second, there is the distinction we make between laughing *at* and laughing *with* someone. These are different distinctions, but they are related in the following way: I cannot really laugh with you, unless I have the right to laugh; and I only have a right to laugh at you if there is a clear possibility of identification with you. Cyrano de Bergerac makes fun of his own nose, but threatens with death anyone who does likewise:

> Je me les sers moi-même avec assez de verve
> Mais je ne permets pas qu'un autre me les serve.[18]

There is often a note of embarrassed reticence in the laughter of white people at the jokes of blacks about themselves. Yet the whites would, perhaps, readily laugh at the blacks, if the blacks weren't laughing at themselves. What causes the unease in the one case is the thought that *they* (who laugh) *have no right to laugh*; what lifts it in the other is the thought that *they* (the others) *won't find out*. The same dynamics can be observed even more commonly nowadays in the jokes of men about women. What is wrong with laughing at someone behind their back, when the same joke would be acceptable face to face? The answer is that if you were face to face, the alienation expressed by the joke itself would be offset by the reality of community signaled by the sharing of it.

An extreme example was related to me by someone who had been brought up among the miners of the Congo. Among these men to laugh at cripples was perfectly normal, and not condemned as especially rude or callous. Part of what the laughter expressed in those circumstances, in which the men were exposed to great danger, is that it could happen to anyone: it had happened to you and *it could have been me, but you are not me and it didn't*. The two movements, identification and alienation, are both clearly present here,[19] and I speculate that each is an essential element, linked with the evocation of some frightening evil, of true phthonic laughter.

I can now add one more layer of understanding to my previous analysis of what is wrong with laughing at a rape joke. It is not merely that it evinces its origins in sexist attitudes. It also involves the presence of a characteristic mix of phthonic fear, identification, and alienation. This combination makes it wrong to laugh, because it in effect involves an important variety of *emotional self-deception.* The identification is hidden by a false front of alienation, or the layer of alienation is hidden— usually all too thinly— by a second false front of identification or sympathy. For in the laughter of put-down or ridicule, the identification is part and parcel of the motivating conditions; but the *aim* of the joke is alienation: it therefore constitutes a kind of denial of reality. (Just such a denial, perhaps, is what we foster when, in our well intentioned way, we try to repress laughter in children.)

A Cognitive Perspective on Laughter

So far, I have argued that the Walberg view couldn't be giving us the right account of phthonic laughter (though it might be right for wit). For such laughter, far from abandoning emotion, presupposes a very definite emotional engagement. If laughter is wrong, it is because this engagement is wrong. I also speculated that certain forms of laughter may be wrong because they represent an act of harmful alienation founded on a distortion or denial of an underlying identification. These two conclusions converge in an unexpected way: the "unethical" in both cases involves a wrong *assessment of reality.* This brings confirmation of the parallels I have been urging between the appropriateness conditions of emotions and the truth of beliefs. The Ethics of Belief form not merely a remote parallel, I contend, but an actual *congeneric* of the Ethics of Laughter. Like belief, laughter is wrong when it is grounded in the deception of self or others. This is what is entailed by viewing the Funny as coming within the quasi-cognitive domain. It allows us to rephrase the title question of this chapter thus:

When is laughter good or bad for the adequacy of our attitudes to the objective world?

That formulation of this chapter's central question suggests yet a *third* line of attack on the question of the incompatibility of the comic with other emotions. Given our limited capacity for attention, humor may distract us from more serious things. The charge of frivolity is often leveled against those who laugh too much, who have too much fun to attend to the serious business of life. But the problem here is one of authority: whom shall we trust to decree the criteria by which some things (the *serious* ones) are more important than others (the *frivolous* ones)? The champion of the Aesthetic says, with Oscar Wilde or Baudelaire, that "To be a useful man has always seemed to me a truly hideous thing."[20] Who is to say that laughing is not intrinsically more important than many of the serious activities with which it is deemed incompatible? (Certainly it's better for your health.)[21] But this should not count as relevant, since we have agreed that the cognitive model of the Ethics of Laughter is inhospitable to considerations of consequences.

Here again, Bergson has another interesting idea, suggesting a *fourth* line of attack against the beleaguered Funny. He defines the difference between Comedy and Tragedy in terms of Tragedy's commitment to the particular, in contrast to Comedy's interest in general types. Indeed he claims that Comedy is "the only one of the arts that aims at the general." (Op. cit. p. 114.) But "the highest ambition of art is to reveal to us nature itself" (p. 119) which is incompatible with the aims of practical living, because "to live is to accept from objects only those impressions that are *useful*, so that we can respond in appropriate ways" (p. 115). In sum, then, Comedy is mid-way between the Utilitarian perception of everyday life, and the essential perception of the world in itself which only art can claim to give us. In these terms we might explain the cognitive defect of laughter not merely as diverting our attention from "more serious things," which in itself is meaningless, but in the necessary distortion and obfuscation of the world it purports to reveal, because of its reliance on generalities and stereotypes. The thesis has some plausibility even from the point of view of a consequentialist Ethics: for if others are screened from our attention by generalities, we are bound to treat them less adequately to who they really are. More generally, insofar as we have a cognitive duty to apprehend the world as clearly as possible, laughter must impede us in the execution of that duty.

Bergson is urging us here to pay attention to the *particularity* of those we encounter, as well as of the situations of life. And it would seem churlish to refuse. Nevertheless, interesting as it is, the proposal must be rejected. It rests on two unwarranted assumptions. One is that by eliminating stereotypes and simplifications, we can have direct access to a correct vision of reality and its singular contents. The second is that simplification acts by cutting out or concealing parts of reality. The assumption is that true reality—as opposed to utilitarian representations of reality—is captured by a direct intuition. If this is to involve art, it must make no use of categories and stereotypes.

But this view is not credible. To be sure, the significant patterns that we find in reality often owe their significance to the importance of practical concerns. But the idea of a reality devoid of salient significant patterns, but perceived through art nevertheless, is the mere shadow of a false contrast. Simplification can be effective in drawing our attention to a pattern, without for all that concealing or obscuring the background. It's just that now we see it *as* background, and we therefore see the whole as differently organized. Insofar as the general types of Comedy do this for us, therefore, they bring us closer to reality, not further away.

Moreover simplification can be a means to knowledge even when it does proceed by exclusion of some elements of reality. This is the normal procedure of science, which—consistently with the views I have cited—Bergson thought powerless to tell us anything about reality. Science standardly considers certain features in isolation, in order to understand them better. If Bergson is right about the Comic, then laughter is revelatory of the nature of reality just in the measure that science is. Those are credentials enough for me. To be sure, elements so isolated need to be reintegrated into their context for the resulting pattern to prove adequate to reality. And it is just so with laughter: a partial view may be required for certain patterns to become salient, but a partial view becomes a distortion when we rest content with it.

So laughter can never be wrong merely because it simplifies. It would only be wrong if one were to remain content to laugh at a single joke forever. (*Idyllic* laughter, too, even if there is no joke, is wrong in being repetitious. That is what is hateful about "angelic" laughter.) Luckily, human laughter seems naturally protected against that particular potential sin. As an avenue to knowledge, it has the great advantage that it is always seeking fresh perspectives. One can be frozen in pomposity, but only angels can be frozen in laughter.

Notes

1. I speak of a Formal Object as *what gives the point* of a representational state, as truth does of belief and good of wanting. I also define a

special sense of *success* for propositional or representational states in which it means the attainment of the relevant formal object: a desire is then successful if its object is indeed good. This contrasts with satisfaction, which is merely the *truth* of the propositional object. For a fuller explanation, see my "The Good and the True," *Mind*, 83 (1974) 534–551.

2. For these and other opinions about laughter, see H.L. Mencken's *Dictionary of Quotations*, s.v. *laughter*. Milan Kundera adds this twist to the theme of ambivalence: the laughter of the angels is fanatical joy, that of the devils sceptical mockery. So there are two forms of laughter, perfectly antagonistic. (Milan Kundera, *The Book of Laughter and Forgetting*, tr. M.H. Heim, (Harmondsworth: Penguin Books, 1981). Which do *you* detest more?

3. For Aristotle on the voluntary and responsibility for character, see *Nicomachean Ethics*, Books II and III.

4. Thomas E. Hill's Manuals of Etiquette, of which selections have been published in facsimile as *Never Give a Lady a Restive Horse* (Berkeley: Diablo Press, 1967). Wilde's advice is from *Phrases and Philosophies for the Use of the Young*.

5. Mary Daly, *Gyn/Ecology: the Metaethics of Radical Feminism* (Boston: Beacon Press, 1978), p. 17.

6. Henri Bergson, a philosopher otherwise best forgotten, wrote a fascinating little book on laughter: *Le Rire; Essai sur la Signification du Comique*. (Paris: Presses Universitaires de France, 1940). See pp. 15, 16.

7. By "bootstrapping" I mean our capacity to "make it so by thinking it so." For example: I take Vitamin C to ward off colds. What I have read about it has convinced me that, *pace* Linus Pauling, vitamin C is a placebo. But *I believe in placebos*. That belief seems entirely rational, because I have read in *Scientific American* that palcebos are surprisingly effective in bringing about improvements.

8. Garrick is said to have remarked in warning to a young actor: "You can fool the town with Tragedy m'boy, but Comedy's a serious business."

9. Plato, *Republic*, Book IV, 436ff. Cf. Terry Penner, "Thought and Desire in Plato", (in G. Vlastos, ed., *Plato*, vol. II (New York: Anchor Books, 1971).

10. See the excellent discussion by Patricia Greenspan, "A Case of Mixed Feelings; Ambivalence and the Logic of Emotions," in Amélie Oksenberg Rorty, ed. *Explaining Emotions* (Berkeley: University of California Press, 1980).

11. Though not, like true and false, as *contradictories*, since as we saw the number of Formal Objects of emotions is large, whereas for belief there is only one. This is one disanalogy which makes the emotional analogue of truth harder than truth. *Good* is already more complicated than True, in that it is subject to the "Monkey's Paw phenomenon": something good can turn out bad because of what it is conjoined with. (see "The Good and the True", art. cit., for details) Nothing true, by contrast, can turn out false because of what *it* is conjoined with. That complication certainly applies here as well. I have a hunch, not worked out as yet, that the multiplicity of Formal Objects may be responsible for yet a further complication to the latter, which might be traced to the possibility of *higher-order motivating aspects.* Even if it is the quality of Pryor's voice that is the relevant motivating aspect, yet perhaps there are two aspects of that quality, or two *aspects of some aspect* of that quality, which evoke the different responses. By this reasoning every situation of type (b), might ultimately be reconstrued as one of type (a).

12. In honor of Hugh Walpole and Henri Bergson. Walpole's quip is often quoted: "This world," he said, "is a comedy to those who think, a tragedy to those who feel." In Bergson's view, "the comical demands . . . something like a momentary anesthesis of the heart. It speaks to pure intelligence . . . Laughter has no greater enemy than emotion." (Op. cit., ch 1, I). In naming it the Walberg view I wish to honor its authors without caring too much about how accurately the version of it which they inspired conforms to their own. For a recent defense of a similar view, see J. Morreall, "Humor and Emotion," *American Philosophical Quarterly*, 20/3 (1983), 297–305. Morreall argues, much like Bergson, that humor and emotion are *incompatible*, and indeed he suggests that it is precisely in this incompatibility that its evolutionary function resides. He writes:

> In [the] development of reason, emotions would have been not a boon but an encumbrance . . . Amusement by contrast, like artistic activities and science, would be helpful in the development of reason because it involves a breaking out of a practical and self-concerned frame of mind . . . The capacity of humor to block emotions would also have facilitated the development of rationality, for emotions would often get in the way of rational thinking . . . (302–3).

These points are unexceptionable in connection with wit or the laughter of incongruity, with which both Bergson and Morreall are chiefly concerned. But I now want to introduce a different species of Funny.

13. For example, Cicero: "laughter has its spring in some kind of meanness or deformity"; Descartes: "The joy that comes from what is good is serious, while that which comes from evil is accompanied by laughter and mockery"; Spinoza: "A man hates what he laughs at."

14. Thomas Hobbes, *Human Nature*, ch. 9, sec. 13.

15. On the "victim or butt" cf. G. Legman, *Rationale of the Dirty Joke, First Series* (New York: Grove Press, 1968) p. 9.

16. This principle was suggested to me in conversation by Birgit Worlidge.

17. I am prompted to suggest a practical application. Most of us are not perturbed by the common charge that philosophy and humor are both useless, because we realize that only the intrinsically worthless can be purely useful. Nevertheless, we might be cheered by a concrete suggestion about how humor, at least, might be of use to philosophy. I am thinking of the task of selecting suitable apprentices to the profession. This is a tedious process, and the usual methods of selection are unsatisfactory, because they concentrate more on such relatively irrelevant facts as talent, intelligence, knowledge, and so forth, when in fact the only important factor is that the candidate should display an appropriately philosophical *attitude*. The best aptitude test is an attitude test. If what I have argued here is right, I can now justify an old dream: philosophical aptitude tests consisting entirely of jokes. The applicants' laughter would be carefully measured. classified, and graded, and since, as I have argued, attitudes cannot be adopted at will for the purposes of finding some joke funny, we need have no qualms of conscience about settling candidates' destiny entirely on the basis of their responses. The main practical obstacle to such a scheme is that the entire scale would have to be calibrated to a given person in a given mood; and the mood induced by the testing conditions would most likely leave all amusement below the threshold of differentiated observable response. But this is merely a technical difficulty — if indeed it is a difficulty at all. For should we really encourage those people to be philosophers who lose their sense of humor under stress?

18. Edmond Rostand, *Cyrano de Bergerac*, I, 3.

19. The element of identification is less obvious than the alienation: so in support I drag in the word of an expert: "The 'only' joke you know how to tell," says G. Legman, "is you." (Legman, op. cit., Second Series, p. 16).

20. Quoted by Hannah Arendt in her Introduction to Walter Benjamin, *Illuminations* (New York: Schocken, 1978). One of Oscar Wilde's *Phrases and Philosophies for the Use of the Young* deplores the "many young men who start out with a beautiful profile and end up adopting a useful profession."

21. Witness Norman Cousins's account of his successful therapeutic program of laughter, in *Anatomy of an Illness as Perceived by the Patient: Reflexions on Healing and Regeneration* (New York: Norton, 1979).

24   Joseph Boskin

Like Bergson and de Sousa, Boskin is concerned with laughter as a form of social communication. Focusing on the Sambo stereotype of blacks created by white Americans, he shows how humor depends on shared beliefs and attitudes, and how it tends to perpetuate those beliefs and attitudes. Whites used the Sambo stereotype, he says, to preserve their illusion of racial superiority and to prolong their subjugation of blacks.

The Complicity of Humor: The Life and Death of Sambo

"The subtlest and most pervasive of all influences," wrote Walter Lippman incisively, "are those which create and maintain the repertory of stereotypes. We are told about the world before we see it. We imagine most things before we experience them. And those perceptions, unless education has made us acutely aware, govern deeply the whole process of perception."[1]

Lippmann's optimism regarding education's potential for offsetting the harmful effects of stereotyping—insofar as minority and ethnic groups are concerned—has not been borne out. Once implanted in popular lore, an image attached to a group, an issue, or an event pervades the deepest senses and profoundly affects behavioral actions. A standardized mental picture representing an oversimplified opinon or an uncritical judgment, a stereotype is tenacious in its hold over rational thinking. It gains its power by repetitive play, presented in different guises, so that the image it projects becomes firmly imbedded in reactive levels of thought and action. As an integral part of the pattern of culture, an image, by its very nature, will operate within and at most levels of society.

Such an image affects the thoughts and actions of those who may even be aware of its existence. More importantly, it influences those who are not. It is not an exaggeration to state that stereotypes are so pertinacious that they can be dislodged only after a series of powerful assaults. This is primarily due to their collective quality but more specifically to their oral and visual passage from one generation to another. The collective aspect of the image also generates a centripetal energy which gives it a strong semblance of reality, a "kernal of truth," as H.R. Trevor-Roper, in his intriguing study of the witch craze of the sixteenth and seventeenth centuries, observed. The stereotype, "once established, creates, as it were, its own folklore, which becomes in itself a centralizing force."[2] Consequently, a stereotype can be reproduced and extended as disparate persons over an extended time period lend credence to it. "And because separate persons attached their illusions to the same imaginary pattern," explained Trevor-Roper, "they made that pattern real to others."[3]

Furthermore, the image may have little relationship to reality at all. Gordon Allport, in his voluminous study, *The Nature of Prejudice*, noted that "It is possible for a stereotype to grow in defiance of *all* evidence."[4] Since stereotyping can proceed virtually unhindered or unchallenged, the image can stand apart from all circumstance, a separable entity, an icon.

While involving multi-dimensional facets, a stereotype possesses a core around which the images flow and change. The constancy of the central image is rarely altered and is repeated in relation to other aspects of the main form. "There is economy in this," wrote Lippman, "For the attempt to see all things freshly and in detail, rather than as types and generalities, is exhausting, and among busy affairs practically out of the question."[5] In Lippmann's view, stereotyping became imperative in modern culture because of the nature of technological society. Contemporary life, being "hurried and multifarious" tends to separate people "who are often in vital contact with each other . . ." Thus, there is "neither time nor opportunity for intimate acquaintance. Instead we notice a trait which marks a well-known type, and fill in the rest of the picture by means of the stereotypes we carry about in our heads."[6]

But everyone's affairs are "busy" and "distant" and probably have always been according to the definitions of time and space at any particular moment in history. Have not events, leaders and places in the past been visually categorized and linguistically typed by the people of the time? Are we to assume that the process of stereotyping began only in the twentieth century? On the contrary, stereotyping has always allowed the individual to compartmentalize and thus to make more comprehensible one's own position in relation to other complexities. Stereotyping simplifies the process of perceiving other people and things.

In the history of race relations in the United States, stereotypes have been particularly pernicious. Of the various images assigned to non-whites, two were developed and flourished almost simultaneously for more than three centuries: Sambo and the Savage. Their functional presence and constant refurbishment in the face of vast social, economic and political changes attests not only to their power but also to the deeply seated prejudices of those who had originated and developed them. To a considerable extent, the view of Sambo and the Savage complemented each other. Both derived from a conception of cultural inferiority.

However, the savage image of blacks was fairly limited in the popular culture and especially in the mass media. It certainly played its part in the oral tradition and was used extensively in political speeches, rallies, and by the press in news stories relating revolts, riots and sexual assaults. Likewise, movies such as D.W. Griffith's early classic, "Birth of a Nation" (1915), and the "Tarzan" series presented blacks as sexual brutes and warriors. But the violent nature of blacks was generally repressed in the mass-oriented media and/or utilized mainly when required for political or related purposes. This was partly due to the fear that a constant portrayal of the Negro as Savage would somehow lead to its realization. Not wishing to encourage black violence and retaliation, the majority generally stressed and stroked the other symbol. By emphasizing Sambo, white America hoped to relate to a figure amenable to subordination whose reaction would be one of shared laughter. The result, however, was one of shared social distance.

What were the essential features of the Sambo stereotype which became so deeply integrated into the popular culture? Southern novelist and poet Robert Penn Warren expressively gathered up the various characteristics:

> He was the supine, grateful, humble, irresponsible, unmanly, banjo-picking, servile, grinning, slack-jawed, docile, dependent, slow-witted, humorous, child-loving, child-like, watermelon-stealing, spiritual-singing, blamelessly fornicating, happy-go-lucky, hedonistic, faithful black servitor who sometimes might step out of character long enough to utter folk wisdom or bury the family silver to save it from the Yankees.[7]

Thus the Sambo figure consisted mainly of two principal divisions. On the one hand, he was childish and comical, given to outlandish gestures, physical gyrations and funny clothes. He could be clever but his cleverness was supposedly unknown to him, a kind of innocent quality. He might be folksmart, displaying little witticisms, but he was not regarded as being wise. Bursts of temper were appropriate, especially if the individual was young, but such behavior was only slightly out of line when older. Irresponsibility was a cardinal characteristic and buffoonery an anticipated act on his part. On the other level was Sambo the natural slave and servant who displayed the qualities of patience, humbleness, nonviolence and sharpness. Here responsibility was expected and smartness rewarded — though both virtues were carefully controlled.

The two separate forms would eventually translate into theatrical forms. The child became the plantation darky called by the name Jim Crow; the servant became the urban mulatto, know as Zip Coon or Jim Dandy. There would be variations on the theme of Sambo but both parts emerged as the national jester, the laughable, smiling, happy-time, natural comic who performed for the folks in the home, streets, at work, and in the theatres. Sambo was mirth.

An appreciation of Sambo's gift of mirth centers on the nature of humor. Of all the ethnic groups in American culture, only the Afro-American was intimately linked to the broad field of humor. Not only were Afro-Americans perceived as the purveyors of laughter but they also served as the butt of comedy. Concomitantly they were initiator and receiver of humor. Other ethnics have found themselves in similar circumstances, but only for relatively short historical durations. The Irish were roundly regarded as a laughable people and as excellent stage performers; and the Poles have been the recipients of countless "stupid" jokes. But the Afro-American has had the unique distinction among American minorities of being on both ends of the humor continuum for over three centuries.

Despite humor's elusive nature, certain of its characteristics help to explain this unusual situation and offer perspective into the historical definition of blacks as humorous and laughable. Humor is a complex arrangement, involving cultural and psychological processes, which moves in external and internal ways: as a means of social control, as an internal fulcrum, as a retaliatory device and as a form of communalism. Humor is clearly ubiquitous. All humans possess a latent sense of humor, meaning a structured way of laughing, and all groups utilize and often institutionalize humor within their social structures.

One of humor's basic functions is as a form of social communication, serving both an individual and a group purpose although not necessarily at the same time or in an identical manner. As an essential form of social communication, humor is integrally connected to the cultural code of society. The code itself is a consequence of diverse yet criss-crossing forces. It devolves from historic patterns recognized and accepted by the populace, and it is buttressed by assumptions about time and space, the values implicitly understood by the majority, and a common consciousness regarding present forces.[8]

The culture code is perhaps the elemental aspect in the structure of social humor. To be understood and possess meaning, humor must in some fashion relate to the experience and awareness of the majority. This does not mean that humor is constantly appreciated or comprehended but that it must relate, in an intimate way, to the scope and direction of society. A primary consequence of this process is the creation of culture and/or sub-culture and a connection to a specific time and place. Sigmund Freud, in his celebrated work on the subject, *Jokes and Their Relation to the Unconscious*, observed that humor is wholly a social process wherein the shared experiences of the participants enable them to aggress and/or regress together.[9] In *Laughter*, Henri Bergson's seminal analysis of the sociality of humor, the complicity of the process was also elaborated. "Our laughter is always the laughter of a group. You would hardly appreciate the comic if you felt yourself isolated from others. Laughter appears to stand in need of an echo." Bergson offered an illustration of the echo: "A man who was asked why he did not weep at a sermon when everybody else was shedding tears replied: 'I don't belong to the parish.' "[10] Konrad Lorenz, in *On Aggression*, offered that "laughter forms a bond" but quickly observed that it also "simultaneously draws a line." Both functions reinforce each other. Laughter produces a "strong fellow feeling among participants and joint aggressiveness against outsiders."[11]

Additionally, humor is vital as a means of creating and maintaining a state of internal equilibrium and stability. Emotions of anxiety and tension are often countered by the protective play of certain mechanisms, especially the act of "humoristic displacement," as Freud termed it. In his own particularistic way, Charlie Chaplin recognized this function. Humor, he stated, "is a kind of gentle and benevolent custodian of the mind which prevents us from being overwhelmed by the apparent seriousness of life."[12]

Humor may well be a form of custodianship but it is clear that it also has aggressive roots which are translated into social meaning. This is due to the fact, Bergson stated, that laughter "must have *social* signification."[13] For Bergson, social signification is inextricably related to aggressive intent. The pleasure caused by laughter, he argued, does not devolve from appreciation of its aesthetic design. Rather, the laugh "always implies a secret or unconscious intent, if not of each one of us, at all events of society as a whole." Comedy and aggression are entwined. "In laughter we always find an unavowed intention to humiliate, and consequently to correct our neighbor, if not in his will, at least in his deed." And this act, Bergson essayed, explains why comedy "is far more like real life than a drama is."[14]

Freud also expounded on the aggressive ends humor serves. In Freud's analysis, humor gives pleasure by permitting a gratification of a forbidden desire. "Humor is not resigned," he observed of its energy, "it is rebellious." Hostility takes the form of "tendentious humor," a veiled attack which satisfies an aggressive motive. For Freud, derogation — assault by joke — is socially acceptable hostility. When expressed through humor, the penalties for aggression are diminished. Consequently, humor that is of hostile design often releases inner tension. Inasmuch as society seeks to exercise some control over the aggressive drives of its members, humor is often utilized as an acceptable social outlet for frustrations and tensions. Humor contains within it "a liberating element."[15]

Since Freud's initial writings and subsequent embellishment by others, contemporary social scientists have amply demonstrated how certain forms of humor are used to ameliorate and regulate sexual and aggressive tendencies. Experimental studies have consistently shown that hostile humor reflects the psychological underpinnings of the verbalizer. Hostile persons prefer caustic forms of humor.

The intimate connection between humor and aggression can be seen in the powerful terminology which has developed over the centuries, words and phrases which reflect hostility. People are

taunted, mocked, ridiculed, twitted, hazed,
heckled, jived, kidded, razzed, japed, jollied,
loshed, roasted, caricatured, parodied, wise-
cracked, ribbed,

poked fun at, made fun of, made merry with,
made butt of the joke, cut up, laughed at.

People are referred to as

> buffoons, idiots, fools, clowns, bumptious,
> slow, dunder-heads, peasants, simpletons, dunces,
> silly, empty-headed, vacuous, thick-brained,
> nincompoop, ignoramus, low-brow, dumb, half-
> brained.

Because of its aggressive aspect, humor is one of the most effective weapons in the repertory of the human mind. It was for this reason that Thomas Hobbes conceived of laughter in relation to power. In his naturalistic account of the origins and purposes of laughter, Hobbes offered an explanation of social rivalry. The passion of laughter was nothing, he argued, save the "sudden glory" emanating from the realization of "some eminency in ourselves, by comparison with the infirmity of others," or with our own former position.[16]

Lorenz likewise conceived of the humor-response as a primal expression and motivation for aggressive behavior. In his observations on geese, for example, Lorenz noted that "laughter resembles militant enthusiasm" and in humans, when directed against an outsider as in scornful mocking, it is "the component of aggressive motivation, and at the same time, the analogy to certain forms of the triumph ceremony become greatly enhanced." In such instances, laughter can become "a very cruel weapon, causing injury if it strikes a defenseless human being undeservedly . . ."[17]

Much of this aggressive behavior, of course, is disguised by the smile, a beguiling physical gesture which makes aggressive humor even more dangerous and undermining. David Singer in his analysis of the cathartic benefit of humor recognized this subterfuge. "The mask of humor's subtlety and its seemingly innocuous character are used by the humorist to conceal his destructive motives and thus to bypass inhibitions in his audience and himself."[18] Since humor at times gives the appearance of unconcern — a false air of seriousness"[19] — the primal aggression from which it arises is held in check by reason. That is the interpretation offered by Lorenz. Lorenz contrasted the expressions of laughter and its close equivalent, enthusiasm. He found laughter a higher sense than enthusiasm, and argued that the former, no matter its intensity, "is never in danger of regressing and causing the primal aggressive

behavior to break through." Lorenz wryly offered an example from
the animal world: "Barking dogs may occasionally bite, but
laughing men hardly ever shoot!" What prevents the laughing individual from doing bodily harm, he maintained, is reason.
Although enthusiasm may eliminate all thought of rational self-
control, laughter relies upon critical judgment; or, as Lorenz put it,
laughter "always remains obedient to reason."[20]

But is Lorenz's optimism justified? Is laughter always "obedient
to reason"? What produces laughter in a comic situation is not
merely the "sudden" response to a new and/or different situation
but rather the recognition of a familiar form. Humor must occur
within a circumstance that has definite, though not necessarily
specific, configurations. The introduction of non-recognizable or
strange comedy often produces puzzlement, as, for example, when
an American attempts to fathom an English joke.

The comic is invariably involved with repetitive play. After all,
if humor possesses an ephemeral quality and its immediate expression is short-lived, then one of its protective qualities is repetition.
Humor is conveyed from one generation to another, from one socio-
economic group to others, by its unending reiteration. And repetition not only erodes reason but also leads to responses in which
critical judgment can be seriously impaired. Psychiatrist Theodore
Reik noted this effect. Reik assumed the correctness of Freud's
theory that the hearer of a joke laughs with the loosened psychic
energy formerly possessed by the inhibition. But Reik further
declared that the laugh is the expression of a manic mood which
derives from the mastery of anxiety and the free expression of impulse. For Reik pleasure in the joke results from the sudden
neutralization of the energy expended in inhibition. Taboos, hitherto held in check, are thus permitted expression.[21]

Bergson explains this process further. Humor can circumvent
reason, he implies, precisely because of its duplicating nature.
Worse yet, the very replication upon which humor depends has the
effect of creating an entity separate from its initial causes. "When a
comic scene has been reproduced a number of times, it reaches the
state of being a classical type or model. It becomes amusing in itself,
quite apart from the causes which render it amusing."[22]

The resultant type or model, Bergson suggested in anxious
tones, turns out to be something mechanical, a type of being who
possesses "movement without life." Here Bergson ties the abstraction

to a physical form. An element of automatism is created when gestures and movements thwart the intuitive vitality of the body. Bergson set down a law which governs phenomena of this kind:

> The attitudes, gestures and movements of the human body are laughable in exact proportion as that body reminds us of a mere machine.

By "mere machine," Bergson meant two things. First, the comic individual has to be viewed with limbs "made rigid as a machine." More importantly, the machine-like appearance has to be that of a living being. *The more these two polar images merge—machine and person—the more striking is the comic effect.*

"Something mechanical encrusted on something living" was a central notion in Bergson's view of the comic. He formulated the image as an axiom of humor: "We laugh every time a person gives us the impression of being a thing." To illustrate his concept, he pointed to the antics of two circus clowns. As they bumped and collided with each other, gradually "one lost sight of the fact that they were men of flesh and blood like ourselves; one began to think of bundles of all sorts, falling and knocking against each other."[23]

The Sambo figure personifies Bergson's conception of the comic machine-person. This, then, is the connection between stereotypes and aggressive humor.

Bergson termed the machine-person a "palpable absurdity." The comic in its extreme form represents the logic of the absurd. Many philosophies of the comic have taken this sense of the contradiction into account. What Bergson meant, however, was that the comic absurdity is of a nature similar to that of a dream. It is not just that illusions are present in both, it is that "the mind . . . seeks in the outer world nothing more than a pretext for realizing its imaginations." The dreamer does not appeal to the whole of his or her recollections for interpretation of what the senses perceive, but rather gives substance only to the favored recollection. In sum, a process of selective and partial illusion is always at work.[24]

What of the obverse side of the comic situation? How do those against whom aggressive humor is directed respond to their circumstance? More to the point, how does the stereotyped individual or group deal with the image thrust upon them? How does the clown react to this demanded role?

One thing is certain: one of the constancies in life is the role of the comic spirit, the use of laughter to ward off pain. Critic Eric Bentley, in *The Life of the Drama*, observed of its process: "The comic sense tries to cope with the daily, hourly inescapable difficulty of being. For if everyday life has an undercurrent or cross-current of the tragic, the main current is material for comedy."[25] George Meredith, in his famous essay on the subject, *An Essay on Comedy* (1877), distinguished between "comedy" and the "comic spirit" and held that the latter provides a necessary ingredient in the development of fellowship. "Sensitiveness to the comic laugh is a step in civilization."[26] Bergson put it more succinctly: "Laughter is, above all, a corrective."[27]

It is, indeed, a *powerful* corrective, for humor permits the offended person an opportunity to create both a space and an opportunity to retaliate. Jacob Levine noted this vital quality of humor. "It is by this protective aggression of others, and many have used this freedom with great effectiveness."[28] Humor creates a wide latitude, often free from counterattack, for victims of hostile laughter. After all, humor can disguise feelings of hatred of the oppressed as well as of the oppressor.

Although the range of response is unlimited for the victims of aggressive humor, there are certain quantitative as well as qualitative differences between the offending and offended parties. Apart from the fact that victims must necessarily disguise their intentions with acute sensitivity, they must also learn to absorb the inflicted blows—"without flinching," as the rules of the child's game dictate—and to cope with their offensiveness. Victims must learn how to accept their situation, ward off its ramifications and then, in some way, humorously retaliate. These processes do not always occur inevitably, or simultaneously, but one or more of the components is critical if a state of personal equilibrium is to be maintained.

Much depends upon the degree to which the assault is accepted by the individual. In his incisive study of the conceptual roles of the self, *The Presentation of Self in Everyday Life*, Erving Goffman suggested there is a continuum of beliefs in the part one plays before an audience. At one end, the performer might become convinced of the role being staged and accept its reality. Conversely, the performer may not assume its existence but the opposite. The one strategy gives rise to "sincerity," the other to "cynicism." Between the two poles, there is also a temporary moment that can be sustained through a small degree of self-illusion. Goffman maintained that

> the individual may attempt to induce the audience to judge him
> and the situation in a particular way, and yet he may not completely believe that he deserves the valuation of self which he asks
> for or that the impression of reality which he fosters is valid.[29]

Both the performer and the audience, then, are involved in a complicity of illusion, and in the case of a stereotype, of a specific kind of illusion. Furthermore, that illusion conveys a sense of reality and perpetuates the action. Levine took cognizance of this "humor illusion" and correctly described its effect of momentarily suspending "the rules of logic, time, place, reality, and proper conduct . . ."[30] That momentary suspension can be extended through repetition so that the illusion becomes "locked in" and typed.

Entrapped within the illusion, the stereotyped person runs the risk of succumbing to it. At what point does an individual begin to accept a portion of an entire role being played? Bergson postulated that deeply-rooted in the comic is an ever-present tendency "to take the line of least resistance." The individual who is forced to perform, who is constantly adapting and readapting to a situation in which he is a party, finally gives in to the role. "He slackens in the attention that is due to life. He more or less resembles the absent-minded."[31]

There is considerable evidence, however, that the opposite can also be true—that the victims understand fully well their emasculated position, and that their response only appears to be one of acceptance. The range of reply is severely limited not in terms of the varieties of humor available but rather in terms of openness. As recipients rather than initiators, stereotyped persons are forced into a diligent disguise in order to prevent their oppressors from understanding their reactions. Goffman noted that one member of a team, performing his part for the special and secret amusement of his teammates, "may throw himself into his part with an affective enthusiasm that is at once exaggerated and precise, but so close to what the audience expects that they do not quite realize, or are sure, that fun is being made of them."[32]

There are many examples of this sort of behavior by those persons who have been typed by their superiors, from elementary and high school students who make faces at their teachers when backs are turned, to military enlisted men who mimic their officers, to prisoners who devise a vocabulary of demeaning expressions directed at the guards, to workers who deride their supervisors in various ways. There are no limits to the humor that is utilized by the stereotyped, particularly those who are locked into a comic role. There is always present the possibility of revenge through a complexity of words, body language and physical disguises. There is also the distinct possibility of role-reversal whereby the stereotyped ascribe to the oppressor the same negative features being used against them. Many of these actions are done in a furtive manner, in a code that is beyond comprehension by those in authority. At the extreme, a mask is devised to conceal thoughts and feelings which might give the game away.

There is, moreover, one brand of humor which distinguishes initiator from subject. It is "gallows humor," the humor of survival. More than one individual who has been interred in an unrelenting situation has observed or used gallows humor. Psychiatrist Viktor Frankl, who spent three years at Auschwitz and other Nazi prisons during World War II, wrote that "humor was another of the soul's weapons in the fight for self-preservation," though he further noted that, under the circumstances, it lasted for only seconds or minutes."[33] An anecdote among prisoners in a camp in which Soviet writer Aleksandr Solzhenitsyn was confined, was in the traditional question-answer joke style: "What is your last word, accused?" "I beg you to send me wherever you please, just as long as it is under the Soviet government and the sun is there!"[34]

Although the victim's laughter may be unrestricted and defiant, it is mostly hidden and defensive in nature. While crucial as a means of survival and for the maintenance of dignity, defensive humor does not alter the structure of the image itself. Rather, it ameliorates the tension between the interacting parties, thus making the stereotype acceptable to both and presentable to the larger society. The illusion continues until one of the two groups either refuses to perpetuate the process, or changes its own role so drastically that the relationship is terminated.

The Sambo stereotype, whose longevity reflected its deeply-rooted functions, was an essential form of hostile humor. Sambo was Bergson's comic "machine-person," the palpable absurdity, subscribed to by whites in their attempt to preserve a social distance between themselves and blacks, to maintain a sense of racial superiority, and to prolong the class structure. The stereotyping of the black as one of the major comics in the popular culture of the United States is an example of psychological and cultural reduction. Sambo, then, illustrates the unique historical relationship between stereotyping and humoring.

Notes

1. Walter Lippmann, *Public Opinion* (Macmillan Co., 1922), pp. 89–90.

2. H.R. Trevor-Roper, *The Crisis of the Seventeenth Century* (Harper & Row, 1956), p. 190.

3. *Ibid.*, p. 191.

4. Gordon Allport, *The Nature of Prejudice* (Doubleday & Co., 1954), p. 185.

5. Lippmann, *Public Opinion*, p. 88.

6. *Ibid.*, pp. 88, 89.

7. Robert Penn Warren, *Who Speaks for the Negro?* (Vintage Books, 1965), p. 52.

8. Arthur Asa Berger and I reached an understanding of the quality and nature of the "cultural code" simultaneously. See his article, "What Makes People Laugh? Cracking the Culture Code," *ETC: A General Review of Semantics*, XXXII, 4 (December, 1975), pp. 427–428.

9. Sigmund Freud, *Jokes and Their Relation to the Unconscious* (Routledge and Kegan Paul, 1922).

10. Henri Bergson, *Laughter*, in Wylie Sypher, ed., *Comedy* (Doubleday & Co., 1956), p. 64.

11. Konrad Lorenz, *On Aggression* (Bantam Books, 1963), p. 284.

12. Robert Payne, *The Great God Pan* (Heritage House, 1952), p. ix.

13. Bergson, *Laughter*, p. 65; Bergson's emphasis.

14. *Ibid.*, p. 148.

15. Sigmund Freud, *International Journal of Psycho-analysis*, IX, Part I (January, 1928), p. 2; Freud's italics.

16. Thomas Hobbes, "Human Nature, or the Fundamental Elements of Policy," in Sir William Molesworth, *The English Works of Thomas Hobbes* (London, 1840), IV, p. 47.

17. Lorenz, *On Aggression*, p. 284.

18. David I. Singer, "Aggression Aroused; Hostile Humor, Catharsis," in Jacob Levine, ed., *Motivation in Humor* (Atherton Press, 1969), p. 104.

19. Fily Dabo Sissoko, "L'Humour Africain," in *Le Monde Noir*, by Theodore Monod (Numero special 8-9 de Presence Africaine, n.d.), p. 227.

20. Lorenz, *On Aggression*, p. 285.

21. Helmuth Plessner, *Laughing and Crying: A Study of the Limits of Human Behavior* (Northwestern University Press, 1970), pp. 162-163.

22. Bergson, *Laughter*, p. 122.

23. *Ibid.*, pp. 79, 80, 97, 98.

24. *Ibid.*, pp. 180-181.

25. Eric Bentley, *The Life of the Drama* (Atheneum, 1970), p. 306.

26. George Meredith, "An Essay on Comedy," in Wylie Sypher, ed., *Comedy*, pp. 48-51.

27. Bergson, *Laughter*, p. 187.

28. Levine, *Motivation in Humor*, p. 11.

29. Ervin Goffman, *The Presentation of Self in Everyday Life* (Doubleday & Co., 1959), pp. 17-18; 21.

30. Levine, *Motivation in Humor*, p. 14.

31. Bergson, *Laughter*, p. 187.

32. Goffman, *The Presentation of Self in Everyday Life*, p. 188.

33. Viktor Frankl, *Man's Search for Meaning* (Beacon Press, 1959), p. 68.

34. Aleksandr I. Solzhenitsyn, *The Gulag Archipelago* (Harper & Row, 1973), pp. 269-270.

Bibliography

This bibliography lists some of the literature on laughter and humor not included in this volume. For a more extensive bibliography on the psychology of laughter and humor, see the one prepared by Jeffrey Goldstein and others in Anthony Chapman and Hugh Foot, eds., *It's a Funny Thing, Humour* (Oxford, N.Y.: Pergamon Press, 1977).

Apte, Mahadev. *Humor and Laughter: an Anthropological Approach.* Ithaca: Cornell University Press, 1985.

Bailey, John. *Intent on Laughter.* New York: Quadrangle, 1976.

Bain, Alexander. *The Emotions and the Will.* 3rd ed. London: Longmans and Green, 1875.

Baudelaire, Charles. *The Essence of Laughter and Other Essays, Journals, and Letters.* Ed Peter Quennell. New York: Meridian Books, 1956.

Beattie, James. "An Essay on Laughter and Ludicrous Composition." In *Essays*, 3rd ed. London, 1779.

Bergler, Edmund. *Laughter and the Sense of Humor.* New York: Intercontinental Medical Book Co., 1956.

Boston, Richard. *An Anatomy of Laughter.* London: Collins, 1974.

Chapman, Anthony, and Foot, Hugh, eds. *Humor and Laughter: Theory, Research and Applications.* New York: Wiley, 1976.

————, eds. *It's a Funny Thing, Humour.* Oxford, N.Y.: Pergamon Press, 1977.

Cooper, Lane. *An Aristotelian Theory of Comedy.* New York: Harcourt Brace, 1922.

Cousins, Norman. *Anatomy of an Illness as Perceived by the Patient.* New York: Norton, 1979.

Darwin, Charles. *The Expression of the Emotions in Man and Animals.* Chicago: University of Chicago Press, 1965.

Dewey, John. "The Theory of Emotion." *Psychological Review*, 1 (1894): 553–69.

Eastman, Max. *Enjoyment of Laughter*. New York: Simon & Schuster, 1936.

———. *The Sense of Humor*. New York: Scribner's, 1921.

Freud, Sigmund. *Jokes and Their Relation to the Unconscious*, trans. and ed. by James Strachey. Harmondsworth: Penguin, 1976.

Froeschels, Emil. *Philosophy of Wit*. New York: Philosophical Library, 1948.

Fry, William. *Sweet Madness*. Palo Alto: Pacific, 1963.

Goldstein, Jeffrey, and McGhee, Paul, eds. *The Psychology of Humor*. New York: Academic Press, 1972.

Gregory, J.C. *The Nature of Laughter*. New York: Harcourt, Brace, 1924.

Grieg, J.Y.T. *The Psychology of Laughter and Comedy*. New York: Dodd & Mead, 1923.

Grotjahn, Martin. *Beyond Laughter: Humor and the Subconscious*. New York: McGraw-Hill, 1966.

Gruner, Charles. *Understanding Laughter: the Workings of Wit and Humor*. Chicago: Nelson-Hall, 1978.

Hayworth, Donald. "The Social Origin and Function of Laughter," *Psychological Review*, 35 (1928): 367–84.

Hertzler, Joyce. *Laughter: A Socio-Scientific Analysis*. New York: Exposition Press, 1970.

Holland, Norman. *Laughing: A Psychology of Humor*. Ithaca: Cornell University Press, 1982.

Huizinga, Johan. *Homo Ludens: A Study of the Play-Element in Human Culture*. London: Routledge & Kegan Paul, 1949.

Hyers, Conrad. *The Comic Vision and the Christian Faith*. New York: Pilgrim Press, 1981.

———, ed. *Holy Laughter: Essays on Religion in the Comic Perspective*. New York: Seabury, 1969.

———. *Zen and the Comic Spirit*. Philadelphia: Westminster, 1973.

Joubert, Laurent. *Treatise on Laughter*, trans. Gregory deRocher. University: University of Alabama Press, 1980.

Kahn, S. *Why and How We Laugh*. New York: Philosophical Library, 1975.

Kallen, Horace. *Liberty, Laughter and Tears*. DeKalb: Northern Illinois University Press, 1968.

Kimmins, Charles. *The Springs of Laughter*. London: Methuen, 1928.

Koestler, Arthur. *The Act of Creation*. London: Hutchinson, 1964.

Krishna Menon, V.K. *A Theory of Laughter*. London: Allen & Unwin, 1931.

Kuhlman, Thomas. *Humor and Psychotherapy*. Homewood, Ill.: Dow Jones-Irwin, 1984.

Leacock, Stephen. *Humor and Humanity*. New York: Holt, 1938.

———. *Humor: Its Theory and Technique*. New York: Dodd, Mead, 1935.

Legman, Gershon. *Rationale of the Dirty Joke*. New York: Grove, 1968.

Levine, Jacob, ed. *Motivation in Humor*. New York: Atherton Press, 1969.

Ludovici, Anthony. *The Secret of Laughter*. New York: Viking, 1933.

McGhee, Paul. *Humor: Its Origin and Development*. San Francisco: W.H. Freeman, 1979.

Mindess, Harvey. *Laughter and Liberation*. Los Angeles: Nash, 1971.

Monro, D.H. *Argument of Laughter*. Melbourne: Melbourne University Press, 1951.

Moody, Raymond. *Laugh After Laugh*. Jacksonville, Fla.: Headwaters Press, 1978.

Morreall, John. "Humor and Aesthetic Education." *Journal of Aesthetic Education*, 15 (1981), 55–70.

———. "Humor and Philosophy." *Metaphilosophy*, 15 (1984), 305–317.

———. *Taking Laughter Seriously*. Albany: State University of New York Press, 1983.

Philips, Michael. "Racist Acts and Racist Humor." *Canadian Journal of Philosophy*, 14 (1984), 75–96.

Piddington, Ralph. *The Psychology of Laughter*. London: Figurehead, 1933.

Plessner, Helmuth. *Laughing and Crying*, trans. James Spence and Margorie Grene. Evanston: Northwestern University Press, 1970.

Rapp, Albert. *The Origins of Wit and Humor.* New York: E.P. Dutton, 1951.

Raskin, Victor. *Semantic Mechanisms of Humor.* Dordrecht, Holland and Boston: Reidel, 1984.

Robinson, Vera. *Humor and the Health Professions.* Thorofare, N.J.: Charles Slack, 1977.

Russell, Olga Webster. *Humor in Pascal.* North Quincy, Mass.: Christopher, 1977.

Seward, Samuel. *The Paradox of the Ludicrous.* Stanford: Stanford University Press, 1930.

Shaftesbury Lord. "The Freedom of Wit and Humour." *Characteristicks,* 4th ed. London, 1727.

Sidis, Boris. *The Psychology of Laughter.* New York: Appleton, 1913.

Stearns, Frederic, *Laughing: Physiology, Pathophysiology, Psychology, Pathopsychology, and Development.* Springfield, Ill.: Thomas, 1972.

Sully, James. *An Essay on Laughter.* London: Longmans, Green, 1902.

———. "Prologomena to a Theory of Laughter." *Philosophical Review,* 9 (1900), 365–83.

Swabey, Marie Taylor. *Comic Laughter: A Philosophical Essay.* New Haven: Yale University Press, 1961.

Thomson, A.A. *Anatomy of Laughter.* London: Epworth, 1966.

Trueblood, Elton. *The Humor of Christ.* New York: Harper & Row, 1964.

Vasey, George. *The Philosophy of Laughter and Smiling.* 2nd ed. London: J. Burns, 1877.

Wilson, Christopher. *Jokes: Form, Content, Use and Function.* New York: Academic Press, 1979.

Wolfenstein, Martha. *Children's Humor.* Glencoe, Ill.: Free Press, 1954.

Wright, M. *What's Funny and Why.* New York: McGraw-Hill, 1939.

Zemach, S. "A Theory of Laughter." *Journal of Aesthetics and Art Criticism,* 17 (1959): 311–29.

Index